THE ECONOMIC METABOLISM

The Economic Metabolism

by

W. J. M. Heijman
Wageningen Agricultural University,
Wageningen, The Netherlands

KLUWER ACADEMIC PUBLISHERS
DORDRECHT / BOSTON / LONDON

A C.I.P. Catalogue record for this book is available from the Library of Congress.

ISBN 0-7923-5039-1

Published by Kluwer Academic Publishers,
P.O. Box 17, 3300 AA Dordrecht, The Netherlands.

Sold and distributed in North, Central and South America
by Kluwer Academic Publishers,
101 Philip Drive, Norwell, MA 02061, U.S.A.

In all other countries, sold and distributed
by Kluwer Academic Publishers,
P.O. Box 322, 3300 AH Dordrecht, The Netherlands.

Printed on acid-free paper

Printed in the Netherlands

CONTENTS

Preface vii

1. Theory of consumption 1
2. Theory of production 13
3. Analysis of costs and supply function 23
4. Market equilibrium, taxation and the market dynamics 31
5. General equilibrium theory 43
6. Welfare economics and cost-benefit analysis 51
7. Market forms 61
8. Production factors 73
9. Income distribution 87
10. Efficiency in resource depletion 97
11. Economic environmental policy instruments 121
12. Macro economic environmental aspects 131
13. Conditions for sustainable resource use 141
14. Economic growth 147
15. Resource depletion and economic growth 155
16. Spatial aspects of environmental problem 163
17. Steady-state economics 175
18. Sustainable growth and economic metabolism 185

Literature 191

Index 195

PREFACE

The concept 'metabolism' used in the title of this book is borrowed from biology. In biology metabolism can be defined as the transformation of inputs (sunlight, nutrients, water, air, etc.) into biomass and waste products by organisms. Here it indicates the transformation of matter and energy into goods and waste by the human economy. The analogy is striking.[1]

The book aims to be a synthesis of general economics, resource economics and environmental economics. Hopefully it will be useful in the teaching of economics especially to university students with a mathematical background (such as physicists and engineers).

I would like to thank Dr S. Loman-Subrahmanyam, Dr P. v. Mouche, Dr R. Haagsma, and Drs A. Leen from the Department of Agricultural Economics and Management of Wageningen Agricultural University for their comments on the draft version of the book.[2]

W.J.M. Heijman,
Wageningen, January 1998.

---

1 Some authors use the concept 'Industrial Metabolism', which indicates a more narrow approach than 'Economic Metabolism' (see: R.U. Ayres and U.E. Simonis, 1994. *Industrial Metabolism: Restructuring for Sustainable Development*. United Nations University Press, Tokyo).
2 For historical details in the footnotes I have made use of: J. Eatwell, M. Milgate, and P. Newman, 1987. *The New Palgrave: a dictionary of economics*. Macmillan, London.

1. THEORY OF CONSUMPTION

Consumer's optimum

Utility is the degree of satisfaction one gains from the consumption of goods. In this respect, two laws are important: *Gossen's first law* or the law of decreasing marginal utility, and *Gossen's second law,* which says that utility is at a maximum if marginal utility per monetary unit in all directions has been equalized.[1]

Assume good X_i with quantity x_i, $i = 1, \ldots, n$. Assume further that I can form utility function u:

$$u = u(x_1, x_2, \ldots, x_i, \ldots, x_n), \qquad \frac{\partial u}{\partial x_i} > 0.$$

Further, I know the budget y and price p_i of good X_i. So, if the entire budget is spent:

$$y = \sum_{i=1}^{n} p_i x_i.$$

The consumer's aim is to reach maximum utility subject to (s.t.) the budget constraint:

$$\text{Max} \quad u, \quad \text{s.t.} \ y = \sum p_i x_i.$$

I can solve this problem by using the Lagrange procedure. The Lagrange function $L(x_1, \ldots, x_n, \lambda)$ is defined as

$$L = u(x_1, \ldots, x_i, \ldots, x_n) + \lambda\left(y - \sum_{i=1}^{n} p_i x_i\right).$$

The first order conditions for a maximum are

$$\frac{\partial L}{\partial x_i} = \frac{\partial u}{\partial x_i} - \lambda p_i = 0,$$

1 H.H. Gossen, 1889 (1853). *Entwickelung der Gesetze des menschlichen Verkehrs, und der daraus fließenden Regeln für menschliches Handeln*. Prager, Berlin. Gossen's idea concerning decreasing marginal utility fits into the cardinal concept of utility. In the ordinal utility concept, the law of decreasing marginal utility must be transformed into the law of decreasing marginal rate of substitution.

$$\frac{\partial L}{\partial \lambda} = y - \sum_{i=1}^{n} p_i x_i = 0.$$

So:

$$\frac{\partial u / \partial x_1}{p_1} = \frac{\partial u / \partial x_2}{p_2} = \ldots = \frac{\partial u / \partial x_i}{p_i} = \lambda,$$

which is Gossen's second law. Now, I will give an example. Suppose:

$$u = 2 x_1^{0.4} x_2^{0.6},$$

$$1000 = x_1 + 2 x_2,$$

$$\text{Max} \quad u.$$

it can be verified that

$$\frac{\partial u / \partial x_1}{\partial u / \partial x_2} = \frac{p_1}{p_2}, \quad \text{so:} \quad \frac{0.8 x_1^{-0.6} x_2^{0.6}}{1.2 x_1^{0.4} x_2^{-0.4}} = \frac{1}{2}, \quad \text{so:} \quad x_2 = 0.75 x_1,$$

$$1000 = x_1 + 2 x_2, \quad \text{so:} \quad x_1 = 400, \quad x_2 = 300.$$

Figure 1.1 illustrates the optimum. In this figure, three *iso-utility curves* are given, of which u_2 is the one on which the optimum lies.[2] For a utility function of the same type with non-specified coefficients, the optimum is calculated as follows:

$$u = \gamma x_1^{\theta} x_2^{1-\theta}, \qquad 0 < \theta < 1,$$

$$\frac{\partial u / \partial x_1}{p_1} = \frac{\partial u / \partial x_2}{p_2},$$

$$y = p_1 x_1 + p_2 x_2, \quad \text{so:} \quad \frac{x_1 p_1}{y} = \theta, \quad \frac{x_2 p_2}{y} = (1 - \theta).$$

This type of utility function is called the *Cobb-Douglas function*. The result above implies that if the budget share of each good is known, the Cobb-Douglas utility function can be constructed. For example, if consumers spend their budgets on three goods X_1, X_2 and X_3 and the relative budget shares are 0.25, 0.50 and 0.25 respectively, then the Cobb-Douglas utility function is:

---

2 An iso-utility curve is a curve showing combinations of goods which represent the same utility.

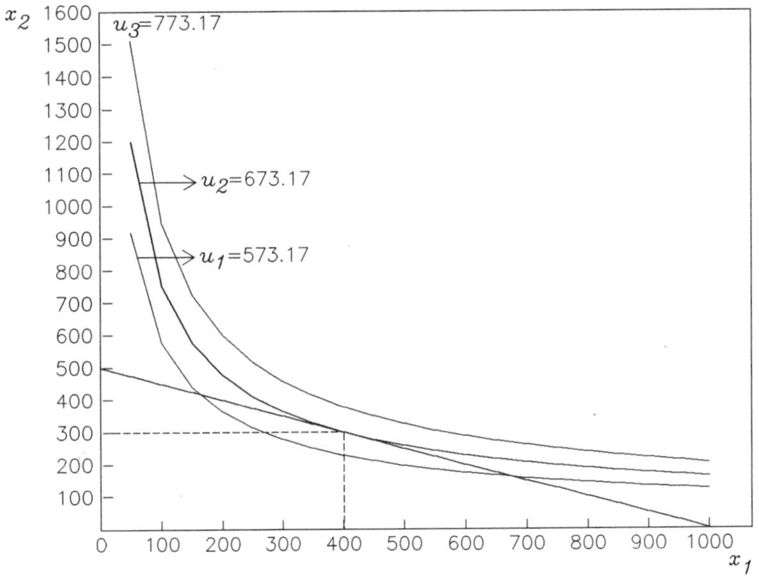

Figure 1.1: Consumer's optimum.

$$u = \gamma x_1^{0.25} x_2^{0.50} x_3^{0.25}.$$

For computing the optimum, γ is not relevant, and besides the utility function, I only have to know budget y and prices p_i.

Demand function and Engel's function

The demand function is the mathematical relation between the volume of a good consumed and its price. This function can be derived from consumer theory by varying the price of a good and determining the effect on the volume consumed. In most instances, there is a negative relation between the price of a good and the volume sold. If the form of the utility function is:

$$u = \gamma x_1^{\theta} x_2^{1-\theta},$$

the demand functions for X_1 and X_2 are:

$$x_1 = \frac{\theta y}{p_1}, \quad x_2 = \frac{(1-\theta)y}{p_2}.$$

So, in this case, x_1 and x_2 are decreasing functions of the respective price levels p_1 and p_2.

The mathematical relation between the individual consumption of a good and the individual's income is called an *income demand* function or *Engel's function*.[3] Again, this function can be derived from consumer theory. From the above it can be observed that, in this case, x_1 and x_2 are linearly rising functions of y.

Market demand

Suppose consumer m $(m = 1 \ldots k)$ has the following individual demand function (with q_d for quantity and p for price):[4]

$$q_d^m = -\alpha^m p + \beta^m \quad \alpha^m, \beta^m > 0,$$

The market demand Q_d is determined by summing up all the individual demand functions:

$$Q_d = \sum_{m=1}^{k} q_d^m = -p \sum_{m=1}^{k} \alpha^m + \sum_{m=1}^{k} \beta^m.$$

Elasticities

The change in demand in response to changes in prices or income is measured by elasticities. Consumer theory distinguishes between three types of elasticities: direct price elasticity, cross-price elasticity and income elasticity.

A direct price elasticity η can be defined as the percentage change in consumption of a good X_i divided by the percentage change in its price p_i. In mathematical terms:

$$\eta_i = \frac{dx_i}{dp_i}\frac{p_i}{x_i}.$$

If $\eta_i < -1$, X_i is said to be a *price elastic good*; If $-1 < \eta_i < 0$, X_i is said to be a *price inelastic good*; if $\eta_i = 0$, X_i is said to be a *completely price inelastic good*; if $\eta_i > 0$, X_i is said to be a *Giffen good*.[5]

3 E. Engel, 1857. *Die Productions und Consumptionsverhaeltnisse des Koenigreichs Sachsen.*
4 Of course, the demand functions are not necessarily linear in every case.
5 This implies that a rising demand is connected with a rising price, which rarely occurs. Though the name of Robert Giffen (1837-1910) is connected to this term, it is not sure whether he ever mentioned it. Marshall started the tradition of calling these types of goods *Giffen* goods in his *Principles* 1920 (1890).

The *turnover elasticity* η_i^t gives us the percentage change in turnover $o_i = p_i x_i$ divided by the percentage change in price:

$$\eta_i^t = \frac{do_i}{dp_i}\frac{p_i}{o_i}.$$

Since $o_i = p_i x_i$ and $x_i = x_i(p_i)$, it holds that:

$$\frac{do_i}{dp_i} = x_i + p_i\frac{dx_i}{dp_i}, \text{ therefore:}$$

$$\eta_i^t = \frac{do_i}{dp_i}\frac{p_i}{o_i} = \left(x_i + p_i\frac{dx_i}{dp_i}\right)\frac{p_i}{p_i x_i} = 1 + \frac{dx_i}{dp_i}\frac{p_i}{x_i} = 1 + \eta_i.$$

Hence, we see that the turnover elasticity equals the price elasticity plus 1.

A cross-price elasticity η_i^j can be defined as the percentage change in consumption of a good X_i divided by the percentage change in the price of another good X_j $(j \neq i)$. In mathematical terms:

$$\eta_i^j = \frac{dx_i}{dp_j}\frac{p_j}{x_i}, \quad i \neq j.$$

If the cross-price elasticity is positive, X_i and X_j are called *substitutes*; if negative, X_i and X_j are *complementary goods*. If the cross-price elasticity is zero, X_i and X_j are said to be *independent* of each other.

The income elasticity η_i^y of a good X_i can be defined as the percentage change in consumption of a good X_i divided by the percentage change in income. In mathematical terms:

$$\eta_i^y = \frac{dx_i}{dy}\frac{y}{x_i}.$$

If $\eta_i^y > 1$, X_i is termed a *good of luxury,* if $0 < \eta_y < 1$, a *primary good*. If $\eta_i^y = 0$, good X_i is said to be completely income inelastic.

Interrelated elasticities

If the utility function does not change, demand for a certain good at time t X_i is a function of its price p_i, prices of other goods p_j $(j = 1 \ldots m,\ j \neq i)$ and income y of the consumer, at time t:

$$x_i = x_i(p_0(t), p_1(t), \ldots, p_i(t), \ldots, p_j(t), \ldots, p_m(t), y(t)).$$

Differentiation with respect to t gives:

$$\frac{dx_i}{dt} = \frac{\partial x_i}{\partial p_i}\frac{dp_i}{dt} + \sum_{j=1}^{m} \frac{\partial x_i}{\partial p_j}\frac{dp_j}{dt} + \frac{\partial x_i}{\partial y}\frac{dy}{dt}, \qquad (j \neq i).$$

The relative change in demand for good X_i can now be determined:

$$\frac{dx_i}{dt}\frac{1}{x_i} = \eta_i \frac{dp_i}{dt}\frac{1}{p_i} + \sum_{j=1}^{m} \eta_i^j \frac{dp_j}{dt}\frac{1}{p_j} + \eta_i^y \frac{dy}{dt}\frac{1}{y},$$

Indicating relative changes with a bar, I can write:

$$\bar{x}_i = \eta_i \bar{p}_i + \sum_{j=1}^{m} \eta_i^j \bar{p}_j + \eta_y \bar{y}.$$

Assuming that income and prices all change by the same positive percentage c, the relative change in the quantity of X_i must be zero, so:

$$0 = c\left(\eta_i + \sum_{j=1}^{m} \eta_i^j + \eta_i^y\right), \quad c \neq 0, \text{ so: } \eta_i + \sum_{j=1}^{m} \eta_i^j + \eta_i^y = 0.$$

So we have the result that the sum of all the elasticities equals 0.

Marshall's rule

Normally, a demand curve is a decreasing curve showing the relation between price and quantity. An example is given in Figure 1.2.

Assume that I have to measure the price elasticity of the demand curve v in point C. The general definition of the price elasticity is:

$$\eta = \frac{dq}{dp}\frac{p}{q}.$$

From Figure 1.2 I can obtain:

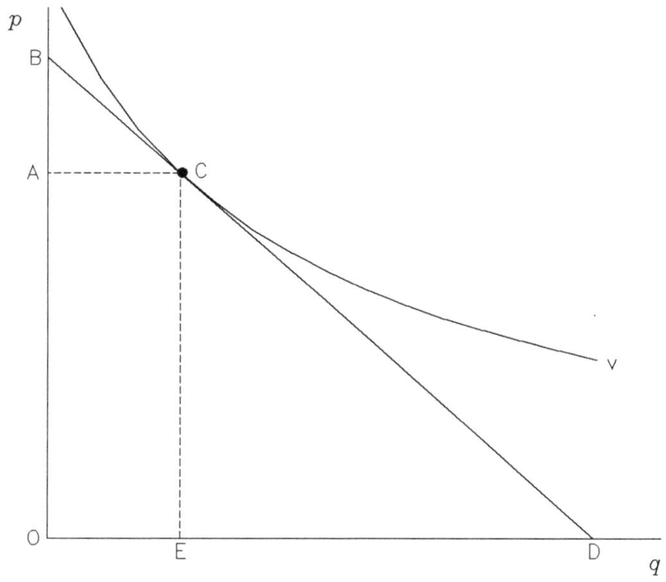

Figure 1.2: Demand curve.

$$\eta = \frac{dq}{dp}\frac{p}{q} = -\frac{\mathrm{ED}}{\mathrm{EC}}\cdot\frac{\mathrm{OA}}{\mathrm{OE}} = -\frac{\mathrm{ED}}{\mathrm{EC}}\cdot\frac{\mathrm{EC}}{\mathrm{OE}} = -\frac{\mathrm{ED}}{\mathrm{OE}} = -\frac{\mathrm{DC}}{\mathrm{BC}}.$$

So, the price elasticity at a point of the demand curve equals the distance to the quantity axis measured along the tangent divided by the distance to the price axis. This result is known as *Marshall's rule*.[6]

This rule can also be applied to Engel's curve. Figure 1.3 shows this curve for a certain commodity. Income elasticity at point D of Engel's curve w equals:

$$\eta_y = \frac{dq}{dy}\frac{y}{q}.$$

From Figure 1.3 I can obtain:

6 A. Marshall, 1920 (1890). *Principles of economics*. MacMillan, London.

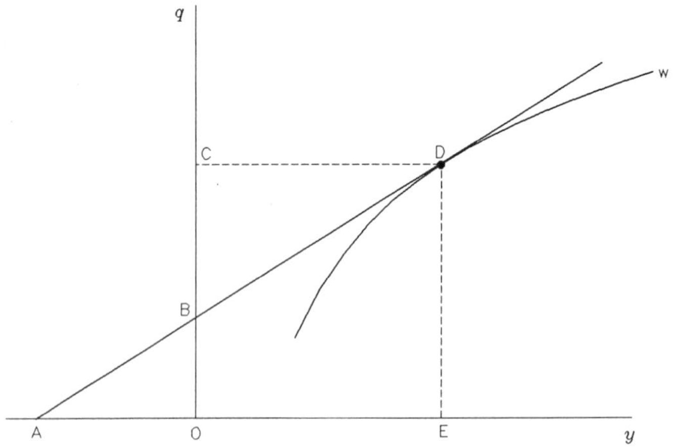

Figure 1.3: Engel's curve.

$$\eta_y = \frac{dq}{dy}\frac{y}{q} = \frac{\text{DE}}{\text{AE}} \cdot \frac{\text{OE}}{\text{OC}} = \frac{\text{DE}}{\text{AE}} \cdot \frac{\text{OE}}{\text{DE}} = \frac{\text{OE}}{\text{AE}} = \frac{\text{BD}}{\text{AD}}.$$

This means that income elasticity at a certain point of the curve equals the distance measured along the tangent to the quantity axis divided by the distance measured along the tangent to the income axis.

Consumer-oriented environmental policy

To influence consumer behaviour, a government may take three types of action: first, changing consumers' attitude; second, imposing penalties for environmentally unfriendly and providing subsidies for environmentally friendly behaviour and third, imposing regulations.[7] In this section I will deal with the first two options.

Changing consumers' attitude means that the utility function changes and that, with the same income, consumers will buy more environmentally friendly goods than previously. For example, assume that X_1 is the environmentally friendly good and that X_2 is the environmentally unfriendly one. Without and with government taking action in this field, the utility function of a consumer looks as follows:

Without: $u = x_1^{0.25} x_2^{0.75}$, with: $u = x_1^{0.75} x_2^{0.25}$.

7 E.S. Mills, 1978. *The economics of environmental quality*. Norton, New York. J.J. Krabbe and W.J.M. Heijman, 1986. *Economische theorie van het milieu*. Van Gorcum, Assen.

Further, assume that income y equals 1000 units and that $p_1 = 5$ and $p_2 = 10$. Now the respective solutions are as follows:

$$\text{without: } x_1 = \frac{0.25 \times 1000}{5} = 50, \quad x_2 = \frac{0.75 \times 1000}{10} = 75,$$

$$\text{with: } x_1 = \frac{0.75 \times 1000}{5} = 150, \quad x_2 = \frac{0.25 \times 1000}{10} = 25.$$

The second type of action is a penalty f imposed on the environmentally unfriendly good. Assuming a Cobb-Douglas utility function of $u = x_1^{\theta} x_2^{1-\theta}$, after this measure, the consumer's optimum is:

$$x_1 = \frac{\theta y}{p_1}, \quad x_2 = \frac{(1-\theta)y}{p_2 + f}.$$

It is also possible that the government subsidizes the environmentally friendly good A by an amount s and imposes taxes on the environmentally unfriendly good of a given amount f, in such a way that, from the government's point of view, the cost of the subsidy equals the benefit from the given penalty. Then, the solution will be:

$$x_1 = \frac{\theta y}{p_1 - s}, \quad x_2 = \frac{(1-\theta)y}{p_2 + f}, \qquad x_1 s = x_2 f, \quad \text{so:}$$

$$x_1 = \frac{y(\theta p_2 + f)}{p_1(p_2 + f)}, \quad x_2 = \frac{(1-\theta)y}{p_2 + f}, \quad s = \frac{p_1(1-\theta)f}{(\theta p_2 + f)}.$$

For example, assume: $\theta = 0.5$, $y = 1000$, $f = 0.25$, $p_1 = 1$, and $p_2 = 2$, then $s = 0.1$, $x_2 = 222.2$ and $x_1 = 555.6$.

Product optimization

A good can be viewed as a typical bundle of attributes, each of them one may value positively or negatively.[8] The starting point of the analysis is the concept of a heterogeneous good. The variants of this good appears very much alike, though the bundles of attributes are not identical. For example, consider two cars of the same price, which look very much alike. On the one hand, the first has been constructed

---

8 K.J. Lancaster, 1966. A new approach to consumer theory. *Journal of Political Economy*, 74, pp. 132-157; J.J. Krabbe and W.J.M. Heijman, 1986. *Economische theorie van het milieu*. Van Gorcum, Assen.

in such a way that it uses less fuel than the second. On the other hand, the first car may have less luxurious seats than the second one. The aim is to find the variant of the heterogeneous good which is best for the fulfilment of the consumer's need.

Total utility of one unit of the heterogeneous good, for which price p must be paid, equals u. The bundle contains attributes a_i that are useful to the individual consumer, and attributes b_i that have a negative influence on the environment and therefore on utility. Of course, the more sensitive the consumer is to the environmental problem, the greater the negative effect upon the consumer's utility.

$$u = u(a_1, a_2, \dots, a_n, b_1, b_2, \dots, b_m), \quad \frac{\partial u}{\partial a_i} > 0, \quad \frac{\partial u}{\partial b_j} < 0.$$

Product price p is made up of prices p_i^a and p_j^b of the attributes, and further, I know that the more environmentally unfriendly the product, the lower its price. In fact, assuming a fixed price, the consumer may choose among products consisting of relative vast bundles of individual attributes a_i together with vast bundles of negative environmental aspects, or products with relatively small bundles of individual attributes combined with relatively small bundles of negative environmental aspects. Perhaps this is not shown by the outward appearance of the product, but only by the way it is produced. An environmentally friendly way of producing is often more expensive than a production process which places less priority on environmental considerations. Now, price can be constructed as:

$$p = \sum_{i=1}^{n} p_i^a a_i - \sum_{j=1}^{m} p_j^b b_j.$$

With the help of the Lagrange procedure, the optimum product can be computed as follows:

$$\frac{\partial u/\partial a_1}{p_1^a} = \dots = \frac{\partial u/\partial a_i}{p_i^a} = \dots = \frac{\partial u/\partial a_n}{p_n^a} = -\frac{\partial u/b_1}{p_1^b} = \dots = -\frac{\partial u/b_j}{p_j^b} = \dots = -\frac{\partial u/b_m}{p_m^b}.$$

Now, I will give an example with only two attributes: a and b:

utility: $u = 10a - b^2,$

price: $20 = a - 2b,$

$p^a = 1, \; p^b = 2.$

According to the optimum rule, the optimum bundle is:

$$\frac{2b}{2} = 10, \text{ so: } b = 10, \ a = 40.$$

The solution is shown in Figure 1.4.

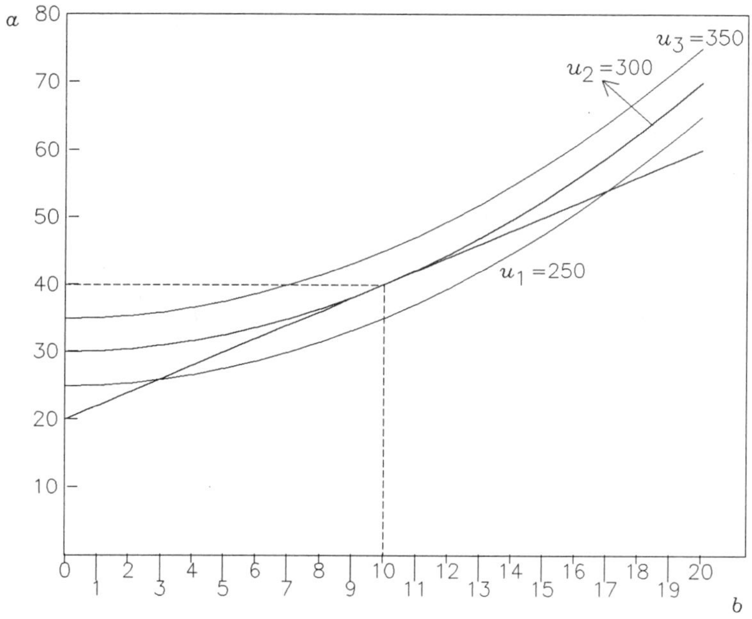

Figure 1.4: Optimum product.

Durability of consumer goods

In general, the durability of durable commodities is influenced by the interest rate. This can be explained as follows.[9] Suppose that two options for building a house are valued equally. The first option is building one house which will last for 30 years. The second one is building two houses (the second being built after the first one has been worn out) which will last for 15 years each. The first option will incur $ 250,000, to be paid now. The second implies opportunity costs of $ 150,000 now and $ 150,000 after 15 years. The present value of the costs of the first option equals 250,000. The present value of the costs of the second option equals: 150,000 + $150{,}000/(1+i)^{15}$. For the builder, there is no difference between the options if:

9 W.J.M. Heijman, Austrian sustainability. In: G. Meijer (ed.), 1995. *New perspectives on Austrian Economics*. Routledge, London. E. von Böhm-Bawerk, 1921 (1889). *Kapital und Kapitalzins II, 1: Positive Theorie des Kapitales,* 4th edition, Fischer, Jena.

$250{,}000 = 150{,}000 + 150{,}000/(1+i)^{15}$, which means that $i \approx 3\%$. Now, if $i < 3\%$, the builder will choose option one, if $i > 3\%$, the builder will choose number two. We see that if the interest rate increases, the house built will be less durable.

The example of buying a house can be generalized. Suppose that the consumer can choose between a house which lasts for $2n$ years (option 1) and two houses (the second being built after the first one has been 'worn out') which last for n years each (option 2). Which option will (s)he choose, if the prices (p_1 for the first option and p_2 for each of the two houses in the second option) are known and if the consumer wants to minimize costs? The solution of this problem depends entirely on the interest rate i. This can be proved as follows. First I calculate the break-even point, which means:

$$p_1 = p_2 + \frac{p_2}{(1+i)^n}, \quad \text{so: } (1+i)^n = \frac{p_2}{p_1 - p_2},$$

with $p_1 > p_2$. This can be written in a continuous form as

$$e^{in} = \frac{p_2}{p_1 - p_2},$$

$$in = \ln\left(\frac{p_2}{p_1 - p_2}\right), \quad \text{so: } i = \frac{\ln\left(\frac{p_2}{p_1 - p_2}\right)}{n}.$$

Now, if

$$i > \frac{\ln\left(\frac{p_2}{p_1 - p_2}\right)}{n},$$

then the consumer chooses option number two (two houses). (S)he chooses option one (one house) if

$$i < \frac{\ln\left(\frac{p_2}{p_1 - p_2}\right)}{n}.$$

Of course, this example can be extended to a choice between more than two houses. The conclusion of this section is that, as far as durable consumer goods are concerned, the durability is determined by the interest rate *ceteris paribus*.

2. THEORY OF PRODUCTION

Aim of a firm and the production function

Production is the transformation of inputs into output. Usually, a firm's aim is to produce in an economically efficient way, which can be defined in two ways:

1. Maximizing production with a given budget;
2. Minimizing the budget for a given amount of output.

The function which represents the technically efficient relation between inputs and output, or production q, is called the *production function*. In a general form with three production factors, labour l, capital c, and nature n, this function can be written as:

$$q = q(l, c, n).$$

A specific form of the production function is the *Cobb-Douglas* production function.[1] This type can be written as:

$$q = \alpha l^{\beta} c^{\gamma} n^{\delta}.$$

Maximum production with a given budget

To reach our aim (economically efficient production), output q is to be maximized under the constraint of a given budget b:

$$b = p_l l + p_c c + p_n n.$$

Finally I need the objective function:

$$\text{Max} \quad q.$$

We have already seen that under certain conditions this type of problems can be solved by a Lagrange procedure. The main condition is a *decreasing marginal product*. This condition can be written as:

1 P.H. Douglas, 1948. Are there laws of production? *American Economic Review,* 38, March, pp. 1-41. Ch. Cobb was a mathematician who was asked, already in 1927, by Douglas to devise a production function that could be handled easily.

$$\frac{\partial q}{\partial l} > 0, \quad \frac{\partial q}{\partial c} > 0, \quad \frac{\partial q}{\partial n} > 0, \quad \frac{\partial^2 q}{\partial l^2} < 0, \quad \frac{\partial^2 q}{\partial c^2} < 0, \quad \frac{\partial^2 q}{\partial n^2} < 0.$$

In fact, this law of decreasing marginal production is the equivalent of Gossen's first law. For a Cobb-Douglas type of production function $q = \alpha l^\beta c^\gamma n^\delta$, this implies:

$$0 < \beta < 1, \quad 0 < \gamma < 1, \quad 0 < \delta < 1.$$

Now I can solve the maximization problem by using the Lagrange procedure. The Lagrange function is given by:

$$L = q(l, c, n) - \lambda(l p_l + c p_c + n p_n - b).$$

First-order conditions for an optimum are:

$$\frac{\partial L}{\partial l} = \frac{\partial q}{\partial l} - \lambda p_l = 0,$$

$$\frac{\partial L}{\partial c} = \frac{\partial q}{\partial c} - \lambda p_c = 0,$$

$$\frac{\partial L}{\partial n} = \frac{\partial q}{\partial n} - \lambda p_n = 0 \quad \text{so:}$$

$$\frac{\partial q / \partial l}{p_l} = \frac{\partial q / \partial c}{p_c} = \frac{\partial q / \partial n}{p_n}.$$

Now I will give an example with the Cobb-Douglas production function $q = \alpha l^\beta c^\gamma n^\delta$.

$$\frac{\partial q / \partial l}{\partial q / \partial c} = \frac{\beta c}{\gamma l} = \frac{p_l}{p_c}, \quad \frac{\partial q / \partial n}{\partial q / \partial c} = \frac{\delta c}{\gamma n} = \frac{p_n}{p_c}, \quad \text{or:}$$

$$\frac{p_l l}{p_c c} = \frac{\beta}{\gamma}, \quad \frac{p_n n}{p_c c} = \frac{\delta}{\gamma}.$$

Together with the budget restriction, I can now deduce:[2]

2 For example: because $(p_l l)/(p_c c) = \beta/\gamma$, $(p_n n)/(p_c c) = \delta/\gamma$ and $p_l l + p_c + p_n n = b$, I can deduce: $\frac{\beta}{\gamma} p_c c + p_c c + \frac{\delta}{\gamma} p_c c = b$, so: $p_c c\left(\frac{\beta}{\gamma} + 1 + \frac{\delta}{\gamma}\right) = b$, so: $p_c c = \frac{\gamma}{\beta + \gamma + \delta} b$.

$$lp_l = \frac{\beta}{\beta+\delta+\gamma}b, \quad cp_c = \frac{\gamma}{\beta+\delta+\gamma}b, \quad np_n = \frac{\delta}{\beta+\delta+\gamma}b.$$

If, for example, it is assumed that: $b = 1000$, $p_l = 2$, $p_c = 1$, $p_n = 4$, $\alpha = 10$, $\beta = 0.25$, $\gamma = 0.50$, and $\delta = 0.25$, then the solution is: $l = 125$, $c = 500$, $n = 62.5$, $q = 2102.25$.

In order to stimulate employment on the one hand and to decrease the input of nature, government may subsidize labour and tax the use of nature in such a way that the tax revenues equal the cost of subsidy. This is called the policy of the *double dividend*. If the tax f upon nature is known, then the available subsidy s per unit labour can be computed as follows:

$$l(p_l - s) = \frac{\beta}{\beta+\delta+\gamma}b, \quad cp_c = \frac{\gamma}{\beta+\delta+\gamma}b, \quad n(p_n + f) = \frac{\delta}{\beta+\delta+\gamma}b, \quad nf = ls.$$

With the given data and an assumed tax of 1 per unit nature, the solution now becomes:

$$l = \frac{0.25 \times 1000}{2-s},$$

$$c = \frac{0.5 \times 1000}{1} = 500,$$

$$n = \frac{0.25 \times 1000}{4+1} = 50,$$

$$sl = nf = 50.$$

So:

$$2l - 50 = 250, \text{ so: } l = 150; \quad s = \frac{50}{150} = 0.33, \quad q = 2080.90.$$

Minimizing costs with given production level

If costs must be minimized, I have to solve the following problem:

$$\text{Min} \quad b = p_l l + p_c c + p_n n,$$

$$\text{s.t.} \quad q = q(l, c, n).$$

To solve this, I will form the following Lagrange function

$$L = b(l,c,n) - \lambda(q(l,c,n) - q).$$

The first-order conditions are:

$$\frac{\partial L}{\partial l} = \frac{\partial b}{\partial l} - \lambda\frac{\partial q}{\partial l} = p_l - \lambda\frac{\partial q}{\partial l} = 0,$$

$$\frac{\partial L}{\partial c} = \frac{\partial b}{\partial c} - \lambda\frac{\partial q}{\partial c} = p_c - \lambda\frac{\partial q}{\partial c} = 0,$$

$$\frac{\partial L}{\partial n} = \frac{\partial b}{\partial n} - \lambda\frac{\partial q}{\partial n} = p_n - \lambda\frac{\partial q}{\partial n} = 0.$$

So, the solution is:

$$\frac{\partial q/\partial l}{p_l} = \frac{\partial q/\partial c}{p_c} = \frac{\partial q/\partial n}{p_n},$$

which is the same solution as that of the related problem of maximizing production under the constraint of a given budget. Now I will give an example using the Cobb-Douglas production function with the same values for the coefficients ($\alpha = 10$, $\beta = 0.25$, $\gamma = 0.50$, and $\delta = 0.25$) Say that the production to be reached equals 500. Because the sum of the coefficients β, γ, and δ equals one, I can say:

$$lp_l = \beta b, \quad cp_c = \gamma b, \quad np_n = \delta b, \quad \text{so:}$$

$$l = \frac{0.25}{2}b = 0.125b, \quad c = \frac{0.50}{1}b = 0.50b, \quad n = \frac{0.25}{4} = 0.0625b.$$

These values and the acquired production level can be substituted into the production function:

$$500 = 10(0.125b)^{0.25}(0.50b)^{0.50}(0.0625b)^{0.25}, \quad \text{so:}$$

$$b = 237.76, \quad l = 29.72, \quad c = 188.88, \quad n = 14.86.$$

Scale of production

An important matter is the *scale of production*, which can be defined as the amount of inputs. If production grows faster than the inputs, there are *increasing returns to scale,* if not as fast, *decreasing returns to scale.* If production grows at the same speed as the inputs, there are *no economies of scale.* I shall discuss this by using the Cobb-Douglas production function:

$$q(l,c,n) = \alpha l^{\beta} c^{\gamma} n^{\delta} \quad \text{and:}$$

$$q(\lambda l, \lambda c, \lambda n) = \lambda^{(\beta+\gamma+\delta)} \alpha l^{\beta} c^{\gamma} n^{\delta}.$$

The coefficients β, γ and δ are called the *elasticity of production* of labour, capital, and nature respectively. One can easily see that if $\beta + \gamma + \delta > 1$, and the growth rate of the three inputs equals 1% $(\lambda = 1.01)$, growth of production will exceed 1%, we have increasing returns to scale. If $\beta + \gamma + \delta < 1$, decreasing returns to scale are the result, and if $\beta + \gamma + \delta = 1$, there are no economies of scale, which means that if the growth rate of the three inputs equals 1%, so will the growth rate of production.

Value of marginal productivity

It is assumed that a firm tries to maximise its profit w with a fixed price p for its final product. Suppose that there is no constraint on the budget nor on production. The firm has to decide how much of every production factor it will use. This means that:

$$\text{Max} \quad w = pq(l,c,n) - (p_l l + p_c c + p_n n).$$

The first-order conditions for maximum profit are:

$$p\frac{\partial q}{\partial l} = p_l, \quad p\frac{\partial q}{\partial c} = p_c, \quad p\frac{\partial q}{\partial n} = p_n.$$

This means that the value of the marginal productivity of each production factor must equal its price.

I take the case of the Cobb-Douglas production function as an example:

$$\frac{\partial q}{\partial l} = \alpha\beta l^{\beta-1} c^{\gamma} n^{\delta} = \frac{p_l}{p},$$

$$\frac{\partial q}{\partial c} = \alpha\gamma l^{\beta} c^{\gamma-1} n^{\delta} = \frac{p_c}{p},$$

$$\frac{\partial q}{\partial n} = \alpha\delta l^{\beta} c^{\gamma} n^{\delta-1} = \frac{p_n}{p}.$$

After multiplying the first equation by l, the second by c, and the third by n and substituting q for $\alpha l^{\beta} c^{\gamma} n^{\delta}$, I can write:

$$l=\frac{\beta pq}{p_l},\qquad c=\frac{\gamma pq}{p_c},\qquad n=\frac{\delta pq}{p_n}.$$

These values can be substituted in the production function, which will give:

$$q=\alpha\left(\frac{\beta pq}{p_l}\right)^{\beta}\left(\frac{\gamma pq}{p_c}\right)^{\gamma}\left(\frac{\delta pq}{p_n}\right)^{\delta},\qquad \text{so:}$$

$$q=\alpha^{\frac{1}{1-\beta-\gamma-\delta}}\left(\frac{\beta p}{p_l}\right)^{\frac{\beta}{1-\beta-\gamma-\delta}}\left(\frac{\gamma p}{p_c}\right)^{\frac{\gamma}{1-\beta-\gamma-\delta}}\left(\frac{\delta p}{p_n}\right)^{\frac{\delta}{1-\beta-\gamma-\delta}}.$$

It can be proved that this q only represents a maximum in the case of decreasing returns to scale $(\beta+\gamma+\delta<1)$.[3]

I will now prove that income distribution, in this case the distribution of income over production factors within a firm, can be explained by the value of the marginal productivity of the production factors only when there are no economies of scale. The shares of labour $\psi=(lp_l)/(pq)$, capital $\chi=(cp_c)/(pq)$ and nature $\upsilon=(np_n)/(pq)$ are, respectively:

$$\psi=\frac{lp(\partial q/\partial l)}{pq}=\frac{lp\alpha\beta l^{\beta-1}c^{\gamma}n^{\delta}}{p\alpha l^{\beta}c^{\gamma}n^{\delta}}=\beta,$$

$$\chi=\frac{cp(\partial q/\partial c)}{pq}=\frac{cp\alpha\gamma l^{\beta}c^{\gamma-1}n^{\delta}}{p\alpha l^{\beta}c^{\gamma}n^{\delta}}=\gamma,$$

$$\upsilon=\frac{np(\partial q/\partial n)}{pq}=\frac{np\alpha\delta l^{\beta}c^{\gamma}n^{\delta-1}}{p\alpha l^{\beta}c^{\gamma}n^{\delta}}=\delta.$$

If $\beta+\gamma+\delta=1$, which means that there are no economies of scale, gross revenue pq is completely distributed over production factors. If $\beta+\gamma+\delta<1$, which means that there are decreasing returns to scale, then, if each production factor is paid for the rest (profit) remains. If $\beta+\gamma+\delta>1$, which means increasing returns to scale, then a loss remains if each production factor is paid according to its value of marginal productivity.

3 In case of increasing returns, one will find a maximum loss. In the case of no economies of scale, the profit will always be 0 in the optimum, because at each scale of production gross revenue (pq) will be completely allocated to the production factors.

Constraint on the use of nature

Environmental problems occur when natural resources are overused. Then two types of policies may be prescribed, namely a directly regulated use of nature or a fee to be paid by the users of nature. I start with the direct regulation. It is assumed that the use of nature is restricted to ω. The problem can be described as follows:

$$\text{Max} \quad q = \alpha l^{\beta} c^{\gamma} \omega^{\delta},$$

$$b = p_l l + p_c c + p_n \omega,$$

The solution to this problem is:

$$l = \frac{\beta}{(\beta + \gamma) p_l}(b - p_n \omega), \quad c = \frac{\gamma}{(\beta + \gamma) p_c}(b - p_n \omega), \quad n = \omega.$$

Assume: $b = 1000$, $p_l = 2$ $p_c = 1$, $p_n = 4$, $\alpha = 10$, $\beta = 0.25$, $\gamma = 0.25$, $\delta = 0.5$, $\omega = 50$. The results of this example are:

$$l = \frac{0.25}{(0.25 + 0.25) \times 2} \times (1000 - 4 \times 50) = 200,$$

$$c = \frac{0.25}{(0.25 + 0.25) \times 1} \times (1000 - 4 \times 50) = 400,$$

$$n = 50, \quad q = 10 \times 200^{0.25} 400^{0.25} 50^{0.5} = 1189.21.$$

When a fee is used to reach the same result, in the absence of economies of scale $(\beta + \gamma + \delta = 1)$, and with f for the fee, the solution is:[4]

$$l = \frac{\beta b}{p_l}, \quad c = \frac{\gamma b}{p_c}, \quad \omega = \frac{\delta b}{(p_n + f)} \quad \text{so:} \quad f = \frac{\delta b - p_n \omega}{\omega}.$$

In my example the results in case of a fee are:

4 This is the double dividend solution.

$$l = \frac{0.25 \times 1000}{2} = 125,$$

$$c = \frac{0.25 \times 1000}{1} = 250,$$

$$n = 50,$$

$$q = 10 \times 125^{0.25} \times 250^{0.25} \times 50^{0.5} = 940.15,$$

$$f = \frac{0.5 \times 1000 - 4 \times 50}{50} = 6.$$

With a compensated fee, which means that the government uses the fee for a subsidy s on, for example, labour, under the condition of budget neutrality, the solution is:

$$l = \frac{\beta b}{p_l - s}, \quad c = \frac{\gamma b}{p_c}, \quad f = \frac{\delta b - p_n \omega}{\omega}, \quad \omega f = s l, \quad \text{so:}$$

$$s l = \delta b - p_n \omega, \quad \text{so:}$$

$$l = \frac{(\beta + \delta) b - p_n \omega}{p_l}, \quad s = \frac{(\delta b - p_n \omega) p_l}{(\beta + \delta) b - p_n \omega}.$$

The results for my example are:

$$l = \frac{(0.25 + 0.50) \times 1000 - 4 \times 50}{2} = 275,$$

$$c = \frac{0.25 \times 1000}{1} = 250, \quad n = 50,$$

$$q = 10 \times 275^{0.25} \times 250^{0.25} \times 50^{0.5} = 1144.99,$$

$$f = \frac{0.5 \times 1000 - 4 \times 50}{50} = 6, \quad s = \frac{(0.5 \times 1000 - 4 \times 50) \times 2}{(0.25 + 0.5) \times 1000 - 4 \times 50} = 1.09.$$

Fee

A fee can be calculated if the monetary value of the environmental damage is known. Assume, for example, that the production function of a certain production process has only one variable production factor: nature. So: $q = q(n)$, with $dq/dn > 0$ and $d^2q/dn^2 < 0$. Price p of the product is assumed to be fixed. The cost k consists of the costs for the use of nature, which equals the fixed price for nature p_n multiplied by n plus the fixed costs c_f for the other production factors, labour and capital. Now profit w equals:

$$w = pq(n) - p_n n - c_f.$$

Profit is maximized if:

$$\frac{dw}{dn} = p\frac{dq}{dn} - p_n = 0, \quad \text{or:} \quad \frac{dq}{dn} = \frac{p_n}{p}.$$

Environmental damage e is assumed to be a linear function of the use of nature n: $e = \upsilon n \ (\upsilon > 0)$. If the firm must pay for environmental damage, the profit function is:

$$w = pq(n) - p_n n - c_f - \upsilon n.$$

Now profit is maximized if:

$$\frac{dw}{dn} = p\frac{dq}{dn} - p_n - \upsilon = 0, \quad \text{so:} \quad \frac{dq}{dn} = \frac{p_n + \upsilon}{p}.$$

This implies that production q will be lower than in a situation where environmental costs are not considered. However, one has to realize that a necessary condition for charging a fee is that the monetary value of the environmental damage has to be known. This assumption is not often met in real life.

As an example, I take:

$$q = -0.25n^2 + 10n, \quad p = 20, \quad c_f = 500, \quad p_n = 50, \quad e = 20n.$$

Now, the profit functions w_1 and w_2 with externalities excluded and included respectively are:

$$w_1 = -5n^2 + 200n - 500 - 50n = -5n^2 + 150n - 500,$$

$$w_2 = -5n^2 + 200n - 500 - 50n - 20n = -5n^2 + 130n - 500.$$

The optimum inputs for the two cases are respectively:

$$\frac{dw_1}{dn} = -10n + 150 = 0, \quad \text{so:} \quad n_1^* = 15,$$

$$\frac{dw_2}{dn} = -10n + 130 = 0, \quad \text{so:} \quad n_2^* = 13.$$

Figure 2.1 presents the two cases.

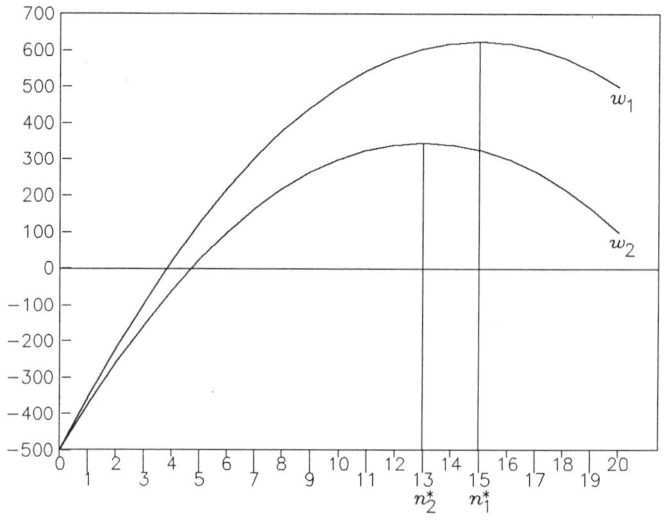

Figure 2.1: Optimum input of nature with externalities excluded and included.

3. ANALYSIS OF COSTS AND SUPPLY FUNCTION

Definition of costs and break-even point

Costs are values sacrificed in order to gain benefits. They can be divided into *fixed costs* c_f and *variable costs* c_v. Fixed costs do not vary with the quantity of production q, while variable costs do. Total costs c are the sum of fixed and variable costs. Now, suppose variable costs are a linear increasing function of production. In this case we can state:

$$c_v = \mu q, \quad c_f = \xi, \quad \text{so:} \quad c = \mu q + \xi, \quad \mu, \ \xi > 0.$$

Turnover o equals price p times production q: [1]

$$o = pq.$$

Profit w equals turnover minus total costs:

$$w = o - c.$$

Now I want to know the minimum volume of production necessary in order to avoid a loss, which means: $w = 0$. I can solve this problem easily by substitution:

$$pq - \mu q - \xi = 0, \quad \text{so:} \quad q = \frac{\xi}{p - \mu}.$$

This value is called *break-even point*. If production is less than this value, the firm will incur a loss; if higher, it will make a profit. Figure 3.1 shows the break-even point indicated by q^*.

Marginal costs and profit maximization

Apart from variable costs and fixed costs, we also have *marginal costs*. Marginal costs are the costs of one extra "unit" of production. In the analysis of costs we generally use a law which says that marginal costs tend to decrease when production is relatively low, and increase when production is relatively large. The following polynomial function of degree three has this necessary property:

---

1 It is assumed that p is independent of q.

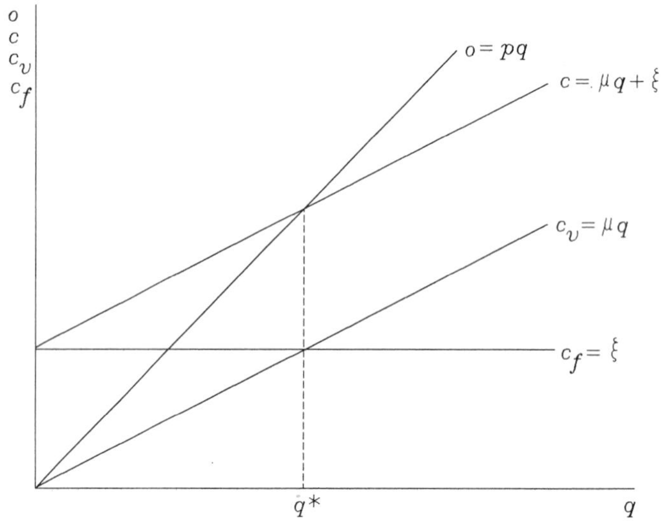

Figure 3.1: Break-even point.

$$c = \alpha q^3 - \beta q^2 + \gamma q + \xi, \quad \alpha, \beta, \gamma > 0.$$

For this function, *average total costs* $\tilde{c}$, *average variable costs* $\tilde{c}_v$, marginal costs c_m, fixed costs c_f and *average fixed costs* $\tilde{c}_f$ are as follows:

$$\tilde{c} = \frac{c}{q} = \alpha q^2 - \beta q + \gamma + \frac{\xi}{q},$$

$$\tilde{c}_v = \frac{c_v}{q} = \alpha q^2 - \beta q + \gamma,$$

$$c_m = \frac{dc}{dq} = 3\alpha q^2 - 2\beta q + \gamma,$$

$$c_f = \xi,$$

$$\tilde{c}_f = \frac{\xi}{q}.$$

We assume a fixed price level p. Assuming that firms are seeking to maximise their profits, the question is at what level of production profit is maximal. I know:

Max $w = o - c$, so:

$$\frac{dw}{dq} = \frac{do}{dq} - \frac{dc}{dq} = 0, \quad \text{or:} \quad \frac{do}{dq} = \frac{dc}{dq}.$$

This means that in order to make maximum profit, marginal revenue o_m (do/dq) must equal marginal costs c_m (dc/dq). Because we assumed a fixed price, it follows that for maximum profit:

$$p = 3\alpha q^2 - 2\beta q + \gamma.$$

This parabolic function has the following roots:

$$q_{1,2} = \frac{2\beta \pm \sqrt{4\beta^2 - 12\alpha(\gamma - p)}}{6\alpha}.$$

Only a positive root has an economic meaning.

Supply function

If the price rises, the volume of production will be greater as well. In fact, the c_m - function represents the mathematical relation between price and quantity for the individual firm. That is why this function can be called the supply function for the individual firm.

The c_m - function intersects the $\tilde{c}_v$ - and $\tilde{c}$ - function at its minimum. For the $\tilde{c}_v$ - function this can be proved as follows. First, it holds that

$$\tilde{c}_v = \frac{c - \xi}{q},$$

$$c_m = \frac{dc}{dq}.$$

Minimizing $\tilde{c}_v$ implies:

$$\frac{d\tilde{c}_v}{dq} = \frac{d\frac{(c-\xi)}{q}}{dq} = \frac{\frac{dc}{dq}q - (c - \xi)}{q^2} = 0, \quad \text{so:}$$

$$\frac{dc}{dq} = \frac{c - \xi}{q} = \tilde{c}_v(\min).$$

For the specified function:

$$\frac{d\tilde{c}_v}{dq} = 2\alpha q - \beta = 0, \quad \text{so:} \quad q^* = \frac{\beta}{2\alpha}.$$

Substitution of this value for q in the c_m – function as well as in the $\tilde{c}_v$ – function gives:

$$\tilde{c}_v = \alpha\left(\frac{\beta}{2\alpha}\right)^2 - \beta\left(\frac{\beta}{2\alpha}\right) + \gamma,$$

$$c_m = 3\alpha\left(\frac{\beta}{2\alpha}\right)^2 - 2\beta\left(\frac{\beta}{2\alpha}\right) + \gamma, \quad \text{so:}$$

$$\tilde{c}_v - c_m = -2\alpha\left(\frac{\beta}{2\alpha}\right)^2 + \beta\left(\frac{\beta}{2\alpha}\right) = \frac{\beta}{2\alpha}\left(\beta - 2\alpha\frac{\beta}{2\alpha}\right) = 0.$$

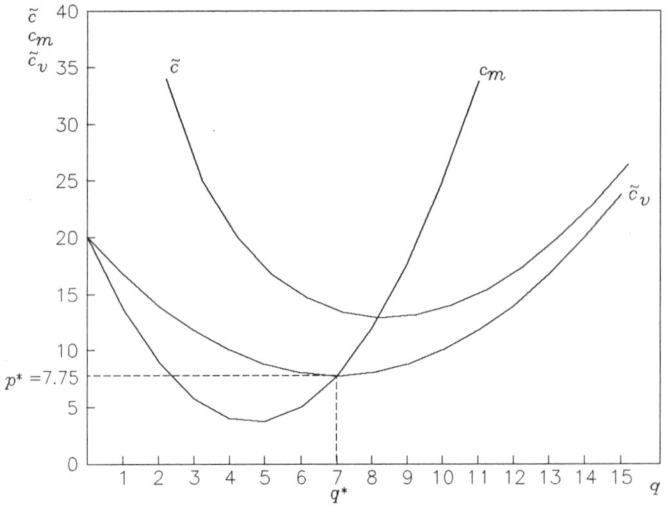

Figure 3.2: Shut-down point and individual supply curve.[2]

2 $\tilde{c} = 0.25q^2 - 3.5q + 20 + \frac{40}{q},$

$\tilde{c}_v = 0.25q^2 - 3.5q + 20,$

$c_m = 0.75q^2 - 7q + 20.$

Now, if price is lower than the average variable cost, the firm will cease production. This point is called the *shut-down point*. Therefore, only the part of the c_m – function above the intersection at the $\tilde{c}_v$ – curve represents the supply function for the individual firm. Figure 3.2 shows the shut-down point, which is indicated by q^* and p^*.

For reasons of simplicity, a linear rising supply curve is often used:

$$q^s = \gamma p + \delta,$$

Here q^s indicates the supply of a good. The collective supply function can be found by totalling all individual supply functions. For example, in the case of only two individual supply functions, the collective one can be found as follows:

$$q_1^s = \gamma_1 p + \delta_1,$$

$$q_2^s = \gamma_2 p + \delta_2, \quad \text{so:}$$

$$q^s = q_1^s + q_2^s = (\gamma_1 + \gamma_2)p + \delta_1 + \delta_2 = \gamma p + \delta,$$

$$\text{with: } \gamma = \gamma_1 + \gamma_2, \quad \delta = \delta_1 + \delta_2.$$

Finally, the price elasticity of a collective supply function can be defined as:

$$\eta^s = \frac{dq^s}{dp}\frac{p}{q^s}.$$

Environmental policy

A government has two strategies available to reduce environmental damage: by reducing the polluting input via direct regulations (command and control measures), or by way of a tax. There are two types of taxes: a *specific* tax that increases marginal costs by a fixed amount, and an *ad valorem* tax that increases marginal costs by a percentage. First, consider two situations with a fixed price p and two supply functions, one without a specific tax f and one with a specific tax. The two optima (q_1, q_2), defined as price (marginal revenue) equals supply function (marginal costs), can be computed as follows:

$$p = \gamma q_1 + \delta, \quad p = \gamma q_2 + \delta + f, \quad p, q_1, q_2, \delta, f > 0,$$

$$q_1 = \frac{p - \delta}{\gamma}, \quad q_2 = \frac{p - \delta - f}{\gamma}, \quad \text{so:} \quad q_1 - q_2 = \frac{f}{\gamma}.$$

So, the producers' reactions depend very much on the value of γ. Figure 3.3 demonstrates how the tax works assuming that price does not change. In this specific case:

$$p = 0.5q + 2, \quad p = 6, \quad f = 2.$$

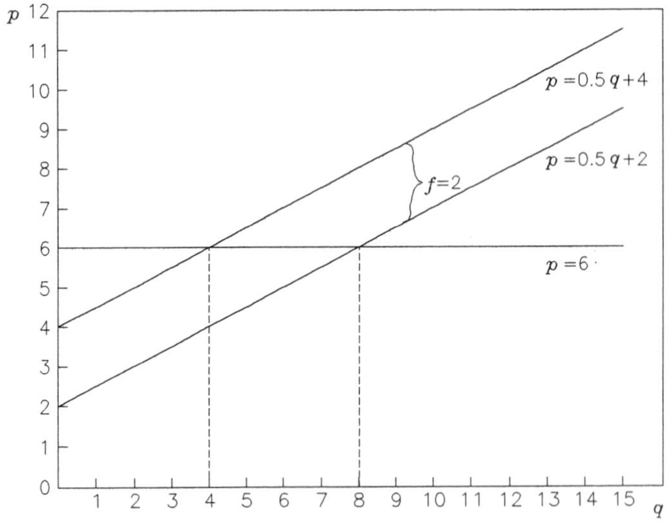

Figure 3.3: Effect of a specific tax.

Second, if the tax is a percentage h of the costs (*ad valorem* tax), then, assuming a zero price change for the consumer, the effect is calculated, with the help of the supply elasticity η^s, as follows (with p_1 and q_1 for the net price and supply without the tax, and p_2 and q_2 for the net price and supply with the tax):

$$\eta^s = \frac{\Delta q}{\Delta p}\frac{p_1}{q_1},$$

$$\Delta p = p_2 - p_1 = (1-h)p_1 - p_1 = -hp_1,$$

$$\Delta q = q_2 - q_1,$$

$$\eta^s = \frac{\Delta q}{q_1}\frac{p_1}{\Delta p} = \frac{\Delta q}{q_1}\left(\frac{p_1}{-hp_1}\right) = \frac{\Delta q}{q_1}\left(\frac{1}{-h}\right), \quad \text{so:} \quad \frac{\Delta q}{q_1} = -\eta^s h.$$

We conclude that the higher the supply elasticity, the greater is the effect of the tax.

The effect of an ad valorum tax is now illustrated with an example. Assume the following supply curve and price: $q = 0.5p + 2,\ \ p = 10$. The equilibrium supply equals: $0.5 \times 10 + 2 = 7$. The supply elasticity at that level equals:

$$\eta^s = \frac{dq}{dp}\frac{p}{q} = 0.5 \times \frac{10}{7} = 0.714.$$

Now, assume a tax for the producer of 10%. This means:

$$\frac{\Delta q}{q} = -0.714 \times 0.1 = -0.071 \ \ (-7.1\%).$$

So, the equilibrium amount will decrease from 7 to $0.929 \times 7 = 6.50$.

4. MARKET EQUILIBRIUM, TAXATION AND MARKET DYNAMICS

Market equilibrium

The collective supply function and the collective demand function together can provide a market equilibrium. Market equilibrium can be defined as a situation in which both consumers and producers are satisfied with price and quantity, so that demand equals supply. In the case of linear demand and supply functions, market equilibrium for good A can be determined as follows:

$$a^d(p_a) = -\alpha p_a + \beta,$$

$$a^s(p_a) = \gamma p_a + \delta,$$

$$a^d(p_a) = a^s(p_a), \quad \text{so:}$$

$$p_a^* = \frac{\beta - \delta}{\gamma + \alpha}, \quad a^* = \frac{\beta\gamma + \alpha\delta}{\gamma + \alpha}.$$

$\beta > \delta, \quad \alpha, \beta, \gamma > 0.$

a^d	Collective demand for A
a^s	Collective supply of A
p_a	Price of A
$\alpha, \beta, \gamma, \delta$	Coefficients

If we assume, for example, that $\alpha = 0.5$, $\beta = 20$, $\gamma = 0.5$, and $\delta = 1$, then the values of a and p_a can be computed: $a^* = 10.5$, $p_a^* = 19$. This is illustrated in Figure 4.1.

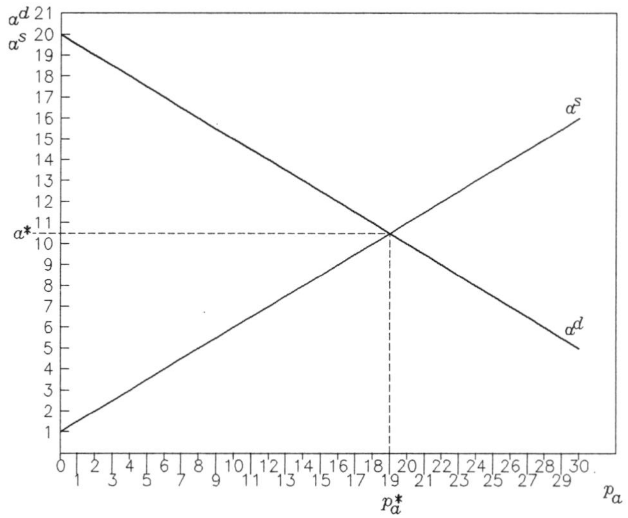

Figure 4.1: Market equilibrium.

Sometimes a government may decide to introduce maximum or minimum prices. Assume, for example, that the minimum price level is fixed at 22. This price level will result in excess supply. This excess c can be computed as follows:

$$c = a^s(22) - a^d(22) = (0.5 \cdot 22 + 1) - (-0.5 \cdot 22 + 20) = 3.$$

This is shown in Figure 4.2.

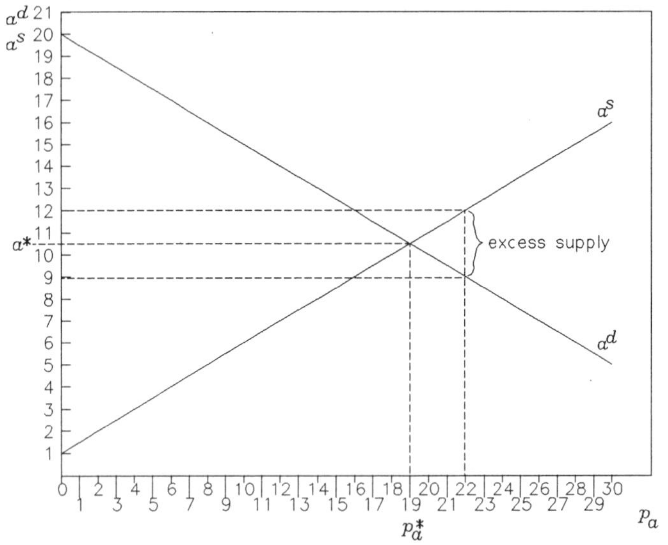

Figure 4.2: Market with fixed minimum price level.

If the maximum price is set below the equilibrium level, there will be excess demand.

Taxation and the Coase theorem

Figure 4.3 shows the effect of a *specific tax* b on equilibrium price and equilibrium quantity. We see that because of the tax b, the supply curve a moves up to a'. As a result price increases from p_0 to p_1 and quantity changes from q_0 to q_1. It appears that price increases by AB and not by AC, which is the entire amount of the tax b. This is because the producers also pay a part of the tax (BC). The proportion of the tax paid by consumers and by producers depends on the steepness of demand and supply curves. If, for example, the demand curve is completely inelastic (v'), price increases by AC, which means that the consumers will pay the whole tax.[1]

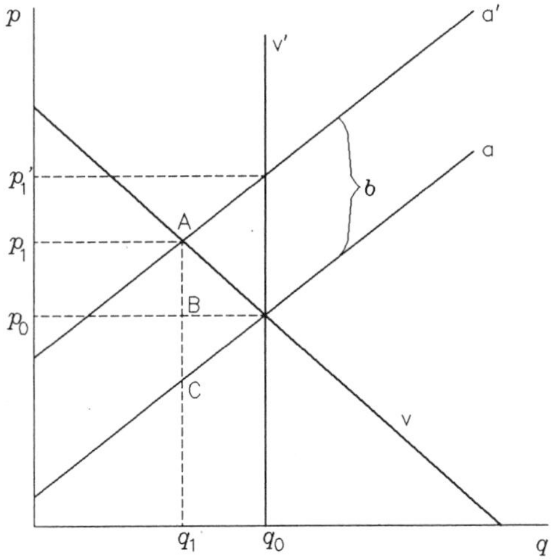

Figure 4.3: Effect of a specific tax.

I continue with the introduction of a cost-increasing *ad valorem* tax in the market system. First, I derive the basis for the analysis, with a^s for the supply of Good A, η^s for the supply elasticity, H for the tax in money units, h for the *ad valorem* tax, and t for time. Further, variables with a bar are indicating relative changes.[2]

$$a^s = a^s(p_a(t), H(t)),$$

$$\frac{da^s}{dt} = \frac{\partial a^s}{\partial p_a}\frac{dp_a}{dt} + \frac{\partial a^s}{\partial H}\frac{dH}{dt},$$

$$\frac{da^s}{dt}\frac{1}{a^s} = \frac{\partial a^s}{\partial p_a}\frac{1}{a^s}\frac{dp_a}{dt} + \frac{\partial a^s}{\partial H}\frac{1}{a^s}\frac{dH}{dt}, \quad \text{so:}$$

$$\bar{a}^s = \eta^s \bar{p}_a + \frac{\partial a^s}{\partial H}\frac{p_a}{a^s}\frac{dH}{dt}\frac{1}{p_a}.$$

1 Now one observes a paradox, if the tax is levied in order to decrease consumption and production of a certain good. On the one hand, if price goes up by the entire amount of the tax, quantity remains the same and the target of the policy is not reached. On the other hand, if price remains the same after tax, quantity will be decreased to the maximum extent. This means that the policy measure is more effective when the price impact is least.

2 $\bar{x} = \frac{dx}{dt}\frac{1}{x}$.

We know that:

$$\frac{\partial a^s}{\partial H} = -\frac{\partial a^s}{\partial p_a}, \text{ and } \frac{dH}{dt}\frac{1}{p_a} = h.$$

So:

$$a^s = \eta^s \bar{p}_a - \eta^s h = \eta^s(\bar{p}_a - h).$$

The effects of an ad valorem tax depend very much upon the elasticities of supply and demand, as is shown in the following analysis with η^s for the price elasticity of supply, η^d for the price elasticity of demand, a^s for the amount supplied of good A, and a^d for the demand for good A.[3] First assume that the producer pays the tax.

$$\bar{a}^s = \eta^s(\bar{p}_a - h), \quad \eta^s > 0,$$

$$\bar{a}^d = \eta^d \bar{p}_a, \quad \eta^d < 0,$$

$$\bar{a}^s = \bar{a}^d, \quad \text{so:}$$

$$\bar{p}_a = \frac{\eta^s}{\eta^s - \eta^d} h, \quad \bar{a} = \bar{a}^s = \bar{a}^d = \frac{\eta^d \eta^s}{\eta^s - \eta^d} h.$$

In the appendix it is shown how high the tax should be if the government wants to reach a certain policy target, assuming that the consumer is not only influenced by the price of the good but also by his income and the price of a substitute.

In the second case assume that the consumer pays the tax:

$$\bar{a}^s = \eta^s \bar{p}_a, \quad \eta^s > 0,$$

$$\bar{a}^d = \eta^d(\bar{p}_a + h), \quad \eta^d < 0,$$

$$\bar{a}^s = \bar{a}^d, \quad \text{so:}$$

$$\bar{p}_a = \frac{\eta^d}{\eta^s - \eta^d} h, \quad \bar{a} = \bar{a}^s = \bar{a}^d = \frac{\eta^d \eta^s}{\eta^s - \eta^d} h.$$

The result implies that the effect of a levy is the same in both cases. It does not make a difference whether the consumer or the producer pays the tax.

---

3 In contrast with the tax in Chapter 3, in this case the demand function is not perfectly elastic.

A similar situation occurs in the case of the so-called *Coase theorem*.[4] Here there are two users of the same resource (for example fishermen and a paper mill using the same lake). If nobody owns the lake, no costs are incurred by the paper mill using the water. This means that the mill will extend its water use till the marginal benefits are zero. If the mill owns the lake, fishermen may buy off part of the pollution. They will do this till the marginal benefit of the less polluted water for the fishermen equals the mill's marginal benefit of polluting the water. If the fishermen own the lake, the mill has to buy the right to pollute the water. In this case the mill will buy pollution rights till the marginal benefits of polluting the water equal the marginal costs of doing so.

The conclusion is that the optimum will be the same in both cases. This means that, speaking from the viewpoint of environmental protection, it does not matter who owns the property rights. It only matters whether property rights exist or not. However, the problem of the transaction costs remains. In the case described there has to be a negotiating process resulting in a transaction between the mill and the fishermen.

The mathematical analysis of the Coase theorem is simple. Assume the marginal benefits of pollution b_p^m to be a decreasing function of the pollution e itself, while marginal benefits of clean water b_c^m is a rising function of pollution e, for example:

$$b_p^m = -\alpha e + \beta \quad \alpha, \beta > 0,$$

$$b_c^m = \gamma e + \delta \quad \gamma > 0, \quad 0 < \delta < \beta.$$

In equilibrium: $b_p^m = b_c^m$, so:

$$e = \frac{\delta - \beta}{-\alpha - \gamma}.$$

If there are no property rights, the mill will pollute the water till $b_p^m = 0$.

$$-\alpha e + \beta = 0, \quad \text{so: } e = \frac{\beta}{\alpha}.$$

In that case, pollution will be much more. Assume, for example, $\alpha = 0.5$, $\beta = 20$, $\gamma = 1$, $\delta = 1$. The optimum pollution point lies at:

$$e = \frac{1 - 20}{-0.5 - 1} = \frac{19}{1.5} = 12.67.$$

---

4 R. Coase, 1960. The problem of social cost. *Journal of law and economics,* 3, October, pp. 1-44.

If there are no property rights:

$$e = \frac{20}{0.5} = 40.$$

In Figure 4.4 this situation is depicted.

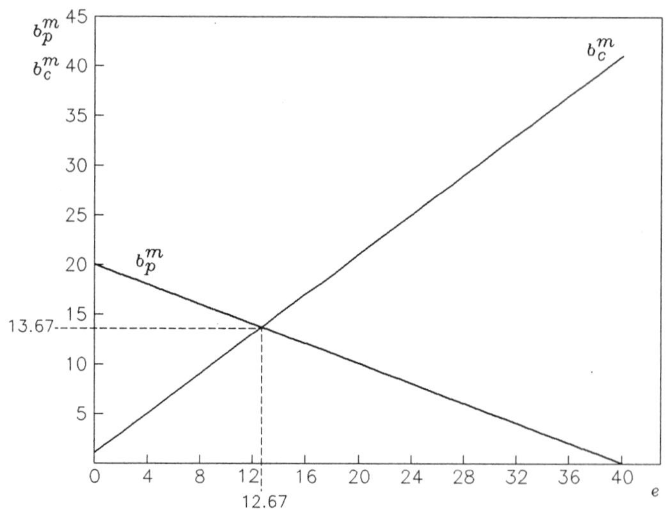

Figure 4.4: Coase theorem.

Market dynamics

To explain price movements I use the following model with q for quantity, p for price and α, β, δ, χ and ρ for coefficients:[5]

$$q_t^d = \alpha p_t + \beta \quad \text{demand} \quad \alpha < 0, \quad \beta > 0.$$

$$q_t^s = \gamma[p_{t-1} - \rho(p_{t-1} - p_{t-2}^x)] + \delta \quad \text{supply} \quad \gamma > 0, \quad \delta < \beta.$$

For a state of equilibrium ($q_t^s = q_t^d$), the following second order difference equation can be derived:

5 R.H. Coase and R.F. Fowler, 1935. Bacon production and the pig-cycle in Great Britain. *Economica,* 2, May, pp. 142-167; J. Tinbergen, 1943. *Economische bewegingsleer*. Noord-Hollandsche Uitgevers Maatschappij, Amsterdam; R.M. Goodwin, 1947. Dynamical coupling with especial reference to markets having production lags. *Econometrica,* 15, nr 3, pp. 181-204; R.G.D. Allen, 1973 (1956). *Mathematical economics*. MacMillan, London.

$$p_t = \frac{\gamma(1-\rho)}{\alpha} p_{t-1} + \frac{\gamma\rho}{\alpha} p_{t-2}^{\chi} + \frac{\delta-\beta}{\alpha}. \tag{1}$$

For the time being $\chi = 1$. If ρ equals zero, the result is a simple cobweb model with the following difference equation relating to price development:

$$p_t = \frac{\gamma}{\alpha} p_{t-1} + \frac{\delta-\beta}{\alpha}. \tag{2}$$

Assume that the values of the coefficients are as follows: $\rho = 0$, $\gamma = 0.5$, $\alpha = -0.8$, $\delta = 10$ and $\beta = 18$. In this case the difference equation is:

$$p_t = -0.625 p_{t-1} + 10.$$

This equation is graphically presented in Figure 4.5.

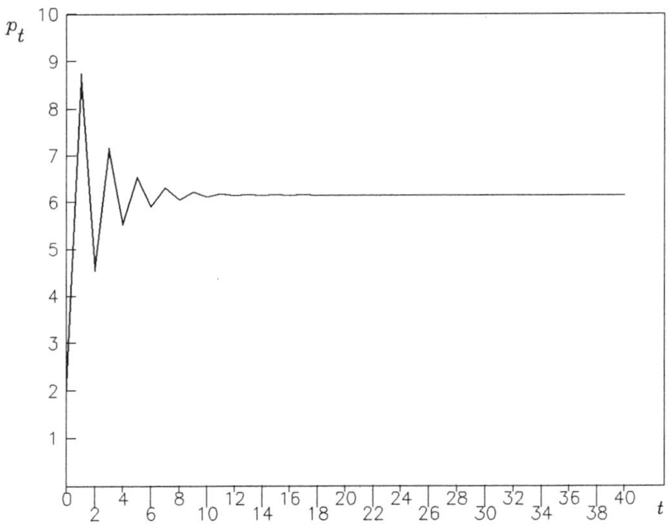

Figure 4.5: Cobweb model with $\rho = 0$, starting value $p_0 = 2$.

As can be seen from Figure 4.5, the difference equation (2) is asymptotically stable. This occurs because $|\gamma/\alpha| < 1$. If $|\gamma/\alpha| = 1$ constant oscillations occur, and if $|\gamma/\alpha| > 1$, there will be an explosion.

In the simple model on the supply side, the price valid in the previous period is expected to continue. In fact it is assumed that suppliers never learn. In the extended model above, the suppliers have a more enduring memory. Here it is assumed that expectations on the supply side are influenced by experience. The *experience coefficient* is ρ. Normally ρ will have a value between zero and one, and then price will move in the direction opposite to that of the previous period. Of course ρ can also be negative, in which case on the supply side a continuation of the price movement is expected. If $\rho \neq 0$, I can write difference equation (1) as follows:

$$p_t = \frac{\gamma(1-\rho)}{\alpha} p_{t-1} + \frac{\gamma\rho}{\alpha} p_{t-2} + \frac{\delta - \beta}{\alpha}. \qquad (3)$$

The result is a second order difference equation. If I substitute $\rho = 0.2$, $\gamma = 0.5$, $\alpha = -0.8$, $\delta = 10$ and $\beta = 18$ equation (3) can be written as:

$$p_t = -0.5 p_{t-1} - 0.125 p_{t-2} + 10.$$

This equation is depicted in Figure 4.6.

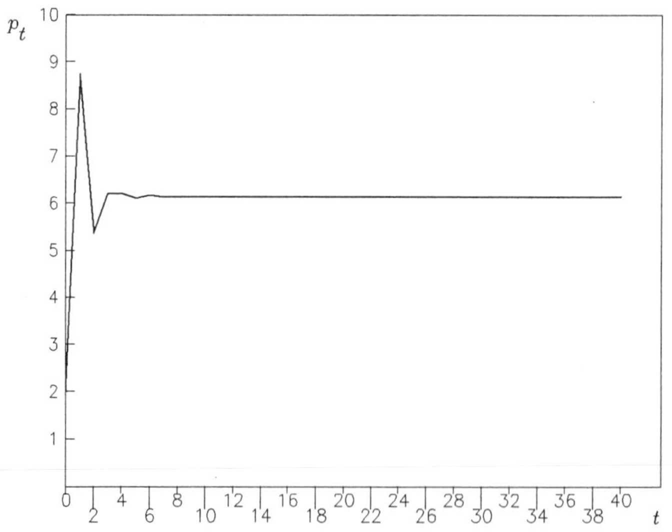

Figure 4.6: Cobweb model with experience coefficient $\rho = 0.2$, starting values p_{-1} and p_0 equal 2.

As can be concluded from Figure 4.6, in this specific case, the difference equation is asymptotically stable. Depending on the values of the coefficients, the equation may be asymptotically stable, explode or show constant oscillations.

Assume that $\chi \neq 1$. Then, we get (1). With $\chi = 2$, $\rho = 0.2$, $\gamma = 0.5$, $\alpha = -0.8$, $\delta = 10$ and $\beta = 18$ the difference equation now becomes quadratic:

$$p_t = -0.5 p_{t-1} - 0.125 p_{t-2}^2 + 10.$$

The graph of this difference equation is presented in Figure 4.7. It can be concluded from this graph that, in this case, price is chaotic. This picture probably gives a fairly adequate description of many real world price patterns.

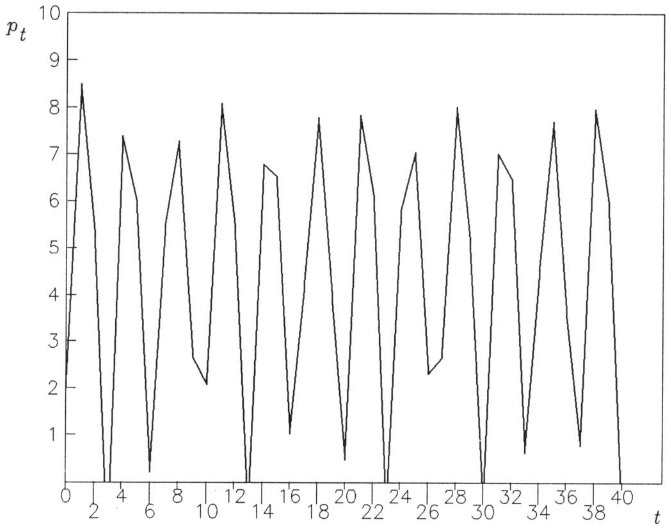

Figure 4.7: Nonlinear cobweb model with experience coefficient $\rho = 0.2$, starting values p_{-1} and p_0 equal 2.

It is also possible to show the effects of a minimum price policy. Assume that the minimum price equals 2.[6] Figure 4.8 shows the ensuing result.

Appendix

Assume the following demand and supply functions (see also Chapter 1 for the demand function) for a good that has only one substitute (for example the private car i versus public transport j):[7]

6 This means that for every price below 2, 2 is substituted for the price.
7 The superfixes d and s refer to demand and supply respectively.

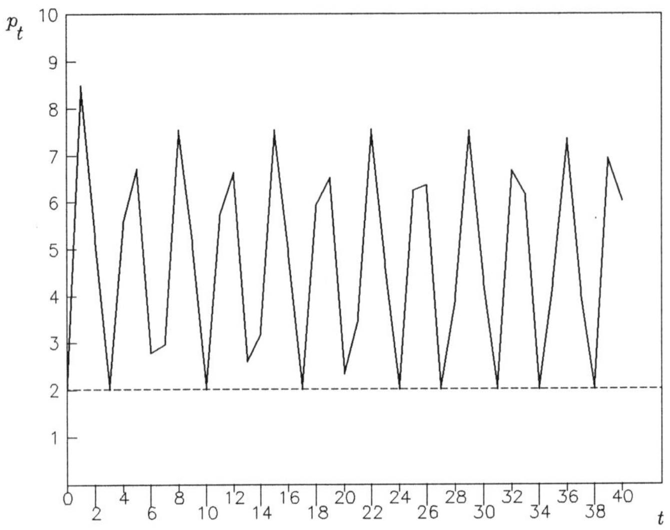

Figure 4.8: Nonlinear cobweb model with experience coefficient $\rho = 0.2$, starting values p_{-1} and p_0 equal 2 and a minimum price of 2.

$$\bar{x}_i^d = \eta_i^d \bar{p}_i + \eta_i^y \bar{y} + \eta_i^j \bar{p}_j, \quad \eta_i^d < 0, \quad \eta_i^y > 0, \eta_i^j > 0,$$

$$\bar{x}_i^s = \eta_i^s (\bar{p}_i - h),$$

$$\bar{x}_i^d = \bar{x}_i^s.$$

So:

$$\bar{p}_i = \frac{\bar{x}_i + \eta_i^s h}{\eta_i^s}, \quad \text{so: } \bar{x}_i = \frac{\eta_i^d \bar{x}_i + \eta_i^d \eta_i^s h}{\eta_i^s} + \eta_i^y \bar{y} + \eta_i^j \bar{p}_j,$$

and:

$$\bar{x}_i = \frac{\eta_i^d \eta_i^s}{\eta_i^s - \eta_i^d} h + \frac{\eta_i^y \eta_i^s}{\eta_i^s - \eta_i^d} \bar{y} + \frac{\eta_i^j \eta_i^s}{\eta_i^s - \eta_i^d} \bar{p}_j.$$

Assume for example that the policy target is to reduce the private car use by 10%, so: $\bar{x}_i = -10\%$. Further we assume the following values:

$$\bar{y} = 3.5\%, \quad \bar{p}_j = 10\%, \quad \eta_i^d = -0.5, \quad \eta_i^s = 0.5, \quad \eta_i^y = 0.25, \quad \eta_i^j = 0.25.$$

Now we can compute:

$-10 = -0.25 \times h + 0.125 \times 3.5 + 0.125 \times 10$, so: $h = 33.25$.

The conclusion is that in this example the government should tax the private car use by 33.25% in order to reduce it by 10%.

5. GENERAL EQUILIBRIUM THEORY[1]

Developing a general equilibrium scheme

A model in which a number of consumers demand a number of goods from a number of producers, and where the quantities of production factors are given, is called a general equilibrium model. Such a model allows the study of how production factors are allocated if the consumer's aim is utility maximization and the producer's aim is profit maximization.

Assume that there are r consumers, s goods and t production factors. A model like that is called an $r \times s \times t$-model.

As an example I take a model with only one consumer, two goods, 1 and 2, with quantities x_1 and x_2, and two production factors: nature n and labour l. These two production factors are considered the original production factors, while capital is only a derivative of labour and nature.[2] The model can now be formulated as follows:

For the utility function, I use a Cobb-Douglas utility function:

$$u = x_1^{0.5} x_2^{0.5}.$$

For the production functions also Cobb-Douglas functions are used:

$$x_1 = 10 l_1^{0.25} n_1^{0.75},$$

$$x_2 = 10 l_2^{0.75} n_2^{0.25}.$$

I know that the consumer has quantities of nature and labour that he/she allocates to the production process of good 1, n_1 and l_1 respectively and good 2, n_2 and l_2 respectively:

$$l = l_1 + l_2,$$

$$n = n_1 + n_2.$$

The quantities of nature and labour are known:

---

1 This chapter leans heavily on: Dietz F.J. (ed.), W.J.M. Heijman and E.P. Kroese, 1996. *Micro-economie: aanvullingen en uitwerkingen,* Aanvulling 7: Constructie van een algemeen evenwichtsmodel. Stenfert Kroese, Houten, the Netherlands.

2 Böhm-Bawerk E., 1921 (1889, 4th ed.). *Kapital und Kapitalzins,* Part II-1: Positive Theorie des Kapitales, and Part II-2: Exkurse. Gustav Fischer, Jena.

$$l = 300,$$

$$n = 600.$$

Then, consumer's income y equals:

$$y = 600\,p_n + 300\,p_l,$$

where p_n and p_l for the price of nature and the price of labour respectively. Utility maximization gives the following demand functions for goods:

$$x_1 = \frac{0.5y}{p_1},$$

$$x_2 = \frac{0.5y}{p_2}.$$

Profit maximization gives the following demand functions for production factors:

$$l_1 = \frac{0.25\,p_1 x_1}{p_l},$$

$$l_2 = \frac{0.75\,p_2 x_2}{p_l},$$

$$n_1 = \frac{0.75\,p_1 x_1}{p_n},$$

$$n_2 = \frac{0.25\,p_2 x_2}{p_n}.$$

From the demand functions for the products, I can derive the consumer's expansion path:

$$\frac{x_1}{x_2} = \frac{p_2}{p_1}.$$

From the demand functions for production factors, I can derive:

$$\frac{n_1}{n_2} = \frac{0.75 p_1 x_1}{0.25 p_2 x_2},$$

$$\frac{l_1}{l_2} = \frac{0.25 p_1 x_1}{0.75 p_2 x_2}.$$

The last two equations together with the consumer's expansion path give:

$$\frac{n_1}{n_2} = \frac{0.75}{0.25} = 3,$$

$$\frac{l_1}{l_2} = \frac{0.25}{0.75} = \frac{1}{3}.$$

Because the amounts of nature and labour are known $(n = n_1 + n_2 = 600,$ $l = l_1 + l_2 = 300)$, it is now possible to allocate the production factors to the two production processes:

$$\frac{n_1}{n_2} = \frac{0.75}{0.25} = 3, \quad n = n_1 + n_2 = 600, \text{ so: } n_1 = 450, \quad n_2 = 150,$$

$$\frac{l_1}{l_2} = \frac{0.25}{0.75} = \frac{1}{3}, \quad l = l_1 + l_2 = 300, \text{ so: } \quad l_1 = 75, \quad l_2 = 225.$$

By using this result together with both production functions, the production of both goods can be computed:

$$x_1 = 10(75)^{0.25}(450)^{0.75} = 2875.2420,$$

$$x_2 = 10(225)^{0.75}(150)^{0.25} = 2033.1054.$$

This and the consumer's expansion path give the price ratio between the two goods:

$$\frac{p_2}{p_1} = \frac{x_1}{x_2} = \frac{2875.2420}{2033.1054} = 1.4142.$$

Absolute prices can only be determined if one price (the so-called *numeraire*) is fixed.[3] Assume that $p_1 = 1$. In that case:

---

3 Walras M.L., 1926. *Éléments d'économie politique pure: Édition Définitive*. Pichon, Paris.

$p_1 = 1,$

$p_2 = 1.4142.$

Then, with the help of the demand functions for the production factors, I can determine prices for nature p_n and labour p_l:

$$p_l = \frac{0.25 p_1 x_1}{l_1} = \frac{0.25 \times 1 \times 2875.2420}{75} = 9.5841,$$

$$p_n = \frac{0.25 p_2 x_2}{n_2} = \frac{0.25 \times 1.4142 \times 2033.1054}{150} = 4.7920.$$

Consumer's income can be computed from the quantities of production factors and factor prices:

$$y = l p_l + n p_n = 300 \times 9.5841 + 600 \times 4.7920 = 5750.43$$

Turnover o, which equals total income, can be computed as follows:

$$o = p_1 x_1 + p_2 x_2 = 1 \times 2875.2420 + 1.4142 \times 2033.1054 = 5750.4597.$$

There appears to be a rounding error of roughly 0.03. Results are now presented by way of an accounts scheme:

Consumer's income

$l p_l = 300 \times 9.5841$	2875	y	5750
$n p_n = 600 \times 4.7920$	2875		
Total:	5750	Total:	5750

Consumption

y	5750	$p_1 x_1 = 1 \times 2875.2420$	2875
		$p_2 x_2 = 1.4142 \times 2033.1054$	2875
Total	5750	Total	5750

Production Good 1

$p_1x_1 = 1 \times 2875.2420$	2875	$l_1p_l = 75 \times 9.5841$	719
		$n_1p_n = 450 \times 4.7920$	2156
Total	2875	Total	2875

Production Good 2

$p_2x_2 = 1.4142 \times 2033.1054$	2875	$l_2p_l = 225 \times 9.5841$	2156
		$n_2p_n = 150 \times 4.7920$	719
Total	2875	Total	2875

Turnover

o	5750	$p_1x_1 = 1 \times 2875.2420$ $p_2x_2 = 1.4142 \times 2033.1054$	2875 2875
Total	5750	Total	5750

Schematically, the solution procedure looks as follows:

1. Derive demand functions for the two goods (two equations).
2. Derive the consumer's expansion path from the demand functions for the two goods (one equation).
3. Determine the individual demand functions for the production factors (four equations).
4. Determine the ratio between input of labour for product 1 and that for product 2 (with the help of the demand functions derived under 3 and the consumer's expansion path). Do the same for nature (two equations).
5. Compute the allocation of production factors by using the results obtained under 4 and the given quantities of production factors.
6. Compute production for both goods (with the help of the production functions and the results under 5)
7. Compute the price ratio between both products (with consumer expansion path (step 2) and the results under 6). Assume the price of good 1 to be the *numeraire* ($p_1 = 1$). Now, compute the price for good 2.
8. Compute factor prices by using the results under 3, 6 and 7.
9. Compute consumer's income using the results under 8 and the given quantities of production factors.
10. Compute total turnover with the help of the results under 6 and 7. Check whether this matches the result under 9.

Application of the scheme

Assume the following $1\times 2\times 2$ general equilibrium model:

$$u = x_1^{0.25} x_2^{0.75},$$

$$x_1 = 10 n_1^{0.4} l_1^{0.6},$$

$$x_2 = 5 n_2^{0.25} l_2^{0.75},$$

$$y = 600 p_n + 400 p_l.$$

The solution to this model according to the scheme is as follows:

Step 1: $x_1 = \frac{0.25y}{p_1}, \quad x_2 = \frac{0.75y}{p_2}.$

Step 2: $\frac{x_1}{x_2} = \frac{0.25}{0.75}\frac{p_2}{p_1} = \frac{1}{3}\frac{p_2}{p_1}, \quad \text{so: } \frac{p_1x_1}{p_2x_2} = \frac{1}{3}.$

Step 3: $n_1 = \frac{0.4p_1x_1}{p_n}, \quad n_2 = \frac{0.25p_2x_2}{p_n},$

$l_1 = \frac{0.6p_1x_1}{p_l}, \quad l_2 = \frac{0.75p_2x_2}{p_l}.$

Step 4: $\frac{n_1}{n_2} = \frac{0.4p_1x_1}{0.25p_2x_2}, \quad \frac{p_1x_1}{p_2x_2} = \frac{1}{3}, \quad \text{so: } \frac{n_1}{n_2} = \frac{0.4}{0.25}\cdot\frac{1}{3} = \frac{0.4}{0.75} = \frac{8}{15},$

$\frac{l_1}{l_2} = \frac{0.6p_1x_1}{0.75p_2x_2}, \quad \frac{p_1x_1}{p_2x_2} = \frac{1}{3}, \quad \text{so: } \frac{l_1}{l_2} = \frac{0.6}{0.75}\cdot\frac{1}{3} = \frac{0.6}{2.25} = \frac{12}{45}.$

Step 5: $n_1 + n_2 = 600, \quad \frac{n_1}{n_2} = \frac{8}{15}, \quad \text{so:}$

$n_1 = \frac{8}{23}\cdot 600 = 208.70, \quad n_2 = \frac{15}{23}\cdot 600 = 391.30,$

$l_1 + l_2 = 400, \quad \frac{l_1}{l_2} = \frac{12}{45}, \quad \text{so:}$

$l_1 = \frac{12}{57}\cdot 400 = 84.21, \quad l_2 = \frac{45}{57}\cdot 400 = 315.79.$

Step 6: $x_1 = 10(208.70)^{0.4}(84.21)^{0.6} = 1210.67,$

$x_2 = 5(391.30)^{0.25}(315.79)^{0.75} = 1665.89.$

Step 7: $\frac{x_1}{x_2} = \frac{0.25}{0.75}\frac{p_2}{p_1}$, so: $\frac{p_2}{p_1} = 3\frac{x_1}{x_2} = 3\frac{1210.67}{1665.89} = 2.1802$.

So if: $p_1 = 1$, then: $p_2 = 2.1802$.

Step 8: $p_n = \frac{0.4 p_1 x_1}{n_1} = \frac{0.4 \times 1210.67}{208.70} = 2.3204$,

$$p_l = \frac{0.6 p_1 x_1}{l_1} = \frac{0.6 \times 1210.67}{84.21} = 8.6261.$$

Step 9: $y = p_l \times 400 + p_n \times 600 = 8.6261 \times 400 + 2.3204 \times 600 = 4842.68$.

Step 10: $p_1 x_1 + p_2 x_2 = 1 \times 1210.67 + 2.1802 \times 1665.89 = 4842.64$.
A comparison between this outcome and income y shows that there is a rounding error of 0.04.

The results of the stepwise procedure are shown in the following accounts.

Consumer's income

$lp_l = 400 \times 8.6261$	3450	y	4842
$np_n = 600 \times 2.3204$	1392		
Total:	4842	Total:	4842

Consumption

y	4843	$p_1 x_1 = 1 \times 1210.67$	1211
		$p_2 x_2 = 2.1802 \times 1665.89$	3632
Total	4843	Total	4843

Production good 1

$p_1 x_1 = 1 \times 1210.67$	1211	$l_1 p_l = 84.21 \times 8.6261$	727
		$n_1 p_n = 208.70 \times 2.3204$	484
Total	1211	Total	1211

Production good 2

$p_2 x_2 = 2.1802 \times 1665.89$	3632	$l_2 p_l = 315.79 \times 8.6261$	2724
		$n_2 p_n = 391.30 \times 2.3204$	908
Total	3632	Total	3632

Turnover

o	4843	$p_1x_1 = 1 \times 1210.67$	1211
		$p_2x_2 = 2.1802 \times 1665.89$	3632
Total	4843	Total	4843

6. WELFARE ECONOMICS AND COST-BENEFIT ANALYSIS

Environmental welfare economics

The foundation for welfare economics has been laid by Marshall, Pigou and Pareto.[1] According to their theory the contribution of a certain good to social welfare is determined by deducting social costs from gross social benefits. The result can be called net social benefits. Gross social benefits can be measured by the consumers' willingness to pay. Figure 6.1 shows the demand curve d and supply curve s. In equilibrium the amount of q^* is supplied at equilibrium price p^*. Total willingness to pay is represented by areas A+B+C. The willingness to pay can be divided into total variable costs (area C), producer surplus (area B) and consumer surplus (area A). Branch turnover is represented by areas B+C. If producer surplus exceeds the fixed costs, there is a profit. If it is less, the branch makes a loss. In a situation of perfect competition, at equilibrium, the producer surplus equals fixed costs, hence no profits will be made. In that situation the contribution to social welfare equals the consumer surplus (area A).

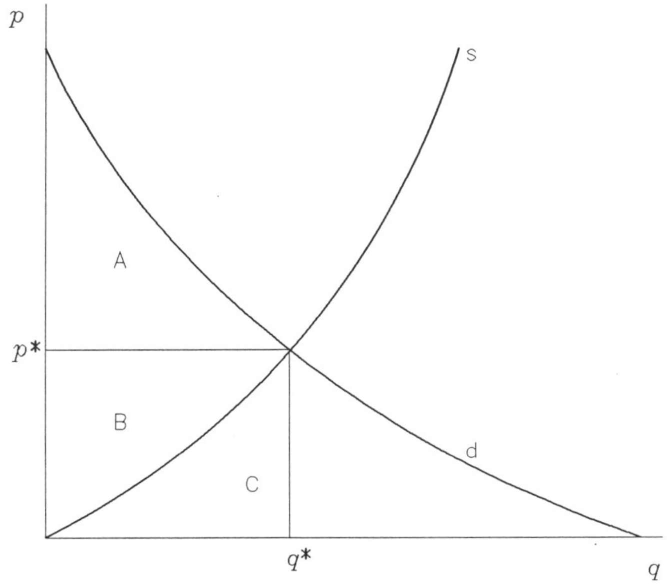

Figure 6.1: Willingness to pay, consumer surplus, producer surplus.

1 A.C. Pigou, 1952 (1920). *The economics of welfare*. MacMillan, London. V.F.D. Pareto, 1966 (1909), *Manuel d'économie politique*. Genève; originally published by Girard et Brière, Paris. A. Marshall, 1920 (1890). *Principles of economics*. MacMillan, London.

The collective demand function represents gross marginal social benefits b_{gm} of a good. Indeed, this function shows how society values one extra unit. The supply function equals marginal private costs c_{pm} of a good. These are the private costs of producing one extra unit. Private costs are costs that have already been valued in money. Those costs that are not valued in money are called externalities. Marginal externalities e_m plus marginal private costs c_{pm} together are called marginal social costs c_m. Gross marginal social benefits b_{gm}, which equal the price of the good, minus marginal social costs c_m are called net marginal social benefits b_{nm}. In order to maximize social welfare, b_{nm} of a good should be 0, in other words b_{gm} must equal c_m. In order to reach this, externalities should be internalized in the money costs of a good. This can be obtained by applying a fee, generally referred to as 'Pigovian tax'. To recapitulate:

$b_{gm} = c_m$, so:

$b_{nm} = b_{gm} - c_m = 0$, or, because $c_m = c_{pm} + e_m$,

$b_{gm} = c_{pm} + e_m$.

The theory above can be demonstrated by an example. Suppose a good with quantity q is characterized by the following collective demand function b_{gm} and cost structure, c_{pm} and e_m:

$b_{gm} = -0.4q + 16$,

$c_{pm} = 0.3q + 2$,

$e_m = 0.2q$.

From the equations above b_{nm} can be derived:

$b_{nm} = b_{gm} - c_{pm} - e_m = -0.9q + 14$.

In order to reach a situation of maximum social welfare, b_{nm} should be zero, so:

$14 - 0.9q = 0$, so: $q = 15.56$,

$p = b_{gm} = -0.4 \times 15.56 + 16 = 9.78$.

Assume that the situation of maximum welfare is to be reached by introducing a fee. In that case, fee f should equal the marginal externality in the optimum, so:

$f = 0.2 \times 15.56 = 3.11$.

In this way externalities are internalized by way of a Pigovian tax f. Figure 6.2 presents a picture of the example above.

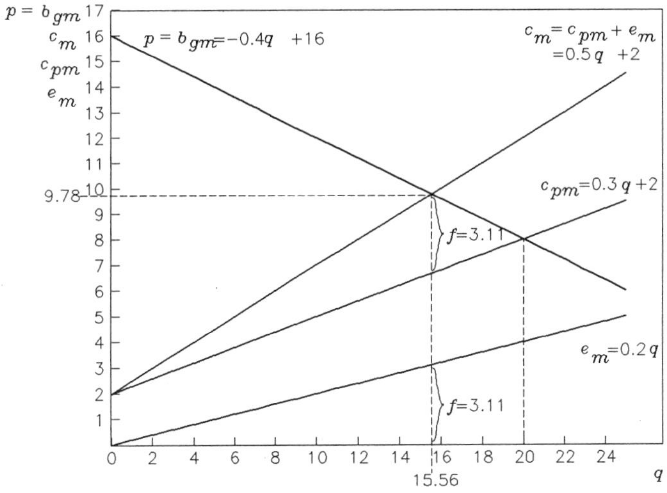

Figure 6.2: Internalization of externalities.

Cost-benefit analysis

Cost-benefit analysis is an application of Paretian and Pigovian welfare theory as explained above.[2] To evaluate a project gross benefits are diminished by total costs. If there is a positive net benefit, the project can be carried out. If you have to choose between projects that are substitutes, the project with the highest positive net benefit should be selected.

Now, suppose I want to determine the net benefits of an environmental project aimed at reducing the externalities of production q of a certain good. I know the values of the function of marginal externalities both without the project $e_m^{without}$ and with the project e_m^{with} being carried out. Costs of the project equal c. For example, if linear externality functions are used, externalities in both situations can be described as:

$$e_m^{without} = \alpha q, \quad e_m^{with} = \beta q \quad \alpha, \beta > 0, \quad \alpha > \beta.$$

2 D.W. Pearce, 1983 (1971). *Cost-Benefit Analysis*. MacMillan, London.

Total net social benefits b^{net} of an environmental project involving q units of production can now be computed by deducting costs c from gross benefits b^{gross}:

$$b^{net} = b^{gross} - c = \int_0^q (e_m^{without} - e_m^{with})dq - c = \int_0^q (\alpha - \beta)q\,dq - c$$

$$= \frac{1}{2}(\alpha - \beta)q^2 - c.$$

Figure 6.3. shows a graphical representation of this principle.

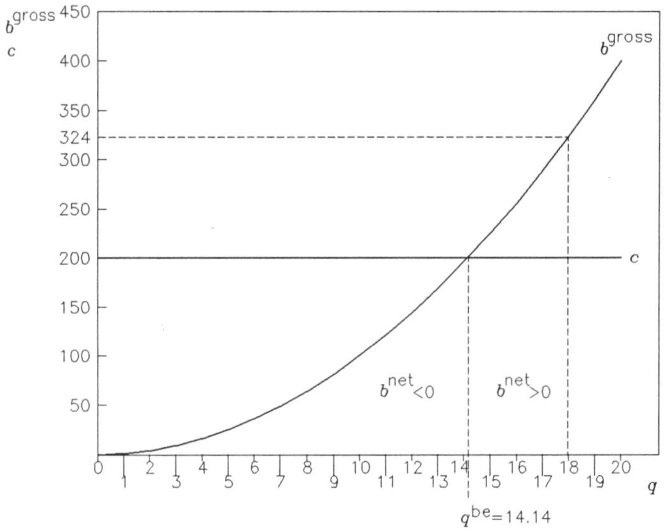

Figure 6.3: Costs and benefits of an environmental project.

In Figure 6.3 b^{net} equals the difference between gross benefits b^{gross} and costs c. To the left of the break-even production q^{be}, b^{net} is negative, to the right b^{net} is positive. If α and β equal 4 and 2, while q and c equal 18 and 200 respectively, then b^{net} equals: $0.5(4\text{-}2)18^2\text{-}200=124$. In Figure 6.3 this situation is depicted.

The explanation above of cost-benefit analysis is based on the assumption that all costs and benefits occur in the same period. If not, costs and benefits should be discounted. In general, the formula to compute present value of net benefits or net present value b^{net} of a project is

$$b^{net} = \sum_{t=0}^{n} \frac{B_t - K_t}{(1+r)^t},$$

where B_t and K_t represent gross benefits and costs in period t, while r and n represent the discount rate and the number of periods respectively. This formula can be illustrated with an example. Assume the following costs and benefits of a project (Table 6.1).

Table 6.1: Costs and benefits of a project.

year	0	1	2	3	4	...	40
benefits	-	50	50	50	50		50
costs	300	10	10	10	10		10
cash flow	-300	40	40	40	40		40

To calculate the cash flow of a certain year undiscounted costs are subtracted from undiscounted benefits. Costs do not include depreciaton and interest, because depreciation is calculated by subtracting the entire amount of investment at once, while the interest costs are calculated by the discounting procedure. If interest equals 10%, the net present value b^{net} can now be computed as follows:

$$b^{net} = -300 + \frac{40}{(1.1)} + \frac{40}{(1.1)^2} + \ldots + \frac{40}{(1.1)^{40}}$$

$$= -300 + 40 \cdot \left(\frac{1}{1.1} + \frac{1}{(1.1)^2} + \ldots + \frac{1}{(1.1)^{40}} \right).$$

The term in brackets is a geometrical progression. The sum of this can be computed, but can also be obtained from a table.[3] In this case the outcome equals 9.78 (rounded).[4] This implies that b^{net} of this project equals -300 + 40 × 9.78 = 91.20.

It is also possible to compute the *internal rate of return* of a project. This can be determined by computing a discount rate such that present value of net benefits b^{net} equals 0. In this example, this gives:[5]

$$b^{net} = -300 + \frac{40}{1+r} + \frac{40}{(1+r)^2} + \ldots + \frac{40}{(1+r)^{40}},$$

$$0 = -300 + 40\left\{ \frac{1}{(1+r)} + \frac{1}{(1+r)^2} + \ldots + \frac{1}{(1+r)^{40}} \right\},$$

$$7.5 = \left\{ \frac{1}{(1+r)} + \ldots + \frac{1}{(1+r)^{40}} \right\}, \quad \text{so:} \quad r \approx 13\%.$$

3 Of course this procedure can only be applied with cash flows that are equal each period.
4 J. Price Gittinger, 1982 (1973). *Compounding and discounting tables for project evaluation*. Johns Hopkins University Press, Baltimore.
5 The problem with the *internal rate of return* is that in some cases there is more than one solution.

If the internal rate of return exceeds the market interest rate (here 10%), carrying out the project is worthwhile.

Instead of a discrete analysis, a continuous analysis can be carried out, which will yield approximately the same results.[6] In that case, the formula of the present value of net benefits equals:

$$b^{net} = \int_{t=1}^{n} s e^{-rt} - I,$$

s is a constant flow of cash flows and I is the investment. This equation can be rewritten as:

$$b^{net} = s\left[-\frac{1}{r}e^{-rt}\right]_0^n - I = \frac{s}{r}(1 - e^{-rn}) - I.$$

This formula can be verified using the example. Net present value according to the new formula equals:

$$b^{net} = \frac{40}{0.1} \times (1 - e^{-0.1\times 40}) - 300 = 400 \times (1 - 0.018) - 300 \approx 92.80.$$

So, there is a small difference in outcome between the discrete and continuous method. In practice, however, this difference is not very significant. Now, if n and r are rather large, as in the example $(n = 40, r = 0.10)$, then, in order to have a rough estimation of the net present value, it is possible to neglect e^{-rn}. So, as an estimation, b^{net} equals: 40/0.1 - 300 = 100. Of course, this always leads to an overestimation of the net present value.

Rate of interest

The rate of interest r may be explained by two factors: productivity of capital ι and time preference υ.[7] With a two period analysis this can be explained as follows. I assume that society has a social utility function which is to be maximized. Total utility u for the two periods is determined by consumption in period 0, c_0, and consumption in period 1, c_1:

---

6 L.H. Klaassen and A.C.P. Verster, 1974. *Kosten-batenanalyse in regionaal perspectief.* Tjeenk Willink, Groningen.
7 E. von Böhm-Bawerk, 1921 (1889). *Kapital und Kapitalzins: Positive Theorie des Kapitales*. Fischer, Jena. K. Wicksell, 1954 (1893). *Value, Capital and Rent.* Allen & Unwin, London. I. Fisher, 1954 (1930). *The theory of interest.* Kelley and Millman, New York. For a critical view on the 'ordinary' discounting procedure with respect to the environment and natural resources see: E. Kula, 1992. *Economics of natural resources and the environment.* Chapman & Hall, London.

$$u = c_0 + \frac{c_1}{1 + \upsilon}.$$

Consumption in period 1 is possible because part of the income y_0 in period 0 is invested. This investment i_0 gives a net productivity ι.[8] Because it is assumed that marginal productivity decreases as investment increases, net productivity ι is a decreasing function of investment i_0. So:

$$c_1 = i_0(1 + \iota) \text{ with } \iota = \iota(i_0), \quad \frac{d\iota}{di_0} < 0.$$

After substitution, this gives:

$$u = (c_0, i_0) = c_0 + \frac{i_0(1 + \iota)}{(1 + \upsilon)}.$$

Further, I know that, in period 0, total income y_0 consists of consumption in period 0 c_0 and investment in this period i_0, so: $y_0 = c_0 + i_0$. Investment is simply defined here as that part of the production of a given period which is not consumed. So, by definition, investment equals savings. Further I know that y_0 is a given quantity, because it is assumed that all production factors are fully used. In order to maximize utility I use a Lagrange procedure, so:

$$\text{Max} \quad L = u(c_0, i_0) - \lambda(c_0 + i_0 - y_0).$$

The first-order conditions are:

$$\frac{\partial L}{\partial c_0} = \frac{\partial u}{\partial c_0} - \lambda = 0,$$

$$\frac{\partial L}{\partial i_0} = \frac{\partial u}{\partial i_0} - \lambda = 0, \quad \text{so:}$$

$$\frac{\partial u}{\partial c_0} = \frac{\partial u}{\partial i_0}.$$

With the specified utility function this means that:

8 This net productivity may also be called *Marginal Efficiency of Capital*. See: J.M. Keynes, 1951 (1936). *The general theory of employment, interest and money*. MacMillan, London.

$$1 = \frac{1+\iota}{1+\upsilon}, \quad \text{so:} \quad \iota = \upsilon.$$

So, the conclusion is that to reach optimum utility net productivity of capital must equal the rate of time preference. In theory, this optimum should be reached through the functioning of the capital market. This is explained as follows.

In equilibrium, the rate of interest r equals net productivity ι. Indeed, if $r > \iota$, r, together with the demand for capital, will decrease because the cost of capital r exceeds net productivity ι. In that case investment results in a loss and the demand for capital will go down. If $r < \iota$, the demand for capital, together with r, will increase, because the net productivity of capital exceeds the cost of capital. In this case, investment results in a profit.

On the supply side of capital, in equilibrium, the rate of interest r equals the rate of time preference υ. If $r > \upsilon$, the supply of capital will increase, causing a decrease in the net productivity of capital. If $r < \upsilon$, the supply of capital will decrease, causing a rise in the net productivity of capital. So, finally, in equilibrium: $r = \iota = \upsilon$. Figure 6.4 depicts this situation.

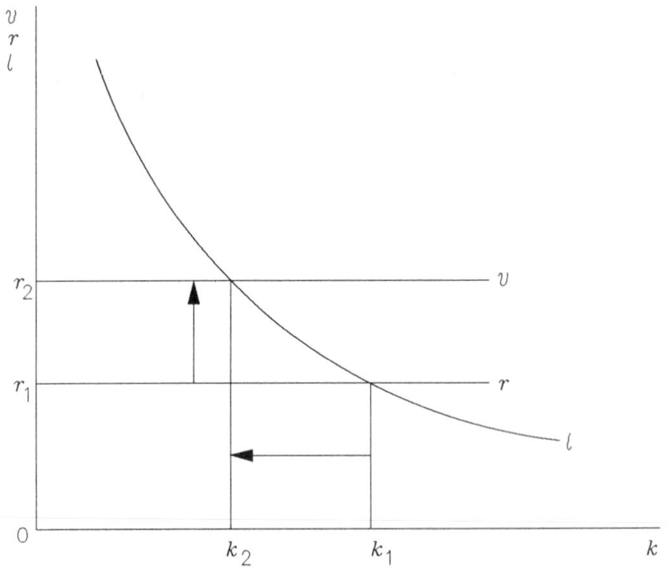

Figure 6.4: Equilibrium on the capital market.

In Figure 6.4 two situations may be observed. In situation 1, k_1 units of capital k are purchased. However the rate of time preference υ exceeds the rate of interest

r, which implies that supply and demand will decrease to k_2, resulting in a higher rate of interest (the rate of interest rises from r_1 to r_2) and also a higher net productivity of capital ι.

Inflation

If the cash flow is measured in constant prices, it is not correct to use the nominal interest rate. The nominal interest also compensates for inflation. So, only if cash flow is nominal may the nominal interest rate be used as the discount rate. If cash flow is measured in real terms, so must be the discount rate. The real rate of interest r^{real} equals nominal interest r^{nom} minus the rate of inflation ϕ: $r^{\text{real}} = r^{\text{nom}} - \phi$. This can be proved as follows. Nominal cash flow for a certain year n, C_n^{nom}, equals real cash flow for this year C_n^{real} multiplied by $e^{\phi n}$. The discounted cash flow C_0 for this year equals:

$$C_0 = C_n^{\text{nom}} e^{-r^{\text{nom}} n} = C_n^{\text{real}} e^{\phi n} e^{-r^{\text{nom}} n}$$

$$= C_n^{\text{real}} e^{-(r^{\text{nom}} - \phi) n} = C_n^{\text{real}} e^{-r^{\text{real}} n}.$$

For discrete time it can be proved that:

$$1 + r^{\text{real}} = \frac{1 + r^{\text{nom}}}{1 + \phi} \approx 1 + r^{\text{nom}} - \phi.$$

Environmental risk management

Risk can be defined as 'the chance of something bad happening'.[9] The expected (environmental) damage $\hat{S}$ connected to the negative uncertain event equals the risk α times the damage S caused by the event when it does happen, so:

$$\hat{S} = \alpha S.$$

Net benefits B of government's risk policy equals the reduction of the expected damage $-\Delta\hat{S}$ minus costs C induced by government's efforts in this field.

$$B = -\Delta\hat{S} - C.$$

---

9 S.J. Callan and J.M. Thomas, 1996. *Environmental Economics and Management.* Irwin, Chicago.

The change in expected damage can be defined as the expected damage with government intervention $\hat{S}_{with}$ minus the expected damage without government intervention $\hat{S}_{without}$:

$$\Delta\hat{S} = S_{with} - S_{without}.$$

The government can take two kinds of actions: actions that are lowering the risk, this effort is indicated as E_α, and actions that are aimed at reducing the damage after the event has taken place, indicated as E_s. Total costs C equal the costs C_α of risk reduction plus the costs C_s of damage reduction, so:

$$C = C_\alpha(E_\alpha) + C_s(E_s).$$

Maximizing net benefits of risk management implies:

$$\begin{aligned} \text{Max } B = -\Delta\hat{S} - C \text{ or } \text{Min } -B &= \Delta\hat{S} + C \\ &= \hat{S}_{with} - \hat{S}_{without} + C_\alpha(E_\alpha) + C_s(E_s) \\ &= \alpha(E_\alpha)S(E_s) - \alpha S + C_\alpha(E_\alpha) + C_s(E_s). \end{aligned}$$

The first order conditons for the minimum are:

$$\frac{\partial(-B)}{\partial E_\alpha} = \alpha'(E_\alpha)S(E_s) + C'_\alpha(E_\alpha) = 0,$$

$$\frac{\partial(-B)}{\partial E_s} = \alpha(E_\alpha)S'(E_s) + C'_s(E_s) = 0.$$

So:

$$\frac{C'_\alpha}{C'_s} = \frac{\alpha'}{\alpha}\frac{S}{S'}.$$

7. MARKET FORMS

Types of market forms

Based upon the number of sellers and the number of buyers, nine market forms can be identified (see Table 7.1).[1]

Table 7.1: Market forms.

		number of sellers:		
		one	few	many
	one	bilateral monopoly	limited monopsony	(pure) monopsony
number of buyers:	few	limited monopoly	bilateral oligopoly	oligopsony
	many	(pure) monopoly	oligopoly	perfect competition (bilateral polypoly)

With perfect competition there is a large number of sellers, with monopoly there is only one seller and with an oligopoly there are just a few sellers. The three market forms monopoly, oligopoly and perfect competition together are called *polipsony* (because there are many buyers). The three market forms pure monopsony, oligopsony and perfect competiton (bilateral polypoly) together may be called *polypoly* (because there are many sellers). The market form with one seller and one buyer is called *bilateral monopoly*, while the market form with few actors on both sides is called *bilateral oligopoly*. The market forms with few sellers and one buyer, and with one seller and few buyers may be called *limited monopsony* and *limited monopoly* respectively. All three market forms with one buyer are together called *monopsony*.

Concentration index

A measure of the concentration on the supply side or on the demand side is the *Herfindahl-Hirschmann-index*.[2] This index h is computed as follows:

$$h = \sum_{i=1}^{n} m_i^2 ,$$

1 A.E. Ott, 1968. *Grundzüge der Preistheorie:* p. 39. Vandenhoeck & Ruprecht, Göttingen.
2 A.O. Hirschmann, 1964. The paternity of an index. *American Economic Review,* 54, September, p. 761.

where n is the number of firms or the number of buyers and m_i is the market share (the share of the firm in the total turnover of the branch) of firm or buyer i. The maximum value for this index is one (in case of a monopoly or a monopsony).[3] In the case of n firms or buyers, with every firm or buyer having a market share of $1/n$, the index will equal $1/n$. If there is a concentration index to be calculated for the demand side and supply side together, the indexes can be multiplied. Assume, for example that in a certain market there are three producers with market shares of 1/4, 1/2, and 1/4; and four buyers with market shares of 1/2, 1/8, 1/8, and 1/4. Now, the concentration index for the supply side is 3/8 and for the demand side 11/32.[4] The overall index will now be: $3/8 \times 11/32 = 33/256$. The maximum value of the index is 1 (in case of a bilateral monopoly). So with the index we can measure the degree of concentration of a certain market not only on the supply side but also on the demand side.[5]

Polipsony

In previous chapters, I have shown how price is determined under conditions of perfect competition. The supply function is nothing more than the summing up of the individual marginal costs functions. This function together with the demand function determines price under conditions of perfect competition.

For a monopoly the conditions are different. There is only one seller who can influence the price level. Also in this case, the rule "marginal revenue must equal marginal cost" applies. However, marginal revenue differs from that in a situation of perfect competition. This can be illustrated with a linear function as follows:

$$p = -\alpha Q + \beta, \quad R = pQ, \quad \text{so:}$$

$$R = -\alpha Q^2 + \beta Q \quad \text{and:} \quad R_m = \frac{dR}{dQ} = -2\alpha Q + \beta,$$

---

3 share $m_i = x_i / x$, with $x_i \geq 0$, $x > 0$. $x = x_1 + x_2 + \ldots + x_n$. From this it follows: $\sum_{i=1}^{n} x_i^2 \leq x^2$, so: $\sum_{i=1}^{n} m_i^2 = \sum_{i=1}^{n} \frac{x_i^2}{x^2} \leq 1$.

4 The index for the supply side is computed as $(1/4)^2+(1/2)^2+(1/4)^2=3/8$. The index for the demand side is computed as $(1/2)^2+(1/8)^2+(1/8)^2+(1/4)^2=11/32$.

5 The formula for this overall concentration index h_{sd} is the concentration index for the supply side $h_s = \sum_{i=1}^{i=n} m_i^2$ multiplied by the concentration index for the demand side $h_d = \sum_{j=1}^{k} m_j^2$, so: $h_{sd} = h_s h_d = \sum_{i=1}^{n} m_i^2 \sum_{j=1}^{k} m_j^2$, with m_i for the market share of firm i and m_j for market share of consumer j.

with R for total revenue, Q for quantity, R_m for marginal revenue and p for price. To find the optimal quantity, we have to confront the marginal revenue function with the marginal cost function:

$$C_m = \gamma,$$

$$R_m = -2\alpha Q + \beta,$$

$$R_m = c_m, \quad \text{so:}$$

$$Q = \frac{\beta - \gamma}{2\alpha}, \quad \beta > \gamma.$$

To find price and total revenue, we have to substitute this value for Q in the appropriate functions. The price will then be:

$$p = 0.5(\gamma + \beta).$$

This point is called the *Cournot point* (see Figure 7.1), named after the French economist.[6] To determine the profit we have to establish the total cost function:[7]

$$C = \int C_m dQ = \gamma Q + \delta,$$

with δ for fixed costs. The expression for profit is:

$$W = R - C = (p - \gamma)Q + \delta = \frac{(\beta - \gamma)(\beta - 0.5\gamma)}{2\alpha} + \delta.$$

In the case of an oligopoly we have several firms, in this example we assume two. Then:[8]

$$r_1 = pq_1, \quad r_2 = pq_2,$$

---

6 A.A. Cournot, 1929 (1838). *Researches into the mathematical principles of the theory of wealth* (translated from the original French into English by N.T. Bacon). MacMillan, New York.

7 A more general approach (with π for profit) implies: $\text{Max} \ \pi(Q) = p(Q)Q - c(Q)$, so: $0 = \pi'(Q) = p'(Q)Q + p(Q) - c'(Q)$, so: $p'(Q)Q + p(Q) = c'(Q)$. This equation generally allows us to determine Q.

8 What is explained here is known in the literature as the 'quasi-competitive solution'. Other possible solutions for this case are: the collusion solution, the Cournot solution for the duopoly, and the Stackelberg solution (see: J.M. Henderson and R.E. Quandt, 1980 (1958), 3rd edition. *Microeconomic theory: a mathematical approach*. Mcgraw-Hill, Auckland).

$p = -\alpha Q + \beta$, so:

$r_1 = (-\alpha Q + \beta)q_1$, $r_2 = (-\alpha Q + \beta)q_2$.

$Q = q_1 + q_2$, so:

$r_1 = (-\alpha q_1 - \alpha q_2 + \beta)q_1$,

$r_2 = (-\alpha q_1 - \alpha q_2 + \beta)q_2$, or:

$r_1 = -\alpha q_1^2 - \alpha q_2 q_1 + \beta q_1$,

$r_2 = -\alpha q_2^2 - \alpha q_2 q_1 + \beta q_2$.

Let us have a look at the costs. Assume that the total cost functions are identical for all firms:

$c_1 = \gamma q_1 + \delta$,

$c_2 = \gamma q_2 + \delta$, so:

$$c_{m1} = \frac{dc_1}{dq_1} = c_{m2} = \frac{dc_2}{dq_2} = \gamma,$$

with δ for the fixed costs per firm. Each particular producer will try to maximize profit. This means that the marginal revenues of the two firms have to be set equal to the marginal costs γ.

$r_{m1} = -2\alpha q_1 - \alpha q_2 + \beta = c_{m_1} = \gamma$,

$r_{m2} = -2\alpha q_2 - \alpha q_1 + \beta = c_{m_2} = \gamma$.

Summing these two functions gives:

$$-3\alpha Q + 2\beta = 2\gamma, \quad \text{so: } Q = \frac{(\beta - \gamma)}{1.5\alpha}.$$

Because $(\beta - \gamma)/1.5\alpha > (\beta - \gamma)/2\alpha$, we can now conclude that production under oligopoly will be larger than under conditions of a monopoly. The general formula for an indefinite number of firms is (see appendix):

$$Q = \frac{\beta - \gamma}{\frac{(n+1)}{n}\alpha}, \quad p = \frac{-\alpha(\beta - \gamma)}{\frac{n+1}{n}\alpha} + \beta = -\frac{n}{n+1}(\beta - \gamma) + \beta.$$

with n for the number of firms. We may conclude that Q will be larger and p will be lower accordingly if n is larger. If $n \to \infty$, we have the perfect competition case with:

$$Q = \frac{\beta + \gamma}{\alpha}, \quad p = \gamma.$$

If $n = 1$, we have a monopoly with:

$$Q = \frac{(\beta - \gamma)}{2\alpha}, \quad p = 0.5(\gamma + \beta).$$

I will give an example. Assume the following values of the coefficients: $\alpha = 0.25$, $\beta = 10$, $\gamma = 5$. We know further that the number of firms n equals 5. This gives the following functions for price p, C_m and R_m:

$$p = 10 - 0.25Q,$$

$$R_m \text{ (monopoly) } = -0.5Q + 10,$$

$$C_m = 5.$$

$$Q = \frac{10-5}{\frac{6}{5} \times 0.25} = 16.67, \text{ so: } p = -\frac{5}{6}(10-5) + 10 = 5.83.$$

This means that for the monopoly: $Q = (10-5)/0.5 = 10$, $p = 0.5(10+5) = 7.5$ (point C in Figure 7.1). In the case of perfect competition (with an infinite number of firms): $p = 5$, $Q = 20$ (point D in Figure 7.1). The bold line segment in Figure 7.1 indicates the combination of p and Q for an industry when the number of firms varies between 1 and infinity.[9]

Of course, in the real world the number of firms will be smaller than infinity. Assuming that under perfect competition profit is zero, the number of firms n can be computed with the following four equations:

9 In fact, what we have here, is the possible set of *'Cournot equilibria'*. A Cournot equilibrium is such that firms who deviate from it will suffer a decrease in their profit.

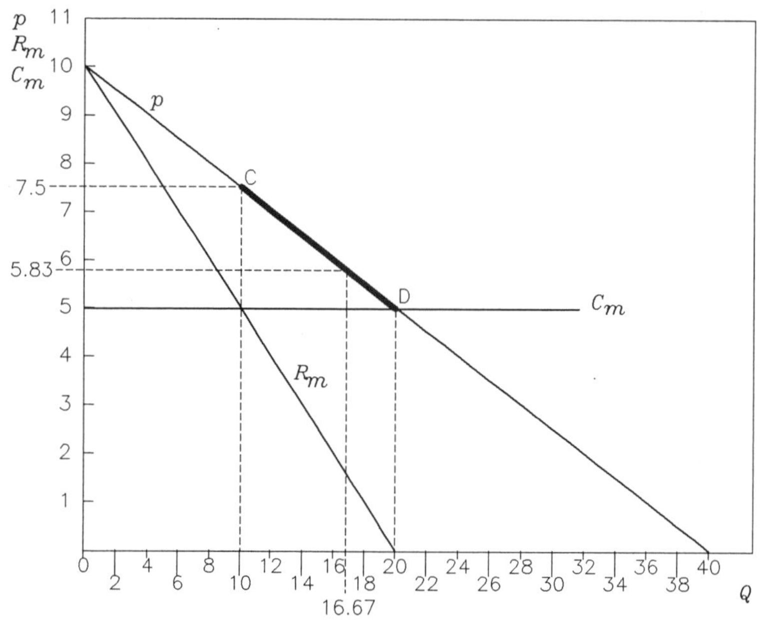

Figure 7.1: Polipsony, with C for the Cournot point and CD for possible combinations of p and Q.

$$R = (-\alpha Q + \beta)Q = -\alpha Q^2 + \beta Q,$$

$$C = \gamma Q + \delta n,$$

$$Q = \frac{\beta}{\frac{n+1}{n}\alpha} = \frac{n}{n+1}\frac{\beta}{\alpha},$$

$$W = R - C = 0.$$

The total number of firms n under perfect competition can be computed from this set of equations.

Monopsony

With a pure monopsony there is only one buyer and a large number of sellers. A monopsony, just like a monopoly, can dictate its price. It wants to obtain a certain number of goods at the lowest possible price. This price depends on the sector's supply function, which, in turn, depends on the number of sellers in the market. Assume that total cost functions for all individual firms are identical, for example for firm i:

$$c_i = \gamma q_i^2 + \beta q_i + \delta, \text{ so: } c_{mi} = \frac{dc_i}{dq_i} = 2\gamma q_i + \beta.$$

The demand function of the monopsonist is given by:

$$p = -\epsilon Q + \phi,$$

with Q for $\sum_{i=1}^{n} q_i$. Assuming that the price is determined by the monopsonist and the quantity supplied is determined by the individual supplier, at the optimum:[10]

$$2\gamma q_i + \beta = -\epsilon Q + \phi.$$

Summing the optimum conditions for n firms gives (with h for Herfindahl-Hirschmann index):

$$2\gamma \sum_{i=1}^{n} q_i + n\beta = -\epsilon n Q + n\phi \text{ or: } 2\gamma Q + \beta n = -\epsilon n Q + n\phi \text{ or:}$$

$$2\frac{\gamma}{n} Q + \beta = -\epsilon Q + \phi, \text{ therefore:}$$

$$Q = \frac{n(\phi - \beta)}{2\gamma + \epsilon n} = \frac{\phi - \beta}{2\frac{\gamma}{n} + \epsilon} \text{ and } p = -\frac{\epsilon(\phi - \beta)}{2\frac{\gamma}{n} + \epsilon} + \phi, \text{ or, if } h = \frac{1}{n}:$$

$$Q = \frac{\phi - \beta}{2\gamma h + \epsilon} \text{ and } p = -\frac{\epsilon(\phi - \beta)}{2\gamma h + \epsilon} + \phi.$$

This result implies that total supply Q increases and price p decreases when the number of firms n increases (see Figure 7.2). From Figure 7.2 it is clear that increasing the number of firms under the given assumptions leads to an increase in total output and a decrease in price. From the last equation it can be deduced:

$$\lim_{n \to \infty} Q(n) = \frac{\phi - \beta}{\epsilon} \text{ and } p = -\frac{\epsilon(\phi - \beta)}{\epsilon} + \phi = \beta.$$

---

10 It is assumed that the monopsonist wants to maximize its consumer surplus. Therefore it wants to set its price as low as possible.

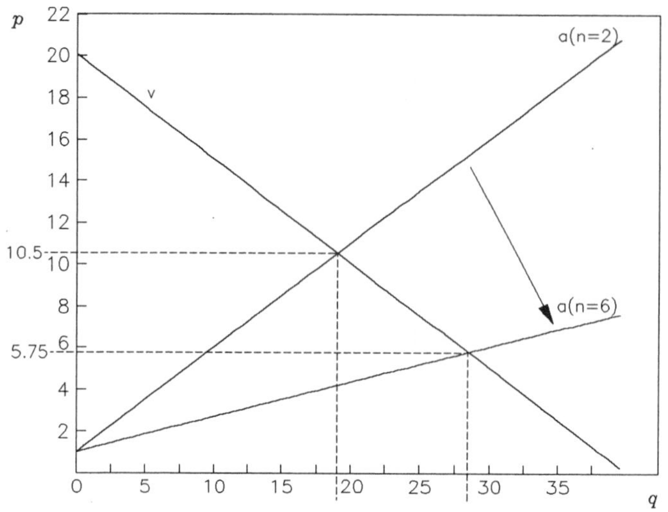

Figure 7.2: Quantities and prices as a result of a change in the number of firms *n*, with: supply functions a(*n*=2), a(*n*=6): $p = \frac{2\gamma Q}{n} + \beta$, demand function (v): $p = -\epsilon Q + \phi$. Values for γ, β and ϕ are respectively: 0.5, 1 and 20. For n the values 2 and 6 have been taken, which lead to the supply functions a($n = 2$) and a($n = 6$) respectively.

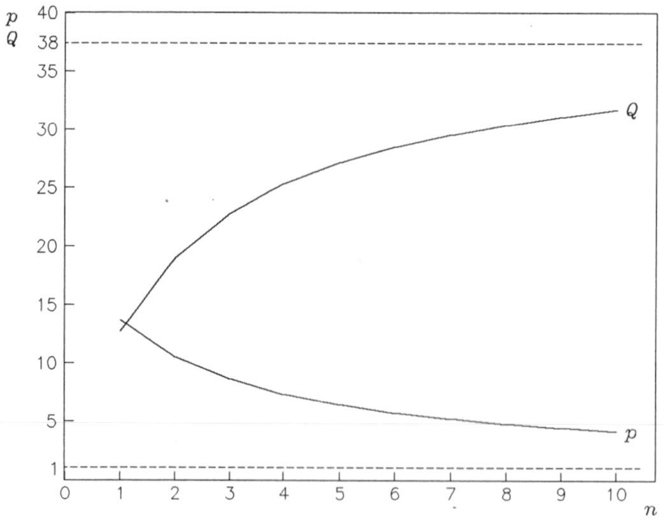

Figure 7.3: Price p and quantity Q as functions of *n*. With: $\beta = 1$, $\gamma = 0.5$, $\phi = 20$ and $\epsilon = 0.5$. Then $\lim_{n\to\infty} Q = 38$ and $\lim_{n\to\infty} p = 1$.

This means that there is a limit to the decrease in price and the increase in amount produced.[11] This is shown in Figure 7.3. Assume that production q_i will be equal for all i, so that $Q = nq_i$. Total costs for the whole sector can be given by:

$$nc_i = n\gamma q_i^2 + \beta n q_i + n\delta, \text{ so: } C = \frac{1}{n}\gamma Q^2 + \beta Q + n\delta.$$

With competition on the supply side and long run profit equal to zero, I can now compute the total number of firms n^* that will be active in this market by:

$$C = R,$$

$$\frac{1}{n}\gamma Q^2 + \beta Q + n\delta = pQ,$$

$$Q = \frac{\phi - \beta}{\frac{2\gamma}{n} + \epsilon}, \quad p = -\frac{\epsilon(\phi - \beta)}{\frac{2\gamma}{n} + \epsilon} + \phi.$$

To solve this for n is analytically difficult. Therefore, a numerical solution is given in Figure 7.4 for $\beta = 1$, $\gamma = 0.5$, $\phi = 20$, $\epsilon = 0.5$ and $\delta = 20$.

In Figure 7.4 costs C, total revenue R, profit W, and profit per firm W/n are shown. Maximum profit for the whole branche is reached when $n \approx 3(2.75)$; maximum profit per firm is reached when $n \approx 2(2.25)$. There are two equilibria, n_1 and n_2. Equilibrium n_1 is not stable, since to the right of this point there is a profit $(R > C)$, which will result in an increase in the number of firms provided that other firms can enter the branch freely. Equilibrium n_2 is stable because at this point an increase in the number of firms results in a loss $(C > R)$, which will cause a decrease in the number of firms. On the left hand side of this point firms are making a profit $(R > C)$, which will cause an increase in the number of firms under perfect competition. The conclusion is that under a pure monopsony (one buyer and many sellers), in this example the maximum number of sellers will be about 6.[12]

Further, it seems strange that in the case of a bilateral monopoly $(n = 1)$ the firm in question is at a loss $(C > R)$. This can be explained by the specification of the cost function and the fact that the monopsonist can dictate its price.[13] In this case the marginal cost function is a strictly rising function for every firm. So in the

---

11 For example, if $\beta = 1$, $\gamma = 0.5$, $\phi = 20$ and $\epsilon = 0.5$, then $\lim_{n\to\infty} Q = 38$ and $\lim_{n\to\infty} p = 1$.

12 I am of the opinion that this case is not different from the situation of perfect competition (many buyers and many sellers). Only the starting point of the analysis is different.

13 So, in this case, there is no bilateral monopoly in the strict sence because the market power is entirely in the hands of the monopsonist.

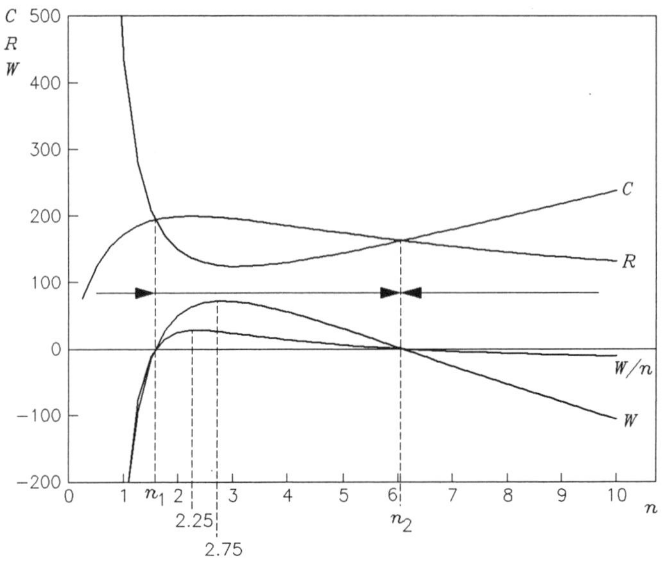

Figure 7.4: Number of firms and equilibrium in the market under competition.

pioneer phase of the branch, total costs may decrease because of the entrance of new firms. Later, when there are more firms, the increase in fixed costs outweighs the decrease in variable costs.[14]

Other market forms

For the other market forms, different types of analyses have proved useful in different circumstances. An important aspect is the side (demand or supply) on which the price is determined. If the price is determined on the demand side, we have a monopsonistic market form. If the price is determined on the supply side, we have a polipsonistic market form. If it is not clear on which side the price is determined, then the market form may be perfect competition.

Market forms and environment

Normally pollution and abuse of natural resources is usually associated with 'big business'. However, from the above analysis it can be concluded that perfect

14 Whether this is a 'real world phenomenon' is questionable.

competition causes an increase of production relative to the market forms oligopoly and monopoly with fewer or even only one firm respectively. *Ceteris paribus*, more production means more pollution and a greater use of natural resources.

With D for pollution and H for the use of a natural resource we can write:

$$D = D(Q), \quad \frac{dD}{dQ} > 0,$$

$$H = H(Q), \quad \frac{dD}{dQ} > 0,$$

$$Q = Q(n), \quad \frac{dQ}{dn} > 0.$$

So:

$$\frac{dD}{dn} = \frac{dD}{dQ}\frac{dQ}{dn} > 0, \quad \frac{dH}{dn} = \frac{dH}{dQ}\frac{dQ}{dn} > 0.$$

The conclusion is that from the point of view of nature conservation and pollution abatement the fewer firms the better.[15] Another argument is that in a few relatively large firms the scale of production is sufficient to implement environmental technological innovations and usually there are sufficient financial means available to finance them. Further it is easier for the authorities to deal with a few big firms than with a lot of small ones. So, contrary to intuition, one might say that small is not always beautiful.[16]

Appendix

For firm i it can be stated:

$$p = -\alpha Q + \beta,$$

$$r_i = pq_i, \text{ therefore:}$$

$$r_i = (-\alpha Q + \beta)q_i, \text{ or: } r_i = -\alpha q_i Q + \beta q_i.$$

---

15 In our analysis fewer firms means less production, but it also means that on average the firms are larger (measured through average production per firm). Proof (see appendix to this chapter):

$$Q = \frac{\beta - \gamma}{\frac{n+1}{n}\alpha}, \text{ so: } \frac{Q}{n} = \frac{\beta - \gamma}{(n+1)\alpha}.$$

16 E.F. Schumacher, 1975 (1973). *Small is beautiful: economics as if people mattered.* Harper and Row, New York.

For n firms $Q = q_i + \sum_{s=1}^{n} q_s (s \neq i)$, therefore

$$r_i = -\alpha q_i \left(q_i + \sum_{s=1}^{n} q_s (s \neq i) \right) + \beta q_i = -\alpha q_i^2 - \alpha q_i \sum_{s=1}^{n} q_s (s \neq i) + \beta q_i .$$

From this total revenue function for firm i, the marginal revenue function can be derived:

$$r_{mi} = \frac{dr_i}{dq_i} = -2\alpha q_i - \alpha \sum_{s=1}^{n} q_s (s \neq i) + \beta .$$

$\sum_{s=1}^{n} q_s (s \neq i) = Q - q_i$ and marginal costs are assumed to be equal to γ, therefore the optimum for firm i can be given by:

$$-2\alpha q_i - \alpha (Q - q_i) + \beta = \gamma .$$

Since $\sum_{i=1}^{n} q_i = Q$, the summing of the optimum conditions for n firms gives:

$$-\alpha Q - n\alpha Q + \beta n = n\gamma , \text{ so: } Q = \frac{\beta - \gamma}{\frac{n+1}{n}\alpha} .$$

8. PRODUCTION FACTORS

Law of increasing and decreasing marginal productivity

Production is influenced by the law of increasing marginal product at relatively low quantities of production and decreasing marginal product at relatively high levels of production. This is reflected in the following production function:

$$q = -\alpha l^3 + \beta l^2 + \gamma l, \text{ with } \alpha, \beta, \gamma > 0.$$

with q for the quantity of production and l for the input of a production factor, for example, labour. Figure 8.1 gives a picture of a specific form of this production function.

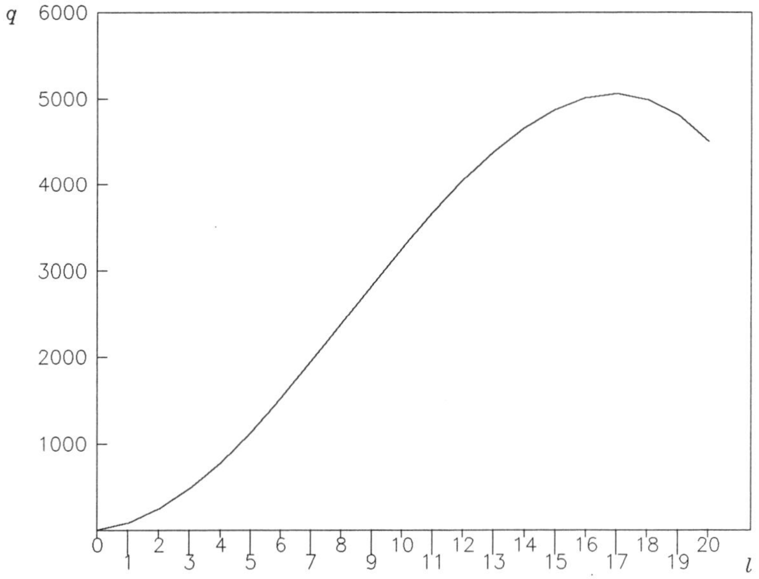

Figure 8.1: Production function with one production factor:
$q = -2l^3 + 50l^2 + 25l$.

If $\alpha = 2$, $\beta = 50$ and $\gamma = 25$, average product q_a equals:

$$q_a = \frac{q}{l} = -2l^2 + 50l + 25.$$

With price of the final product p, value of average product pq_a equals:

$$pq_a = p\frac{q}{l} = -2pl^2 + 50pl + 25p.$$

Marginal product q_m equals:

$$q_m = \frac{dq}{dl} = -6l^2 + 100l + 25.$$

The value of the marginal product pq_m equals:

$$pq_m = p\frac{dq}{dl} = -6pl^2 + 100pl + 25p,$$

If $p = 5$, pq_a and pq_m are respectively:

$$pq_a = p\frac{q}{l} = -10l^2 + 250l + 125,$$

$$pq_m = p\frac{dq}{dl} = -30l^2 + 500l + 125,$$

Figure 8.2 shows these curves. Now, if the price for labour p_l is fixed, then in order to maximize profit w, the firm is going to hire so much labour that q_m equals p_l. This can be proved as follows:

$$q = q(l),$$

$$w = pq(l) - p_l l,$$

$$\frac{dw}{dl} = p\frac{dq}{dl} - p_l = 0, \text{ so: } p\frac{dq}{dl} = pq_m = p_l.$$

So:

$$p_l = pq_m = p\frac{dq}{dl} = -3p\alpha l^2 + 2p\beta l + p\gamma.$$

Assume $p_l = 500$. With our assumed values for the coefficients α, β and γ, and price p it follows:

$$500 = -30l^2 + 500l + 125, \quad \text{so: } l_1 = 15.9, \; l_2 = 0.8.$$

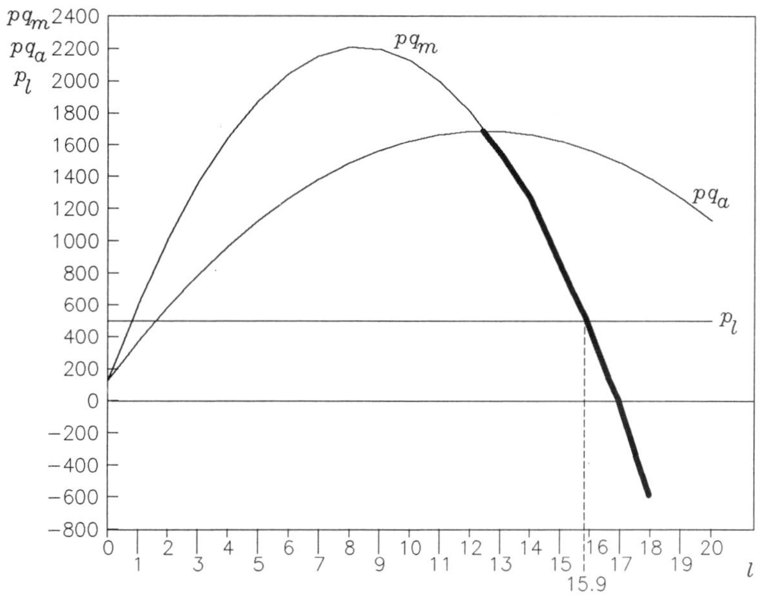

Figure 8.2: Demand for labour.

It can be seen from Figure 8.2 how much labour the firm is going to hire. In fact, we may look upon the pq_m-function under the pq_a-function as the demand function for the production factor concerned (the bold line in Figure 8.2), in this case: labour. The part of the pq_m-curve above the pq_a-curve should not be considered, because in that part wage will always be higher than the value of the average product, so the firm will always operate at a loss. The conclusion is that the firm will hire 15.9 units of labour at a price of 500.

Capital

Price for capital equals interest and depreciation, or interest only, depending on the definition of productivity of capital. For the sake of simplicity, I assume the other production factors (land, labour) to be fixed. To establish the optimum amount of capital to be attracted by a firm, I have to maximize gross revenue $pq(k)$ minus costs: interest rk and depreciation δk. It is assumed that depreciation is a fixed portion of capital stock.

$$\text{Max} \quad w(k) = pq(k) - rk - \delta k,$$

with w for profit, k for capital (expressed in money), p for price, q for production, r for the rate of interest, and δ for the depreciation rate. To gain maximum profit, the first derivative with respect to capital must be set equal to 0, so:

$$\frac{dw}{dk} = p\frac{dq}{dk} - r - \delta = 0.$$

Thus, in case of 'gross productivity of capital', the optimum rule is:

$$p\frac{dq}{dk} = r + \delta,$$

with $p(dq/dk)$ for gross productivity of capital. In terms of 'net productivity of capital' (with q_n for 'net product') the optimum rule is:

$$p\frac{dq_n}{dk} = r,$$

with:[1]

$$q_n(k) = q(k) - \frac{\delta k}{p}.$$

The second version of the optimum rule can be called the *Marginal Efficiency of Capital* theory.

Duration of capital goods

What determines the average duration n of a capital good? The choice for the firm is characterized by three equations. The first one is:

$$q = s\left\{\frac{1}{(1+i)} + \frac{1}{(1+i)^2} + \ldots + \frac{1}{(1+i)^n}\right\}.$$

---

1 The following result can be derived: $w(k) = pq(k) - rk - \delta k$, $w(k) = pq_n(k) - rk$, so: $q_n(k) = q(k) - \frac{\delta k}{p}$.

In this equation, q represents the discounted cash flows of a capital good. Annual cash flow is represented by s. The interest rate is represented by i. It is assumed here that the cash flow per unit output equals 1, so that, in this case, s equals the production per period. Further it is assumed that this capacity is constant.

A continuous form for this equation is:

$$q = s\int_0^n e^{-it}dt$$

$$q = \frac{s}{i} - \frac{se^{-in}}{i}.$$

It can be seen as a 'production function'and be shown with the help of iso-production curves. In Figure 8.3, a field of six possible iso-production curves is shown, the rate of interest being equal to 0.06. It is also clear from this figure that the iso-production curves are convex.

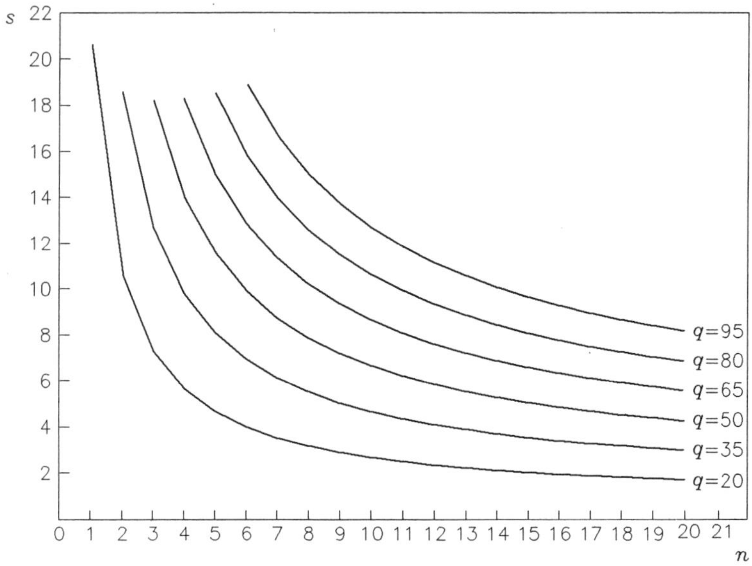

Figure 8.3: iso-production curves combining s and n $(i = 0.06)$.

The second equation is the budget function:

$$B = p_s s + p_n n.$$

Total budget B for one capital good can be spent on either a good with a high production per period s and a relatively short duration n or a capital good with a low production per period and a long lifetime. It is assumed that the budget, as well as the shadow prices for duration p_n per period (for example, per year) and capacity (production per year) p_s are fixed parameters. So, with the given prices of duration and capacity, a machine will be expensive if it has a long duration combined with a high capacity. Finally, the last equation represents the optimum condition: maximize the total of the discounted cash flows under the constraint of the given budget.

$$\text{Max } q,$$

$$s.t.\ B = p_s s + p_n n.$$

Through a Lagrange procedure we arrive at the third equation, the optimum condition:

$$\frac{\partial q/\partial s}{p_s} = \frac{\partial q/\partial n}{p_n}.$$

From this equation it can be deduced that the capacity of a capital good and the duration of this capital good are two quality attributes of the capital good. In order to gain maximum discounted production q with a given budget B the ratio between marginal productivity and price must be equal for each quality attribute.

Partial differentiation of q with respect to s and n gives:

$$\frac{\partial q}{\partial s} = \frac{1 - e^{-in}}{i},$$

$$\frac{\partial q}{\partial n} = s e^{-in}.$$

Substitution of these equations into the optimum condition yields an equation for the producer's expansion path:

$$s = \frac{p_n(e^{in} - 1)}{i p_s}.$$

Differentiation of s with respect to n yields the tangent of the angle of inclination of the expansion path:

$$\frac{ds}{dn} = \frac{p_n}{p_s} e^{in}.$$

It appears that the expansion path is steeper in proportion to the rate of interest i, which means that with a given budget, a high interest rate provides a short duration n of the capital good and a high capacity s, while a low interest rate causes a long duration of capital goods and a low capacity, which seems favourable for nature conservation.[2]

Land rent

Land rent R equals gross revenue pq per square unit per period diminished by the costs K: $R = pq - K$. Production q is a function of the input of production factors and the quality of the soil θ.[3] Assume there is only one production factor: labour l. Costs K equal the return on labour $p_l l$ and transportation costs $p_a q A$, with p_a for the costs of transporting one weight unit over one distance unit (*e.g.* transport costs per kilo kilometre) and A for the distance to the market. Now:

$$R = pq(l,\theta) - p_l l - p_a q(l,\theta) A,$$

$$\frac{\partial q}{\partial l} > 0, \quad \frac{\partial q}{\partial \theta} > 0, \quad \frac{\partial^2 q}{\partial l^2} < 0, \quad \frac{\partial^2 q}{\partial \theta^2} < 0, \quad \frac{\partial^2 q}{\partial \theta \partial l} > 0.$$

The first-order condition for maximizing R is:

$$\frac{\partial R}{\partial l} = (p - p_a A)\frac{\partial q}{\partial l} - p_l = 0,$$

$$(p - p_a A)\frac{\partial q}{\partial l} = p_l.$$

Assuming $p > p_a A$ and from the assumption already made that $\frac{\partial q}{\partial l}$ is a positive function of θ, we can deduce that the higher the quality of the soil and shorter the distance to the market, the more labour will be hired. Further, we can state:

---

2 However, one might wonder whether a long duration of capital goods is always favourable to the conservation of natural resources. If the duration of capital goods is relatively long, then the introduction of nature-sparing technological innovations will take relatively more time. Indeed, many (nature-sparing) innovations are bound to new capital goods. In other words, many technological innovations are *embodied* (see: Heijman W.J.M., 1995. Austrian sustainability. In: Meijer G. (ed.), *New perspectives on austrian economics*. Routledge, London).

3 D. Ricardo, 1978 (1817). *The principles of political economy and taxation*. Everyman's library, London. J.H. von Thünen, 1921 (1826). *Der isolierte Staat*. Fischer, Jena.

$$\frac{\partial R}{\partial \theta} = p\frac{\partial q}{\partial \theta} - p_a A\frac{\partial q}{\partial \theta} = (p - p_a A)\frac{\partial q}{\partial \theta} > 0,$$

$$\frac{\partial R}{\partial A} = -p_a q < 0.$$

This means that in order to gain a maximum rent, distance A must be minimized and the quality of the soil must be maximized. I will illustrate the previous analysis with an example. Assume the following Cobb-Douglas production function:

$$q = l^{\beta}\theta^{1-\beta}.$$

First-order condition for maximum rent is:

$$\frac{\partial R}{\partial l} = (p - p_a A)\beta l^{\beta-1}\theta^{1-\beta} = p_l \quad \text{so:} \quad l = \left\{\frac{\beta(p - p_a A)}{p_l}\right\}^{\frac{1}{1-\beta}}\theta.$$

Now, assume the values for A and θ mentioned in columns 1 and 2 of Table 8.1. Further it is assumed that: $p_a = 2$, $p_l = 5$, $\beta = 0.75$, $p = 30$. The value of the rent for every distance from the marketplace is computed in Table 8.1. Figure 8.4 gives a picture of the values of labour, production and rent.

Table 8.1: Labour, production and rent, per square unit, for distance A to a marketplace and given quality θ of the land (quality is measured on a scale from 1-10).

Distance A	Quality θ	labour per square unit $l = (4.5 - 0.3A)^4\theta$	production per square unit $q = l^{0.75}\theta^{0.25}$	Rent $R = 30q - 5l - 2qA$
0	4	1640.25	364.50	2733.75
1	6	1867.02	444.53	3111.70
2	3	694.03	177.96	1156.72
3	2	335.92	93.31	559.87
4	7	830.15	251.56	1383.57
5	9	729.00	243.00	1215.00
6	10	531.44	196.83	885.74
7	8	265.42	110.59	442.37
8	7	136.14	64.83	226.90
9	8	83.98	46.66	139.97
10	3	15.19	10.13	25.31

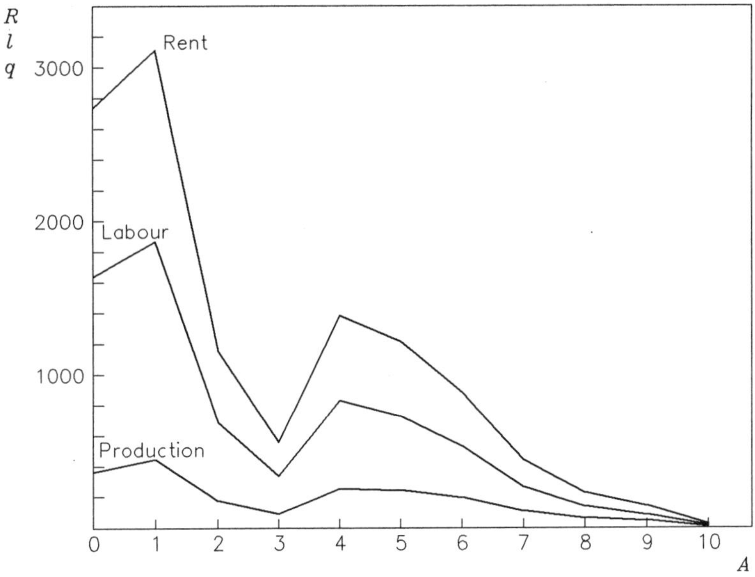

Figure 8.4: labour, production and rent, per square unit.

Value of land

The value of land is determined by the rent and the interest rate. In general one can say that if the rent equals an amount of R per year per hectare, and the rate of interest equals r, then the value of the hectare v equals:

$$v = \frac{R}{r}.$$

This can be proved as follows. Assume t for time and n for the lifetime of land. The net present value of the land v equals:

$$v = \int_{t=0}^{n} R e^{-rt} dt = R \left[-\frac{1}{r} e^{-rt} \right]_0^n, \quad \text{or:} \quad \frac{R}{r}(1 - e^{-rn}).$$

Because, where land is concerned, n is large (sometimes even infinite), I can state: $v = R / r$.

Industrial location

The neoclassical industrial location theory follows naturally from Alfred Weber's classical industrial location theory.[4] The main difference between Weber's location theory, as far as the minimization of transport costs is concerned, and the neoclassical location theory can be found in the structure of the firm's production function. In the Weber model substitution of input factors is not possible. In neoclassical analysis of the locational problem of the firm, substitution of production inputs is assumed. To illustrate the neoclassical location theory, I will present a simplified example. On a line two locations of inputs, L for labour l and G for raw material g, and a marketplace M for a certain commodity are assumed (see Figure 8.5). The question is what should be the location V of a firm producing this commodity and seeking to maximize its profit.

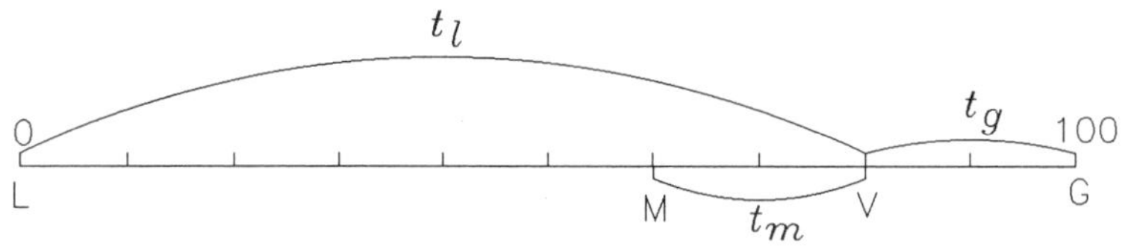

Figure 8.5: Location of a firm along a line.

Total length of the line is T distance units. In Figure 8.5 $T = 100$. The distance from L to V, the location of the firm, is represented by t_l, the distance from G to V by t_g, and the distance from V to M by t_m. Because total length of the line equals T, I know that $t_g = T - t_l$. Transport cost of one unit of labour over one distance unit equals p_{tl}, transport cost for one unit of raw material per distance unit equals p_{tg}, and transport cost for one unit of product per distance unit equals p_{tm}. I will deal with two cases. In the first case transportation costs for the final product are 0 ($p_{tm} = 0$). In the second case transportation costs for the final product exceed 0 ($p_{tm} > 0$). I assume the following Cobb-Douglas production function with production q and the two inputs l and g:

$$q = l^{\alpha} g^{(1-\alpha)}.$$

Further I assume a budget B, to be spent entirely on the buying of the two inputs, including its transportation costs:

4 A. Weber, 1929 (1909). *Theory of the Location of Industries*. Chicago Press, Chicago. A. Predöhl, 1925. Das Standortsproblem in der Wirtschaftstheorie, *Weltwirtschaftliches Archiv* 21, pp. 294-331. W. Isard, 1956. *Location and Space-Economy*. John Wiley, New York. J.H.P Paelinck and P. Nijkamp, 1975. *Operational theory and method in regional economics*. Saxon House, Westmead.

$$B = (p_l + p_{tl} t_l) l + (p_g + p_{tg} t_g) g,$$

$$= (p_l + p_{tl} t_l) l + [p_g + p_{tg}(T - t_l)] g.$$

So, at the optimum:[5]

$$l = \frac{\alpha B}{p_l + p_{tl} t_l},$$

$$g = \frac{(1-\alpha) B}{p_g + p_{tg}(T - t_l)}.$$

Now, assume that $\alpha = 0.5$, $T = 100$, $B = 500$, $p_l = 2$, $p_g = 5$, $p_{tl} = 0.1$, $p_{tg} = 0.2$. Then:

$$l = \frac{250}{2 + 0.1 t_l},$$

$$g = \frac{250}{5 + 0.2(100 - t_l)}.$$

In Table 8.2 it is shown what the inputs and production are on every location of the line.

Table 8.2: Inputs and production along a line.

t_l	l	g	q
0	125.00	10.00	35.36
10	83.33	10.87	30.10
20	62.50	11.91	27.28
30	50.00	13.16	25.65
40	41.67	14.71	24.75
50	35.71	16.67	24.40
60	31.25	19.23	24.52
70	27.78	22.73	25.13
80	25.00	27.78	26.35
90	22.73	35.71	28.49
100	20.83	50.00	32.27

5 See 'Maximum production with a given budget' in Chapter 2: Theory of production.

In Figure 8.6 the last column of Table 8.2 is shown as a graph. This graph may be called the spatial production curve.[6]

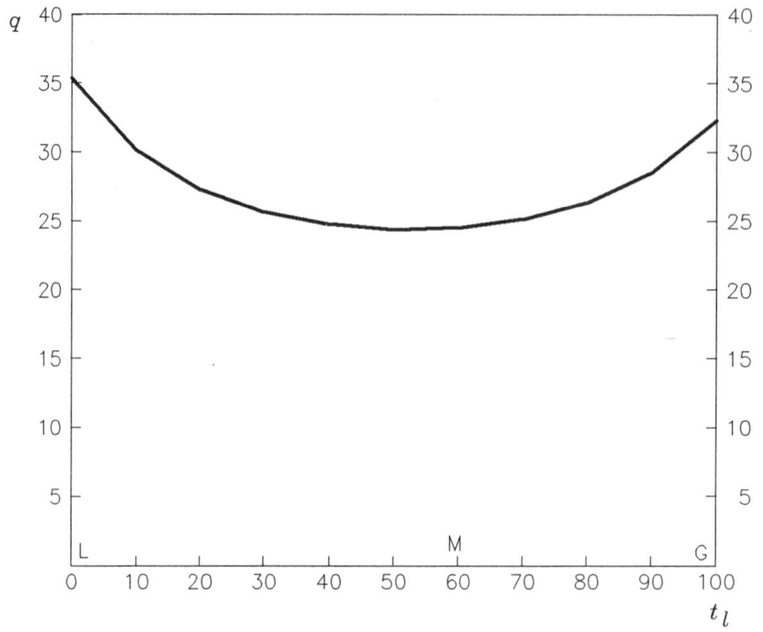

Figure 8.6: Spatial production function.

From Figure 8.6 and Table 8.2 it can be concluded that the best location for this firm will be at the location L of the labour force. Because the budget is given, it can now be concluded that in this model, with a fixed price of the final product and in absence of transportation costs of the final product, the location of the firm will always be at the location of the labour force, or at the location of the raw material.[7] Which location it will be depends on the production function, prices of the inputs, and transportation costs of the inputs.

Turning to Case 2, I will take into account the transportation costs of the commodity, while all the other assumptions remain the same. This means that the net price p_q for the commodity will be:

$$p_q = p - p_{tm} t_m,$$

6 W.J.M. Heijman, 1990. The neoclassical location model of firms. In: F. Dietz, W. Heijman and D. Shefer, *Location and Labor considerations for regional development*. Avebury, Aldershot.
7 It can be proved that the spatial production curve of this kind derived from a Cobb-Douglas production function is always convex.

with p for the fixed price for the commodity. The distance from the location of the firm to the market place equals:

$t_m = | T_m - t_l |$, so:

$p_q = p - p_{tm} | T_m - t_l |$,

with T_m for the distance LM in Figure 8.5. Assume that $T_m = 60$ (like in Figure 8.5) and $p = 25$. Further I know that total revenue o excluding transportation costs for the final product equals $p_q q$ and that profit R equals total revenue o minus the budget B, that equals 500, so: $R = o - B = p_q q - B$. Now, two situations are distinguished. In the first situation, transportation costs for the final product are relatively low: $p_{tm} = 0.1$, whereas in the second situation transportation costs of the final product are relatively high: $p_{tm} = 0.2$. In Table 8.3 it can be observed what the consequences are of this difference in transportation costs.[8]

Table 8.3: Location of the firm when transportation costs of final product are taken into account.

t_l	q	p_q $p_{tm} = 0.1$	p_q $p_{tm} = 0.2$	$o = p_q q$ $p_{tm} = 0.1$	$o = p_q q$ $p_{tm} = 0.1$	R $p_{tm} = 0.1$	R $p_{tm} = 0.2$
0	35.36	19	13	671.84	459.68	171.84	-40.32
10	30.10	20	15	602.00	451.50	102.00	-48.50
20	27.28	21	17	572.88	463.76	72.88	-36.24
30	25.65	22	19	564.30	487.35	64.30	-12.65
40	24.75	23	21	569.25	519.75	69.25	19.75
50	24.40	24	23	585.60	561.20	85.60	61.20
60	24.52	25	25	613.00	613.00	113.00	113.00
70	25.13	24	23	603.12	577.99	103.12	77.99
80	26.35	23	21	606.05	553.35	106.05	53.35
90	28.49	22	19	626.78	541.31	126.78	41.31
100	32.27	21	17	677.67	548.59	177.67	48.59

Figure 8.7 shows the spatial profit curves for the two situations. The outcomes imply that in the case of constant prices and in the absence of transportation costs for the final product, one of the locations of the inputs must be chosen (L or G). In the case described it should be L. The choice of location depends on the value of these transportation costs. With relatively low transportation costs of the commodity, location G should be chosen. With relatively high transportation costs of the commodity, location M should be chosen.

8 Because the production function for q, the budget B and the values of all the other coefficients is the same as in Case 1, the column with production q in Table 8.3 is the same as in Table 8.2. With given price p and the transport costs for the final product p_{tm} all the other values can be computed.

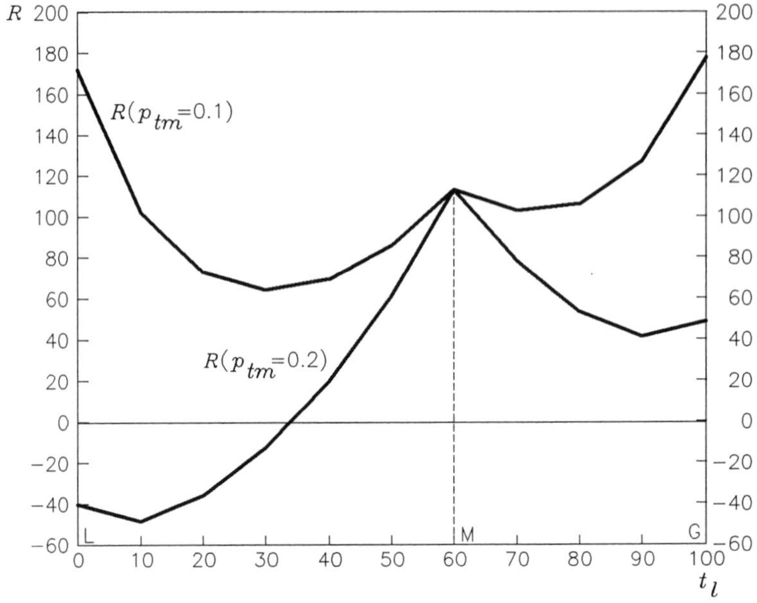

Figure 8.7: Spatial profit curves for two cases.

9. INCOME DISTRIBUTION

Lorenz curve

An indicator of the income distribution of a country is the *Gini coefficient*.[1] This coefficient can be computed with the help of the *Lorenz curve*.[2] First we shall show how this curve is constructed. Suppose the following distribution of income:

Table 9.1: distribution of income.

(1)	(2)	(3)	(4)	(5)	(6)	(7)
income class	number of people	total income	% people	% people acc. x_i	% income	% income acc. y_i
0-10	2	10	20	20	5.0	5.0
10-20	3	45	30	50	22.5	27.5
20-30	3	75	30	80	37.5	65.0
30-40	2	70	20	100	35.0	100.0
Total	10	200	100		100.0	

The Lorenz curve is deduced from columns 5 and 7 (see Figure 9.1 with x for cumulated percentage people and y for cumulated percentage of total income). The greater the surface of the area ODCBA related to area ODE ($0.5 \times 100 \times 100 = 5000$), the more unequal is the income distribution.

Gini coefficient

The Gini coefficient g is calculated as follows (with m for the number of observations):

$$g = \frac{\mathrm{OABCD}}{\mathrm{OED}} = \frac{\mathrm{OED} - \mathrm{OEDCBA}}{\mathrm{OED}}$$

$$g = \frac{0.5 \cdot 100 \cdot 100 - \sum_{i=1}^{m} (x_i - x_{i-1}) y_{i-1} - 0.5 \sum_{i=1}^{m} (x_i - x_{i-1})(y_i - y_{i-1})}{0.5 \cdot 100 \cdot 100}.$$

1 C. Gini, 1912. Variabilità e mutibilità. In: C. Gini, 1955. *Memorie di metodologia statistica: Vol. 1: Variabilità e concentrazione*. Libreria Eredi Virgilio Veschi, Rome.
2 M.O. Lorenz, 1905. Methods for measuring concentration of wealth. *Journal of the American Statistical Association,* 9, pp. 209-219. The Lorenz curve is also called Lorenz-Gini curve, because both authors developed the idea independently.

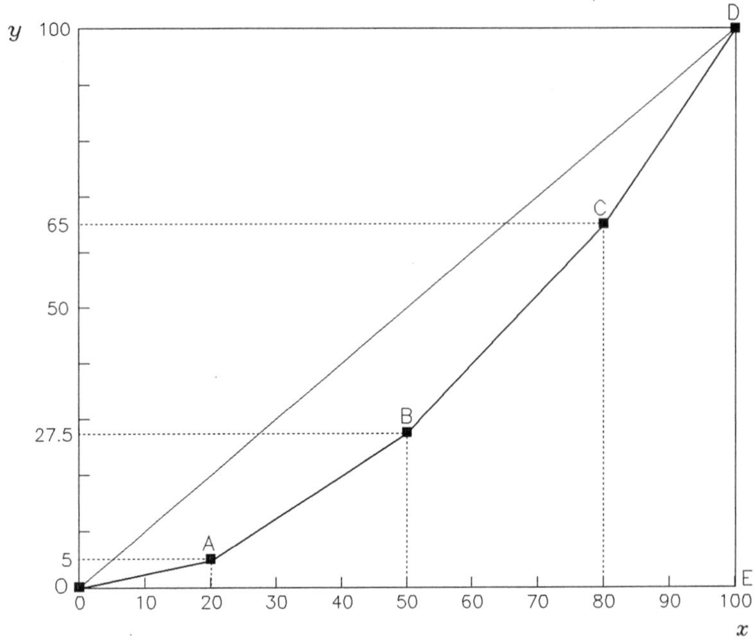

Figure 9.1: Lorenz curve.

In the case of the income distribution of Table 9.1, the Gini coefficient is computed as follows:

$$g = \frac{0.5\times 100\times 100 - 0.5\times 20\times 5 - 5\times 30 - 0.5\times 22.5\times 30 - 30\times 27.5 - 0.5\times 37.5\times 30 - 20\times 65 - 0.5\times 35\times 20}{0.5\times 100\times 100}$$

$$= \frac{5000 - 3575}{5000} = 0.285.$$

If we have only one observation: one share of total population x and share of total income y, $g = x - y$. This can be proved as follows:

$$g = \frac{0.5 - 0.5xy - (1-x)y - 0.5(1-y)(1-x)}{0.5},$$

$$g = 1 - xy - 2(y - xy) - (1 - y - x + xy) = -2y + y + x = x - y.$$

Optimum income distribution

Generally speaking, social welfare u can be considered as a function of total production q. Production is realized from the input of production factors. Now, I assume only one production factor: labour l. However, this production factor is not homogenous, but heterogenous. In our case there are two types of labour l_1 and l_2, so that $l_1 + l_2 = l$. The aim is to maximize total welfare. This problem may be formulated as follows:

$$u = u(q),$$

$$q = q(l_1, l_2)$$

$$l = l_1 + l_2,$$

$$\text{Max} \quad u.$$

To solve the problem, I form the following Lagrange function:

$$L = u(q(l_1, l_2)) - \lambda(l - l_1 - l_2).$$

The first-order conditions are:

$$\frac{\partial u}{\partial l_1} = \frac{du}{dq}\frac{\partial q}{\partial l_1} + \lambda = 0,$$

$$\frac{\partial u}{\partial l_2} = \frac{du}{dq}\frac{\partial q}{\partial l_2} + \lambda = 0.$$

The conclusion is that, at the optimum:

$$p\frac{\partial q}{\partial l_1} = p\frac{\partial q}{\partial l_2}.$$

If labour is valued according to the value of its marginal product, then:

$$w_1 = w_2 = p\frac{\partial q}{\partial l_1} = p\frac{\partial q}{\partial l_2},$$

with w_1 and w_2 for the wages of the two types of labour. The conclusion is that, at the optimum, the value of the marginal product of each kind of labour is equalized. This implies that if real wage equals the value of the marginal product at the optimum, wages are equal.

As an example, I take a Cobb-Douglas production function:

$$q = \alpha l_1^{\beta} l_2^{1-\beta}.$$

I know that, at the optimum:

$$\frac{\partial q}{\partial l_1} = w_1 = \frac{\partial q}{\partial l_2} = w_2, \text{ so: } \alpha\beta l_1^{\beta-1} l_2^{1-\beta} = \alpha(1-\beta) l_2^{-\beta} l_1^{\beta}.$$

This means that:

$$\frac{l_1^{\beta-1} l_2^{1-\beta}}{l_1^{\beta} l_2^{-\beta}} = \frac{1-\beta}{\beta}, \text{ so: } \frac{l_2}{l_1} = \frac{1-\beta}{\beta}.$$

If, for example, the total amount of labour equals 100, and $\beta = 0.4$, then $l_2/l_1 = 0.6/0.4$. This implies that 60% of the total labour force should be in category 1, and that 40% of the total labour force should be in category 2.

The Gini coefficient of primary wages (wages before taxation and social security payments) is an indicator for the vicinity of the optimum. If $g = 0$, the welfare optimum has been reached.[3] This means that the total amount of labour l should be allocated over the two categories, l_1 and l_2, such that their marginal productivity is equal.[4]

In this case the Gini coefficient can be calculated as follows. Because β represents the share of category 1 labour in total income, the Gini coefficient equals (see the beginning of this chapter):

$$g = \left| \frac{l_1}{l} - \beta \right|.$$

Because the Gini coefficient is always positive, I have to use absolute value strips here.[5]

In this case, the idea of optimum income distribution has been applied with only one product. I can extend the previous idea to more products, for example two. In that case the model is (with u for utility or welfare):

---

3 An important thing to notice here is that, in this case, the Gini coefficient has to measure the distribution of *primary wages*. One cannot maximize welfare by equalizing *secondary wages* (by taxing or otherwise). The important point to stress is that marginal products of different kinds of labour are equal in the optimum. A tool that may contribute to this end is education.

4 In the real world this can only be approached, for example, by adapting the education system such that students are guided toward the specialization with high marginal productivity. The market itself is a tool to that end. Higher wages in certain sectors attract more labour than sectors with relatively low wages. However, differences in wages will always exist. Certain types of labour remain scarce because they require relatively more skill and/or natural talents (football players, musicians *etc.*)

5 I derived before: $\frac{\beta}{1-\beta} = \frac{l_1}{l_2}$. This is the same as $g = 0$. Proof: $g = 0$, so: $\beta = \frac{l_1}{l}$ and $1 - \beta = \frac{l_2}{l}$.

So: $\frac{\beta}{1-\beta} = \frac{l_1}{l_2}$.

$$\text{Max } u = u(q_1, q_2),$$

$$q_1 = q_1(l_{11}, l_{21}),$$

$$q_2 = q_2(l_{12}, l_{22}),$$

$$l = l_{11} + l_{21} + l_{12} + l_{22},$$

with l_{ij} for type of labour i allocated to production process j.

The solution is reached by forming the Lagrange equation:

$$L = u(q_1(l_{11}, l_{21}), q_2(l_{12}, l_{22})) - \lambda(l - l_{11} - l_{21} - l_{12} - l_{22}).$$

The first order conditions for a maximum are:

$$\frac{\partial L}{\partial l_{11}} = \frac{\partial u}{\partial q_1}\frac{\partial q_1}{\partial l_{11}} - \lambda = 0,$$

$$\frac{\partial L}{\partial l_{21}} = \frac{\partial u}{\partial q_1}\frac{\partial q_1}{\partial l_{21}} - \lambda = 0,$$

$$\frac{\partial L}{\partial l_{12}} = \frac{\partial u}{\partial q_2}\frac{\partial q_2}{\partial l_{12}} - \lambda = 0,$$

$$\frac{\partial L}{\partial l_{22}} = \frac{\partial u}{\partial q_2}\frac{\partial q_2}{\partial l_{22}} - \lambda = 0.$$

The conclusion is that at the optimum:

$$\frac{\partial u}{\partial q_1}\frac{\partial q_1}{\partial l_{11}} = \frac{\partial u}{\partial q_1}\frac{\partial q_1}{\partial l_{21}} = \frac{\partial u}{\partial q_2}\frac{\partial q_2}{\partial l_{12}} = \frac{\partial u}{\partial q_2}\frac{\partial q_2}{\partial l_{22}}$$

and that:

$$p_1\frac{\partial q_1}{\partial l_{11}} = p_1\frac{\partial q_1}{\partial l_{21}} = p_2\frac{\partial q_2}{\partial l_{12}} = p_2\frac{\partial q_2}{\partial l_{22}}, \quad \text{so: } w_{11} = w_{21} = w_{12} = w_{22}.$$

This means that, if in every branch labour is valued according to the value of its marginal product, in order to reach a welfare optimum, primary wages should be equal.[6]

---

6 Of course this proof can be extended to an unspecified number of branches and types of labour.

Income distribution and environment

When trying to maximize welfare taking into account the state of the environment, income distribution can have a profound influence as the following analysis shows. Here it is assumed that society consists of two persons or groups (1 and 2) and that welfare u is determined by a given income y minus diseconomies D, which are a function of income and pollution abatement A.[7] Abatement is assumed to be a positive function of income.[8] This means that the persons with a higher income tend to abate pollution more than persons with a low income. Recapitulating:

$$\text{Max} \quad u = y - D(y, A), \quad \frac{\partial D}{\partial y} > 0, \quad \frac{\partial D}{\partial A} < 0,$$

$$y = y_1 + y_2,$$

$$A = A_1 + A_2,$$

$$A_1 = A_1(y_1), \quad \frac{dA_1}{dy_1} > 0,$$

$$A_2 = A_2(y_2), \quad \frac{dA_2}{dy_2} > 0.$$

The Lagrange function connected with this maximization problem is:

$$L = y_1 + y_2 - D((y_1 + y_2), (A_1(y_1) + A_2(y_2))) + \lambda(y - y_1 - y_2).$$

The first order conditions are:

$$\frac{\partial L}{\partial y_1} = 1 - \frac{\partial D}{\partial y_1} - \frac{\partial D}{\partial A_1}\frac{dA_1}{dy_1} - \lambda = 0,$$

$$\frac{\partial L}{\partial y_2} = 1 - \frac{\partial D}{\partial y_2} - \frac{\partial D}{\partial A_2}\frac{dA_2}{dy_2} - \lambda = 0.$$

So:

7 Of course it is possible to extend the analysis to more than two persons.
8 For the positive relation between income and environmental research and development, see: Komen R., S. Gerkin and H. Folmer, 1997. Income and environmental RD: some empirical evidence from OECD countries. Accepted for *Environment and Development Economics*.

$$\frac{\partial D}{\partial y_1}+\frac{\partial D}{\partial A_1}\frac{dA_1}{dy_1}=\frac{\partial D}{\partial y_2}+\frac{\partial D}{\partial A_2}\frac{dA_2}{dy_2}.$$

Assume:

$$\frac{\partial D}{\partial A_1}=\delta_1,\quad \frac{\partial D}{\partial A_2}=\delta_2,\quad \frac{dA_1}{dy_1}=\alpha_1 y_1,$$

$$\frac{dA_2}{dy_2}=\alpha_2 y_2,\quad \frac{\partial D}{\partial y_1}=\gamma_1 y_1,\quad \frac{\partial D}{\partial y_2}=\gamma_2 y_2,$$

$$\delta_1<0,\ \delta_2<0,\ \alpha_1>0,\ \alpha_2>0,\ \gamma_1>0,\ \gamma_2>0.$$

Then:

$$y_1=\frac{(\gamma_2+\delta_2\alpha_2)}{(\gamma_1+\delta_1\alpha_1)}y_2.$$

If the number of persons in the two groups are equal then the optimum gini coefficient g equals:[9]

$$g^*=\left|0.50-\frac{\frac{(\gamma_2+\delta_2\alpha_2)}{(\gamma_1+\delta_1\alpha_1)}}{\frac{(\gamma_2+\delta_2\alpha_2)}{(\gamma_1+\delta_1\alpha_1)}+1}\right|=\left|0.50-\frac{\gamma_2+\delta_2\alpha_2}{\gamma_2+\delta_2\alpha_2+\gamma_1+\delta_1\alpha_1}\right|.$$

So, if $\gamma_2+\delta_2\alpha_2=\gamma_1+\delta_1\alpha_1$, then $g=0$, which means that in that case the income distribution is completely equal.

The Environmental Kuznets curve

The Kuznets curve is a inverse-U curve, with average income $\underline{y}$ on the horizontal axis and the income distribution (measured for example by the Gini coefficient g) on the vertical axis.[10] It concerns the empirical phenomenon that, with increasing average income, income distribution tends to become more unequal in the first stages

---

9 If $y_1=\beta y_2$, then $y_1=\frac{\beta}{1+\beta}\underline{y}$. Now, if the number of the groupes is equal the gini coefficient is: $\left|0.5-\frac{\beta}{1+\beta}\right|$ (see the beginning of this chapter).

10 M. Blaug, 1985. *Great Economists since Keynes*. Wheatsheaf, Brighton.

of the economic growth process and more equal in the later stages. With the maximum of the inverse-U curve lying at $\underline{y}^*$, I can now formulate the Kuznets function as follows:

$$g = g(\underline{y}), \text{ with } \frac{dg}{d\underline{y}} > 0 \text{ if } 0 < \underline{y} < \underline{y}^*, \ \frac{dg}{d\underline{y}} = 0 \text{ if } \underline{y} = \underline{y}^*,$$

$$\frac{dg}{d\underline{y}} < 0 \text{ if } \underline{y} > \underline{y}^*, \ g, \underline{y} \geq 0.$$

Assuming that the optimum gini coefficient g from the viewpoint of the environment equals 0, we can now derive the following relationships (with p for population):[11]

$$D = D(y, A), \ \frac{\partial D}{\partial y} > 0, \ \frac{\partial D}{\partial A} < 0,$$

$$A = A(\underline{y}, g), \ \frac{\partial A}{\partial \underline{y}} > 0, \ \frac{\partial A}{\partial g} < 0,$$

$$g = g(\underline{y}), \text{ see above},$$

$$y = \underline{y} p.$$

From this model the environmental Kuznetscurve can be derived. The following example shows this. Assume the following explicit model:

$$D = \alpha y - \beta A, \ \alpha, \beta > 0,$$

$$A = \gamma \underline{y} - \delta g, \ \gamma, \delta > 0,$$

$$g = -\epsilon \underline{y}^2 + \mu \underline{y}, \ \epsilon, \mu > 0 \text{ (Kuznets curve)},$$

$$y = p\underline{y}.$$

Now the environmental Kuznetscurve can be derived:

$$D = -\epsilon\beta\delta \underline{y}^2 + (\mu\beta\delta + \alpha p - \beta\gamma)\underline{y}.$$

---

11 The first order conditions for minimum diseconomies are the same as for maximum welfare in the previous section. Further it is assumed that all agents are identical. In that case, in terms of the previous section: $\gamma_2 + \delta_2 \alpha_2 = \gamma_1 + \delta_1 \alpha_1$. This means that in the optimum the gini coefficient g must be 0 and that D is an increasing function of g.

Figure 9.2 gives a picture of both the Kuznetscurve and the Environmental Kuznetscurve.

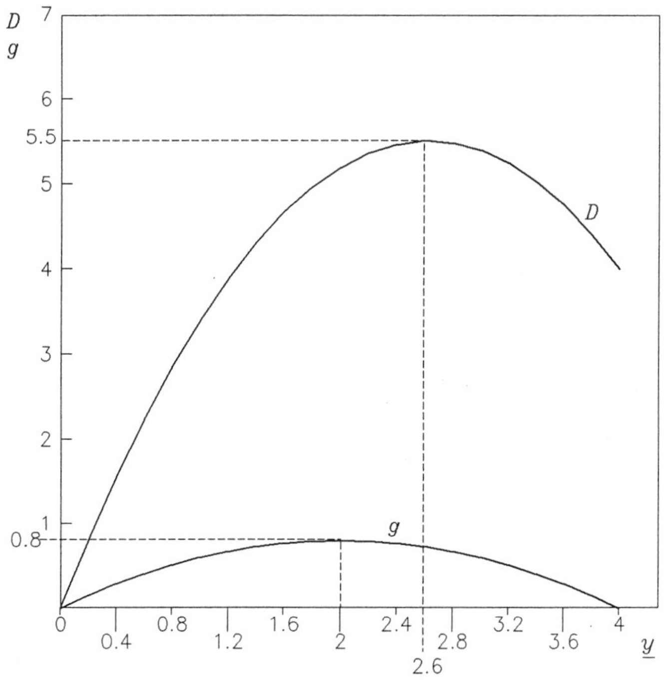

Figure 9.2: Environmental Kuznetscurve. With: $\epsilon = 0.2$, $\beta = 2$, $\delta = 2$, $\mu = 0.8$, $\alpha = 1$, $p = 2$. and $\gamma = 0.5$. So: $g = -0.2\underline{y}^2 + 0.8\underline{y}$, and $D = -0.8\underline{y}^2 + 4.2\underline{y}$.

10. EFFICIENCY IN RESOURCE DEPLETION

Hotelling rule

Original Hotelling rule: non-renewable resource, perfect competition

This chapter deals with the question of how to deplete a stock of resources in an efficient way.[1] In this respect efficiency means maximizing social utility or welfare U, given a resource stock Q, while in every period t $(0,\ldots,T)$ an amount q_t is depleted. The first case is the case of a non-renewable resource (*e.g.* a stock of iron ore). Then, the problem may be put as:

$$\text{Max} \quad U = U(q_0, q_1, \ldots, q_t, \ldots, q_T)$$

$$= U_0(q_0) + \frac{U_1(q_1)}{1+i} + \ldots + \frac{U_t(q_t)}{(1+i)^t} + \ldots + \frac{U_T(q_T)}{(1+i)^T},$$

$$Q = q_0 + q_1 + \ldots + q_t + \ldots + q_T.$$

To solve it, I use the following Lagrange function:

$$L = U(q_0, q_1, \ldots, q_t, \ldots q_n) + \lambda(q_1 + q_2 + \ldots + q_t + \ldots + q_n - Q).$$

The first-order conditions are: $\frac{\partial L}{\partial q_t} = \frac{\partial U_t / \partial q_t}{(1+i)^t} + \lambda = 0.$

Because the definition of the shadow price of the resource is (see chapter 6):

$$\frac{\partial U_t}{\partial q_t} = p_t, \quad \text{so:} \quad p_t = (1+i)^t p_0.$$

with p_t for the resource *rent* in period t.[2] This result, which says that for an efficient depletion of a non-renewable resource the rent of the resource should increase by the rate of interest, is called the Hotelling rule.[3]

---

1 W.J.M. Heijman, 1991. *Depletable resources and the economy*. Wageningen Economic Studies (WES), nr 21, Wageningen Agricultural University, Wageningen.
2 As has been explained in Chapter 6, the price of a good equals gross marginal benefits. Gross marginal benefits minus marginal costs equals the *rent* of the resource.
3 Hotelling H., 1931. The economics of exhaustible resources. *The journal of political economy* 39, nr 2, pp. 137-175.

Adaptation 1: Hotelling efficiency rule for a renewable resource
The second case deals with renewable resources (*e.g.* fish, wood). Then, the original Hotelling rule has to be adapted. The problem can now be formulated as follows (with a for the constant rate of renewal):

$$\text{Max} \quad U = U(q_0, q_1, \ldots, q_t, \ldots, q_n)$$

$$= U_0(q_0) + \frac{U_1(q_1(1+a))}{1+i} + \ldots + \frac{U_t(q_t(1+a)^t)}{(1+i)^t} + \ldots + \frac{U_n(q_n(1+a)^n)}{(1+i)^n},$$

$$Q = q_0 + q_1 + \ldots + q_t + \ldots + q_n.$$

Lagrange function:

$$L = U(q_0, q_1, \ldots, q_t, \ldots, q_n) + \lambda(q_0 + q_1 + \ldots + q_t + \ldots + q_n - Q).$$

First-order conditions:

$$\frac{\partial L}{\partial q_t} = \frac{(\partial U_t / \partial q_t)(1+a)^t}{(1+i)^t} + \lambda = 0, \quad \text{so:}$$

$$p_t = p_0 \frac{(1+i)^t}{(1+a)^t}.$$

According to this result, for an efficient depletion of a renewable resource the rent of the resource should increase by the rate of interest corrected for the (constant) rate of growth. This is the Hotelling rule for renewable resources.[4]

Adaptation 2: Market forms
Assume s firms, each firm m depleting a well-defined part Q^m of a reserve of Q units of a non-renewable resource. So: $Q = Q^1 + \ldots + Q^s$. Further I know that rent p_t for period t depends on the supply $Q_t = q_t^1 + \ldots + q_t^m + \ldots + q_t^s$, of all the firms together, where q_t^m is the depletion of firm m in period t. Every firm m $(m = 1, \ldots, s)$ tries to maximize its total profit W^m. So:

$$\text{Max} \quad W^m = p_0 q_0^m + \frac{p_1 q_1^m}{(1+i)} + \ldots + \frac{p_T q_T^m}{(1+i)^T},$$

$$\text{s.t.} \quad Q^m = q_0^m + q_1^m + \ldots + q_T^m,$$

4 This is the case for a renewable resource with a constant growth rate.

$$p_t = p_t(Q_t) = p_t(q_t^1 + q_t^2 + q_t^3 + \ldots + q_t^m + \ldots + q_t^s).$$

I solve this with the help of the following Lagrange function:

$$L^m = W^m(q_0^m, \ldots, q_T^m) - \lambda^m(q_0^m + q_1^m + \ldots + q_T^m - Q^m).$$

First-order conditions are:

$$\frac{\partial L^m}{\partial q_t^m} = \frac{\left\{\frac{dp_t}{dQ_t} q_t^m + p_t\right\}}{(1+i)^t} - \lambda^m = 0 \quad (*), \quad \text{so:}$$

$$\frac{dp_t}{dQ_t} q_t^m + p_t = \left\{\frac{dp_0}{dQ_0} q_0^m + p_0\right\}(1+i)^t,$$

which means that the marginal rent of each firm m is to increase by the rate of interest. The solution (*) represents a so-called Cournot-Nash equilibrium.[5] Adding up all individual optimum rules yields:

$$\frac{dp_t}{dQ_t} q_t^1 + p_t = \left\{\frac{dp_0}{dQ_0} q_0^1 + p_0\right\}(1+i)^t$$

$$\frac{dp_t}{dQ_t} q_t^2 + p_t = \left\{\frac{dp_0}{dQ_0} q_0^2 + p_0\right\}(1+i)^t$$

...

$$\frac{dp_t}{dQ_t} q_t^m + p_t = \left\{\frac{dp_0}{dQ_0} q_0^m + p_0\right\}(1+i)^t$$

...

$$\frac{dp_t}{dQ_t} q_t^s + p_t = \left\{\frac{dp_0}{dQ_0} q_0^s + p_0\right\}(1+i)^t \qquad +$$

$$\frac{dp_t}{dQ_t} Q_t + s p_t = \left\{\frac{dp_0}{dQ_0} Q_0 + s p_0\right\}(1+i)^t$$

$$\text{So:} \quad \left(\frac{1}{s}\right)\frac{dp_t}{dQ_t} Q_t + p_t = \left\{\left(\frac{1}{s}\right)\frac{dp_0}{dQ_0} Q_0 + p_0\right\}(1+i)^t.$$

---

5 In the Cournot-Nash equilibrium each firm m takes in each period t an action q_t^m that is such that deviation of any firm alone from this equilibrium will yield a lower profit to this firm.

If $s \to \infty$, there is perfect competition and the Hotelling rule applies. If $s = 1$, there is a monopoly. In that case marginal rent of the whole sector will increase by the rate of interest. If $1 < s < \infty$, the case of an oligopoly arises. The situation approaches perfect competition or monopoly depending on the value of s.

I will illustrate the former theory with the following case for two periods and two firms using a specific demand function:[6]

$$p_t(Q_t) = 10 - Q_t, \quad \text{so: } \frac{dp_t}{dQ_t} = -1.$$

I can derive:

$$\frac{dp_t}{dQ_t} q_t^m + p_t = \lambda^m (1+i)^t, \quad \text{so:}$$

$$-q_t^m + 10 - Q_t = \lambda^m (1+i)^t, \quad \text{or: } -q_t^m + 10 - q_t^1 - q_t^2 = \lambda^m (1+i)^t.$$

For two periods this gives the following set of equations:

$$10 - 2q_0^1 - q_0^2 = \lambda^1,$$

$$10 - 2q_0^2 - q_0^1 = \lambda^2,$$

$$10 - 2q_1^1 - q_1^2 = \lambda^1 (1+i),$$

$$10 - 2q_1^2 - q_1^1 = \lambda^2 (1+i),$$

$$Q^1 = q_0^1 + q_1^1,$$

$$Q^2 = q_0^2 + q_1^2.$$

The solutions of this set with q_0^1, q_0^2, q_1^1 q_1^2, λ^1 and λ^2 as unknown values are:

---

6 Of course, it is possible to prove that the Cournot equilibrium also exists in the case of s firms and T periods.

$$q_0^1 = \frac{Q^1 + 3.33i}{2+i}, \quad q_1^1 = \frac{(1+i)Q^1 - 3.33i}{2+i},$$

$$q_0^2 = \frac{Q^2 + 3.33i}{2+i}, \quad q_1^2 = \frac{(1+i)Q^2 - 3.33i}{2+i},$$

$$\lambda^1 = \frac{20 - 2Q^1 - Q^2}{2+i}, \quad \lambda^2 = \frac{20 - 2Q^2 - Q^1}{2+i}.$$

General equation

Including the effects of renewability and market forms, the Hotelling equation is:[7]

$$\frac{dp_t}{dQ_t} q_t^m + p_t = \left\{ \frac{dp_0}{dQ_0} q_0^m + p_0 \right\} \frac{(1+i)^t}{(1+a)^t}.$$

Adding up all individual optima gives the general Hotelling equation:[8]

$$\sum_{m=1}^{s} \left\{ \frac{dp_t}{dQ_t} q_t^m + p_t \right\} = \sum_{m=1}^{s} \left\{ \frac{dp_0}{dQ_0} q_0^m + p_0 \right\} \frac{(1+i)^t}{(1+a)^t}, \quad \text{so:}$$

$$\left(\frac{1}{s} \right) \frac{dp_t}{dQ_t} Q_t + p_t = \left\{ \left(\frac{1}{s} \right) \frac{dp_0}{dQ_0} Q_0 + p_0 \right\} \frac{(1+i)^t}{(1+a)^t}.$$

If $a = 0$ and $s \to \infty$, for reasonable demand functions, the original Hotelling rule applies.

Depletion time of a resource stock with a linear demand function

In this section I determine the depletion time T of an exhaustible resource under the assumptions of perfect competition, well-defined property rights and a specified linear demand function. To determine the depletion time it is possible to use the Hotelling efficiency rule. This rule is that the price of an exhaustible resource should increase by the rate of interest if the social value of the resource is to be maximized. The price of the resource p is the net price after paying the marginal costs of extraction and placing the amount of resource on the market. As we know, this 'price' is referred to as the *rent* of the resource.

According to the Hotelling rule, the royalty of the exhaustible resource (p_t) should increase each period by the rate of interest (i), which means:

---

7 This goes without proof.

8 Of course, it can be proved here that this general Hotelling equation implies a Cournot equilibrium.

$$p_t = p_0 e^{it}.$$

I assume the following demand function:

$$p_t = \alpha q_t + \beta, \quad \alpha < 0, \ \beta > 0.$$

Total stock Q equals the sum of all depletions, or:

$$Q = \int_0^T q_t dt.$$

Because I know that the firm exploiting the resource is assumed to maximize its profit, it follows that $q_T = 0$, or:

$$p_T = p_0 e^{iT} = \beta.$$

Now, depletion time T is derived as follows:

$$\begin{aligned}
Q = \int_0^T q_t dt &= \int_0^T \frac{p_t - \beta}{\alpha} dt, \\
&= \int_0^T \frac{p_t}{\alpha} dt + \int_0^T \frac{-\beta}{\alpha} dt, \\
&= \frac{1}{\alpha} \int_0^T p_t dt - \frac{\beta}{\alpha} T, \\
&= \frac{1}{\alpha} \int_0^T p_0 e^{it} dt - \frac{\beta}{\alpha} T, \\
&= \frac{p_0}{\alpha} \left[\frac{1}{i} e^{it} \right]_0^T - \frac{\beta}{\alpha} T, \\
&= \frac{p_0}{\alpha i} (e^{iT} - 1) - \frac{\beta}{\alpha} T.
\end{aligned}$$

Because $p_0 = \beta e^{-iT}$, I can now deduce:

$$Q = \frac{\beta e^{-iT}}{\alpha i} (e^{iT} - 1) - \frac{\beta}{\alpha} T = \frac{\beta}{\alpha i} - \frac{\beta e^{-iT}}{\alpha i} - \frac{\beta}{\alpha} T,$$

$$= \frac{\beta}{\alpha} \left(\frac{1}{i} - e^{-iT} - T \right).$$

When T is rather large, we can assume e^{-iT} to be 0. This implies that

$$T \approx \frac{1}{i} - \frac{Q\alpha}{\beta}.$$

This outcome means that as the rate of interest increases, the depletion time decreases. Further, it can be computed that in case of a monopoly, depletion time will be longer than under perfect competition. Then, because marginal revenue equals $2\alpha q_t + \beta$, depletion time T_m equals:[9]

$$T_m \approx \frac{1}{i} - \frac{2Q\alpha}{\beta}.$$

Figure 10.1 gives a picture of these relations when $\alpha = -0.5$, $Q = 1000$ and $\beta = 20$.

Depletion time of a resource with a non-linear demand function

In this section I determine the depletion time of an exhaustible resource within the given constraints of perfect competition, well-defined property rights and a specified non-linear demand function, which is probably more realistic than a linear demand curve.

According to the Hotelling rule, the royalty of the exhaustible resource (p_t) should increase each period by the rate of interest i, which means:

$$p_t = p_0 e^{it}.$$

The following specified demand function:[10]

$$p = Ke^{-\alpha q},$$

implies that p approaches zero when q approaches infinity and that p equals K when q equals 0. The total stock of the exhaustible resource is known to be equal to ω units. The question is to determinate the time (T) during which the stock of the exhaustible resource will completely be depleted. Since we know that, in the end, p_t must equal K, this means that $K = p_0 e^{iT}$, or, written a little differently:

---

9 It is also possible to determine the optimum depletion time in case of an oligopoly. Then I will have to use the results of the previous section.

10 This specific demand curve stems from: Heijman W.J.M., 1990. Natural resources and market forms. *Wageningen Economic Papers*. Wageningen Agricultural University. This specification is also used in Perman *et al.*, 1996. *Natural resources and environmental economics*. Longman, New York.

$$p_0 = K e^{-iT}.$$

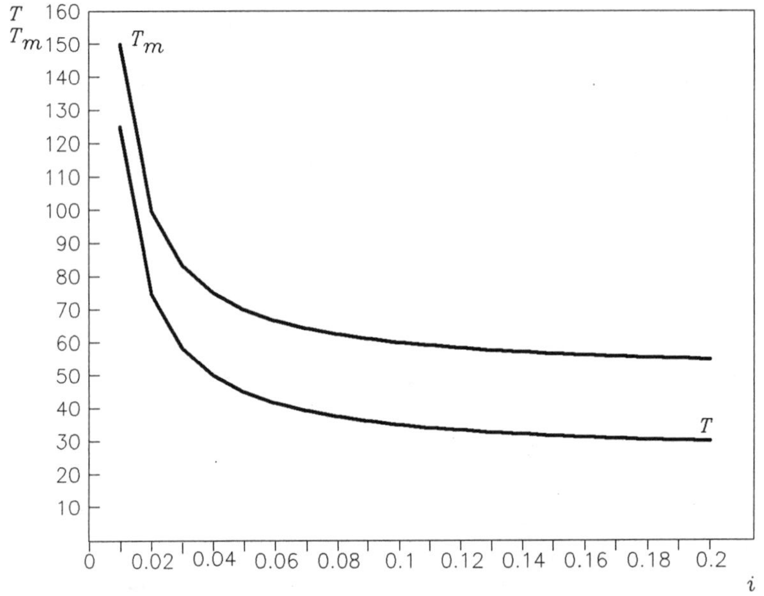

Figure 10.1: Relation between depletion time T and rate of interest i.

From the last three equations it follows:

$$K e^{-\alpha q} = K e^{i(t-T)}, \quad \alpha q = i(T-t), \quad q_t = \frac{i}{\alpha}(T-t).$$

So: $$\int_0^T q_t dt = \int_0^T \frac{i}{\alpha}(T-t) dt.$$

Because $\int_0^T q_t dt$ equals ω:

$$\omega = \frac{i}{\alpha}[Tt - \frac{1}{2}t^2]_0^T = \frac{1}{2}\frac{i}{\alpha}T^2.$$

From this the following expression for T follows:

$$T^2 = \frac{2\omega\alpha}{i}, \quad \text{so: } T = \sqrt{\frac{2\omega\alpha}{i}}.$$

Now it is possible to compute p_0 and q_0:

$$p_0 = Ke^{-\sqrt{2i\omega\alpha}},$$

$$q_0 = \frac{\sqrt{2i\omega\alpha}}{\alpha}.$$

The goal of a monopolist is usually to maximize profits or royalties over time. When r stands for the total amount of royalties, p for the royalty per unit of product and q for the total production, a monopolist tries to maximize the following function:

$$r = p(q)q,$$

subject to the condition:

$$\int_0^T q_t dt = \omega.$$

Taking into account a discount rate i, the function (J) to be maximized changes into:

$$J = \int_0^T qp(q)e^{-it}dt.$$

The discounted marginal revenue must be equal for each period, because, if this were not so, the monopolist could increase total discounted royalty by moving an extracted unit from a period with a relatively low discounted marginal revenue to a period with a relatively high discounted marginal revenue. In other words:

$$MR_t e^{-it} = c$$

$$MR_t = ce^{it}$$

$$MR_t = MR_0 e^{it}.$$

The marginal revenue (MR) function connected with the specified demand function is:

$$MR = -\alpha q K e^{-\alpha q} + K e^{-\alpha q}.$$

From this it can be concluded that marginal revenue equals K when q equals 0. This leads to the following expression for the marginal revenue:

$$MR_t = MR_0 e^{it}$$

$$K = MR_0 e^{iT}$$

$$MR_t = K e^{i(t-T)}.$$

The specified marginal revenue function of equation does not enable an easy solution to the dynamic programming problem. Therefore I use a function which is a fairly precise approximation of the marginal revenue function, through which the problem can be elegantly solved:[11]

$$MR = K e^{-h\alpha q}, \qquad \text{with} \qquad h \approx 2.49.$$

Once this simplified expression for marginal revenue is known, it is possible to solve the dynamic programming problem in the same way as was done in the perfect competition case:

$$K e^{-h\alpha q} = K e^{i(t-T)}.$$

This means that:

$$h\alpha q = i(T-t),$$

$$q = \frac{i}{h\alpha}(T-t).$$

Integration of this equation gives:

---

11 See: Heijman W.J.M, 1990. Natural resource depletion and market forms. *Wageningen Economic Papers 1990-1*. Wageningen Agricultural University. Also: Perman R., Y. Ma and J. McGilvray, 1996. *Natural resource and environmental economics*. Longman, London.

$$\int_0^T q\,dt = \int_0^T \frac{i}{h\alpha}(T-t)\,dt.$$

Because total stock equals ω, this equation can be rewritten as:

$$\omega = \int_0^T \frac{i}{h\alpha}(T-t)\,dt.$$

Computing the integrand of this equation from 0 to T gives:

$$\omega = \frac{i}{h\alpha}\left[Tt - \frac{1}{2}t^2\right]_0^T dt$$

$$\omega = \frac{1}{2}\frac{i}{h\alpha}T^2$$

$$T = \sqrt{\frac{2\omega h\alpha}{i}}.$$

Now it is possible to determine q_0 and p_0:

$$q_0 = \frac{\sqrt{2i\omega h\alpha}}{h\alpha}$$

$$p_0 = Ke^{\frac{-\sqrt{2i\omega h\alpha}}{h}}.$$

Table 10.1: Perfect competition and monopoly compared

perfect competition	**monopoly**
$T = \sqrt{\frac{2\omega\alpha}{i}}$	$T = \sqrt{\frac{2\omega h\alpha}{i}}$
$p_0 = Ke^{-\sqrt{2i\omega\alpha}}$	$p_0 = Ke^{\frac{-\sqrt{2i\omega h\alpha}}{h}}$
$q_0 = \frac{\sqrt{2i\omega\alpha}}{\alpha}$	$q_0 = \frac{\sqrt{2i\omega h\alpha}}{h\alpha}$

In Table 10.1, the results of the perfect competition situation are compared with the results obtained from the situation with a monopoly. From this table it is clear that a monopolist is more careful about depletion of an exhaustible resource than the joint firms acting under perfect competition. Using the specified non-linear demand function, a monopolist multiplies $\sqrt{h}$ (≈ 1.6) by the time the firms under perfect competition take to deplete the resource stock completely. In a monopoly, prices will be higher and the quantities put on the market each period will be smaller than they are with perfect competition. This is a remarkable aspect, because a monopoly is generally considered to be working against the common interest and the environment. It was this result that forced Solow to make the following much-quoted comment:[12]

> The amusing thing is that if a conservationist is someone who would like to see resources conserved *beyond* the pace that competition would adopt, then the monopolist is the conservationist's friend. No doubt they would be surprised to know it.

Optimum rotation period in forestry

One rotation period

A rotation period is the period of growth of a forest. The question is: how long should a forest grow from an economic point of view. The net present value $V(t)$ of the forest is to be maximized with q_t for the amount of wood in time t, p_t for the price of wood in time t, c for the cost of planting the trees, i for the rate of interest and t for the time of the rotation period (for example, the number of years). Now:

$$V(t) = -c + p(t)q(t)e^{-it}.$$

Maximizing the net present value of the forest means:

$$\frac{dV}{dt} = p\frac{dq}{dt}e^{-it} + \frac{dp}{dt}qe^{-it} - ipqe^{-it} = 0,$$

or:

$$\frac{1}{q}\frac{dq}{dt} + \frac{1}{p}\frac{dp}{dt} = i.$$

12 Solow R.M., The economics of resources or the resources of economics. *The American Economic Review* 78 (1988), nr 2, pp.1-14.

So the rate of renewal of the forest plus the rate of the expected rise in the price of wood should be equal to the rate of interest. This rule may be called the *Faustmann rule.*[13] If the functions $q(t)$ and $p(t)$ are known, then the optimum rotation time can be determined. For example:

$$q(t) = q_0 e^{-\alpha t^2 + \beta t}, \text{ then:}$$

$$\frac{dq}{dt} = q_0(-2\alpha t + \beta)e^{-\alpha t^2 + \beta t}, \text{ so: } \bar{q} = \frac{dq}{dt}\frac{1}{q} = -2\alpha t + \beta \quad 0 \le t \le \frac{\beta}{2\alpha}.$$

and:

$$p(t) = p_0 e^{\gamma t}, \text{ so: } \frac{dp}{dt} = p_0 \gamma e^{\gamma t} \text{ and } \bar{p} = \frac{dp}{dt}\frac{1}{p} = \gamma.$$

Now assume that $\beta = 0.4$, $\alpha = 0.1$, $\gamma = -0.05$, $q_0 = 10$ and $i = 0.10$. The growth curve of this forest is shown in Figure 10.2.

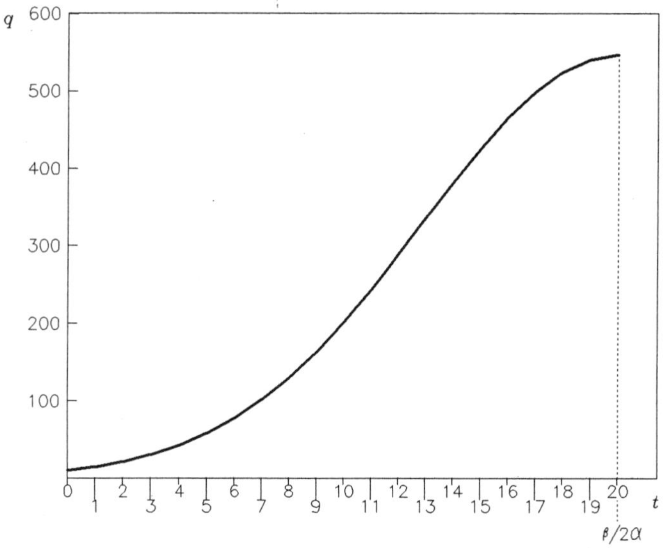

Figure 10.2: Growth curve of a forest.

13 Faustmann M., 1968 (1849). *Calculation of the value which forest land and immature stands possess for forestry.* Commonwealth Forestry Institute (CFI), Institute paper nr 42. Translation from the original German article. Notice that if the rate of renewal equals 0, the Hotelling rule applies.

The curve of the relative growth speed $\overline{q}$ and the curves of interest i and relative price change $\overline{p}$ are shown in Figure 10.3. The optimum harvesting time t^* appears to be 12.5 years.

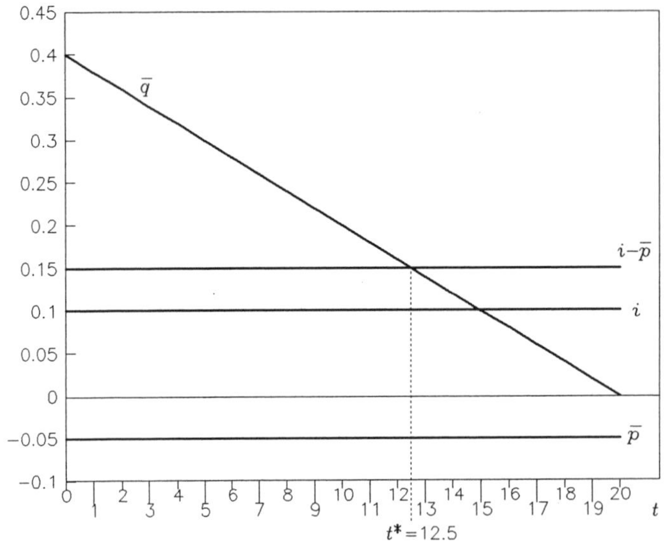

Figure 10.3: Optimum harvesting time for a forest with one rotation period.

In the previous model, I did not take into account the opportunity costs of land. This means that the land used for forestry could be used for alternative purposes. To make the right decision we must include the market price M (as a measure for the opportunity costs of land) in the equation. So, before starting to grow the forest we have to buy the land and after felling the trees we sell it again. Assuming the market price M of the land does not change over time:[14]

$$V(t) = -c - M + (pq + M)e^{-it}.$$

The optimum rotation time can now be computed as follows:

$$\frac{dV}{dt} = p\frac{dq}{dt}e^{-it} + \frac{dp}{dt}qe^{-it} - i(pq + M)e^{-it} = 0,$$

$$\frac{dq}{dt}\frac{1}{q} + \frac{dp}{dt}\frac{1}{p} = i + \frac{iM}{pq}.$$

14 Even if we own the land ourselves we have to take into account its (virtual) buying and selling value of land.

Because $iM/pq > 0$, this rotation time will be shorter than the rotation time computed according to the previous method.

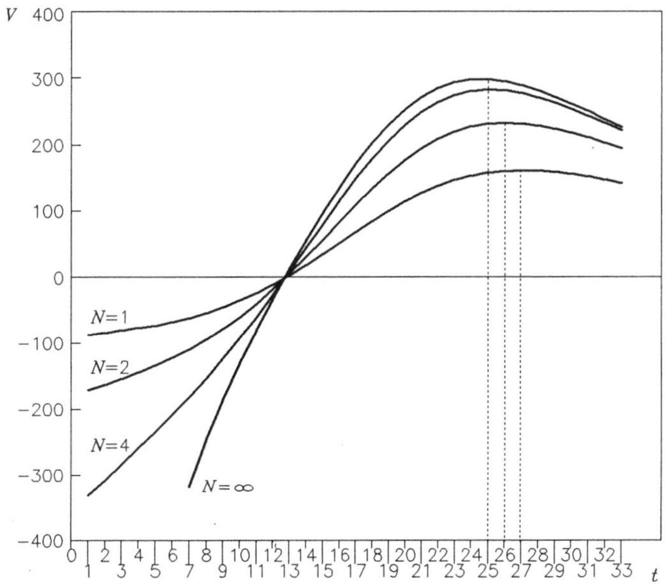

Figure 10.4: Optimum rotation time for different numbers of rotations.

More rotation periods

The optimum rotation time also depends also on the number of rotation periods. In general (with fixed prices and $M = 0$):[15]

$$V(t) = -c + (pq_t - c)e^{-it} + (pq_t - c)e^{-2it} + (pq_t - c)e^{-3it} + \ldots + (pq_t - c)e^{-Nit} + ce^{-Nit},$$

with N for the number of rotations. From this it follows:

$$V(t) = -c + (pq_t - c)\left(\frac{1 - e^{-iNt}}{1 - e^{-it}}\right)e^{-it} + ce^{-iNt}.$$

Generally speaking, the rotation period is shortened when the number of rotations is increased. With an explicit function for q_t, this can be shown. Assume, for example, that

15 When $N \to \infty$, the value of M does not matter anymore.

$$q_t = \frac{340}{1 + 60e^{-0.22t}}.$$

This function is a specific form of a logistic function. Further, I assume $p = 2$, $i = 0.03$ and $c = 100$. In Figure 10.4 the optimum rotation time is shown for $N = 1$, $N = 2$, and $N = 4$.

When $N \to \infty$, then

$$V(t) = -c + (pq_t - c)\left(\frac{e^{-it}}{1 - e^{-it}}\right).$$

Maximizing V implies:

$$\frac{dV}{dt} = 0,$$

Finally, this gives

$$\frac{1}{q}\frac{dq}{dt} = \bar{q} = \frac{i\left(1 - \frac{c}{pq_t}\right)}{1 - e^{-it}}.$$

The rotation time for $N \to \infty$ is also shown in Figure 10.4. It appears that, in this case, the rotation time lies between 25 years (for $N = \infty$) and 27 years (for $N = 1$).

Fishery model

If the condition of *well-described property rights* is not fulfilled, we are dealing with an open access resource. Often this is the case in the fishery sector. With this fishery model I try to analyze such a situation. First I assume that the catch H is a function of total population of fish Q and fishery effort (number of boats, number of fishermen *etcetera*) E. For example: $H = \alpha QE$, with α for a coefficient. Further I assume the natural increase of population of fish ΔQ to be a quadratic function of population, for example: $\Delta Q = \beta Q(1 - Q/K) - H$, with β for a coefficient and K for the climax population[16]. Further I assume price P to be fixed and costs C to be a linear

16 The climax population of a species is the maximum attainable population given the availability of food, space, and other natural circumstances.

function of the fishery effort E, so that total revenue R equals PH and total costs equal γE, with γ for the cost per unit of effort. Now, in the steady-state situation, in which $\Delta Q = 0$, the whole model can be read as follows:[17]

$$H = \beta Q\left(1 - \frac{Q}{K}\right) = \beta Q - \frac{\beta Q^2}{K},$$

$$R = PH = P\beta Q\left(1 - \frac{Q}{K}\right) = P\beta Q - \frac{P\beta Q^2}{K},$$

$$E = \frac{H}{\alpha Q} = \frac{\beta Q\left(1 - \frac{Q}{K}\right)}{\alpha Q} = \frac{\beta}{\alpha} - \frac{\beta Q}{\alpha K},$$

$$C = \gamma E = \frac{\gamma\beta}{\alpha} - \frac{\gamma\beta Q}{\alpha K}.$$

Now three kinds of equilibrium can be computed. First, the equilibrium of the *maximum sustainable yield (msy)*. In this equilibrium the catch is at a maximum, so:

$$\frac{dH}{dQ} = \beta - \frac{2\beta Q}{K} = 0, \quad \text{so:} \quad Q_{msy} = \frac{1}{2}K.$$

The equilibrium in the case of *perfect competition (pc)*. This means:

$$R - C = 0, \quad \text{so:} \quad P\beta Q - \frac{P\beta Q^2}{K} - \frac{\gamma\beta}{\alpha} + \frac{\gamma\beta Q}{\alpha K} = 0.$$

From this equation Q can be solved. In the case of a *monopoly* (*m*) the optimum rule equals:

$$\frac{d(R - C)}{dQ} = P\beta - \frac{2P\beta}{K}Q + \frac{\gamma\beta}{\alpha K} = 0,$$

$$\text{so:} \quad Q_m = \frac{1}{2}\left(K + \frac{\gamma}{\alpha P}\right).$$

For example, if $\alpha = \beta = 0.1$, $\gamma = 10$, $K = 100$ and $P = 10$, the results are: $Q_{msy} = 50$, $Q_{pc} = 10$, $Q_m = 55$. Figure 10.5 gives a picture of this case.

17 See for example: Clark C.W., 1990. *Mathematical bioeconomics*. John Wiley, New York. Kula E., 1992. *Economics of natural resources and the environment*. Chapman and Hall, London.

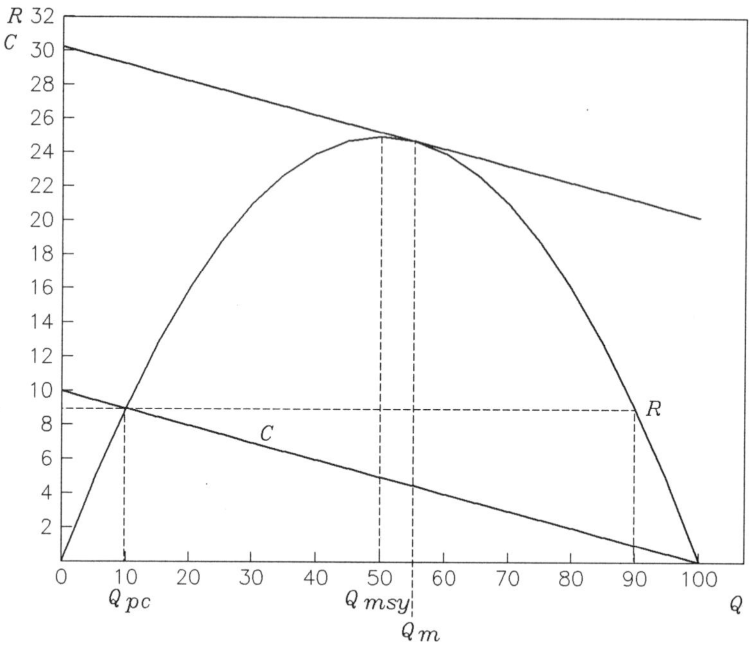

Figure 10.5: Population of fish under perfect competition, maximum sustainable yield and monopoly.

It can be observed from Figure 10.6 that, in the absence of property rights, perfect competition is not an efficient market form. Indeed, the same catch can be reached at lower costs (the catch at $Q = 10$ equals the catch at $Q = 90$). To avoid these kinds of inefficiencies a government could impose a tax t on the catch. Now revenue R' becomes:

$$R = (P - t)\beta Q - \frac{P\beta Q^2}{K},$$

or with the given values for price and coefficients:

$$R = 0.1(10 - t)Q - \frac{0.1(10 - t)Q^2}{100}$$

Assume that fee t equals 5. This gives the revenue function R' in Figure 10.6.

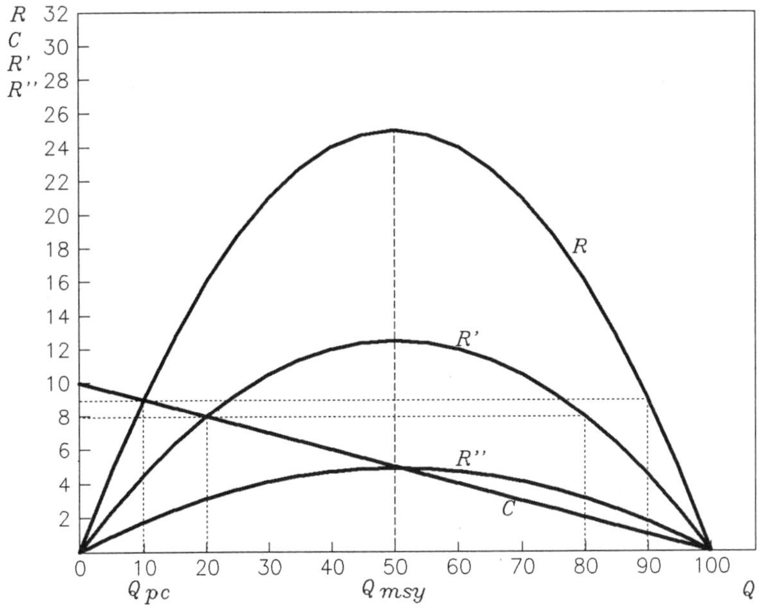

Figure 10.6: A fee in the fishery model.

I may conclude that in that case perfect competition is not efficient. Still the equilibrium amount can be obtained at lower cost and a higher population of fish. The conclusion is that, to avoid inefficiencies of the kind described (a given catch is efficient when one cannot get it at a lower cost), the fee t should be such that the equilibrium stock of fish equals at least the maximum sustainable yield at $Q = 50$. In my example this means that fee t equals at least 8, which gives revenue function R'' in Figure 10.6. This fee can be computed as follows:

$$R - C = 0, \quad \text{so:} \quad (P-t)\beta Q - \frac{(P-t)\beta Q^2}{K} - \frac{\gamma\beta}{\alpha} + \frac{\gamma\beta Q}{\alpha K} = 0 \quad \text{so:}$$

$$0.1(10-t)50 - \frac{0.1(10-t)50^2}{100} - \frac{10\times 0.1}{0.1} + \frac{0.1\times 10\times 50}{0.1\times 100} = 0, \quad \text{so: } t = 8.$$

From the viewpoint of the society, Q_{msy} is only the optimum stock of fish when total costs are fixed, which means that marginal costs equal 0. If efficiency is defined as maximizing utility U, then, in general, in the optimum, the marginal utility of the catch should equal the marginal cost of catching the fish:

$$\frac{dU}{dH}\frac{dH}{dQ}=\frac{dC}{dH}\frac{dH}{dQ}, \text{ so: } P\frac{dH}{dQ}=\frac{-\gamma\beta}{\alpha K}, \text{ or: } P\beta-\frac{2P\beta Q}{K}+\frac{\gamma\beta}{\alpha K}=0, \text{ so: } Q=Q_m=\frac{1}{2}\left(K+\frac{\gamma}{2\alpha P}\right).$$

which implies that from the viewpoint of society the optimum lies at Q_m. (Figure 10.5).[18]

In the previous static model I did not take into account the discounting of future harvests.[19] In the following dynamic model, net present value of the fishery sector Y is maximized in the case of a constant rent (price minus marginal costs) p.

$$Y=-Q_0 p+\frac{pH_1(Q_0)}{(1+i)}+\frac{pH_2(Q_1)}{(1+i)^2}+\ldots+\frac{pH_n(Q_{n-1})}{(1+i)^n}, \quad (n\to\infty).$$

In the steady-state situation: $Q_0=Q_1=\ldots=Q_n$, $H_1=H_2=\ldots=H_n=\Delta Q$. So:

$$Y=-pQ+\frac{p\Delta Q(Q)}{(1+i)}+\frac{p\Delta Q(Q)}{(1+i)^2}+\ldots+\frac{p\Delta Q(Q)}{(1+i)^n}, \quad (n\to\infty).$$

The first-order condition to gain a maximum is:

$$\frac{dY}{dQ}=-p+p\frac{d\Delta Q/dQ}{(1+i)}+p\frac{d\Delta Q/dQ}{(1+i)^2}+\ldots+p\frac{d\Delta Q/dQ}{(1+i)^n}=0, \quad (n\to\infty),$$

$$\frac{dY}{dQ}=-p+p\frac{d\Delta Q}{dQ}\left\{\frac{1}{(1+i)}+\frac{1}{(1+i)^2}+\ldots+\frac{1}{(1+i)^n}\right\}=0, \quad (n\to\infty),$$

$$0=-p+p\frac{d\Delta Q}{dQ}\left(\frac{1}{i}\right), \quad \text{so:} \quad \frac{d\Delta Q}{dQ}=\frac{dH}{dQ}=i.$$

This is shown in figure 10.7. In the example, with $i=0.1$:

$$\frac{d(R-C)}{dQ}=P\beta-\frac{2P\beta}{K}Q+\frac{\gamma\beta}{\alpha K}=i,$$

$$10\times 0.1-\frac{2\times 10\times 0.1}{100}Q+\frac{10\times 0.1}{0.1\times 100}=0.1, \text{ so: } Q=50,$$

18 This is remarkable because normally, in economic theory, the social optimum is found under conditions of perfect competition.

19 See Hartwick J.M. and N.D. Olewiler, 1986. *The economics of natural resource use*. Harper Collins, New York. Also: Perman R., Y. Ma and J. McGilvray, 1996. *Natural resource and environmental economics*. Longman, London.

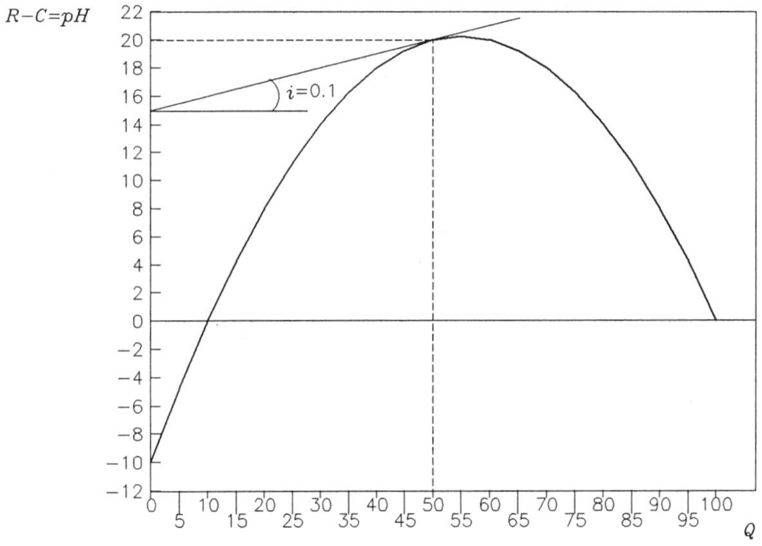

Figure 10.7: Optimum catch under time preference.

$$H = \beta Q - \frac{\beta Q^2}{K}$$

$$= 0.1 \times 50 - \frac{0.1 \times 50^2}{100} = 2.5,$$

$$R = PH = 10 \times 2.5 = 25,$$

$$C = \frac{\gamma\beta}{\alpha} - \frac{\gamma\beta Q}{\alpha K} = \frac{10 \times 0.1}{0.1} - \frac{10 \times 0.1 \times 50}{0.1 \times 100} = 5,$$

$pH = R - C = 25 - 5 = 20$ (see Figure 10.7).

Recycling

I want to conclude this chapter with some remarks about recycling. Most economists rightly think of depletable resources as capital assets to society. However, more should be said about the nature of these capital assets. The difference between exhaustible and renewable resources has already been dealt with extensively.

Depletable resources can also be divided into recyclable and non-recyclable resources. An example of a recyclable resource is copper, an example of a non-recyclable resource is oil.[20]

There are three advantages of recycling and re-use techniques. First, large energy savings arise in cases where waste or scrap can be used as fuel or can provide raw material at a lower cost than the primary source. Second, recycling decreases the need for all kinds of ore, and third, it has a favourable impact on the environmental quality, since it helps to reduce the need for extraction from increasingly poor grade ore, and since in most cases the recycling process itself hardly pollutes the natural environment. Of course, because of the second law of thermodynamics, account has to be taken of a leakage in every round of recycling.

Suppose there is a stock of ore S. During each period n, this stock is depleted by S_n. S_n is a fraction o_n of the inital stock of ore S, so that:

$$S_n = o_n S$$

and:

$$\sum_{n=1}^{\omega} S_n = S,$$

in which ω denotes the number of periods during which the initial stock of ore is exhausted. Now it follows:

$$\sum_{n=1}^{\omega} o_n = 1.$$

Suppose that M represents the total generation of the raw material (for instance copper or iron) out of the initial stock of ore (S), and that M_n represents the generation of raw material out of one year's extraction of ore. Further suppose that π represents the raw material-ore ratio (for instance, the copper grade of the ore) and ι the fractional loss of iron when it is recycled. Then:

20 This distinction is based upon a technical concept of recycling. However, the possibility of recycling in the economic sense might be a feature of all resources, including energy resources. If, for example, the recycling of a unit of output requires less energy than to produce a new unit, then this is in fact caused by the recycling of the input of energy present in the old product.

$$M_n = \pi o_n S\{1 + (1-\iota) + (1-\iota)^2 + \ldots + (1-\iota)^m + \ldots + (1-\iota)^\infty\},$$

$$M_n = \pi o_n S \sum_{m=0}^{\infty} (1-\iota)^m \quad \text{so:} \quad M_n = \frac{1}{\iota}\pi o_n S.$$

Further it is known that:

$$M = \sum_{n=1}^{\omega} M_n.$$

This leads to the conclusion that:

$$M = \frac{\pi}{\iota} S.$$

So, the recycling multiplier, dM/dS, equals π/ι, where total use out of the endowment of a non-recycleable resource is represented by πS (in that case $dM/dS = \pi$). By using the multiplier formula the total possible use of copper out of the initial endowment of copper can be computed.

The conclusion must be that, compared with a non-recyclable resource, total use out of an endowment of a recyclable resource will be higher and that with the given assumptions, though the initial endowment of a recyclable resource is exhaustible, the raw material made out of this resource is not.

11. ECONOMIC ENVIRONMENTAL POLICY INSTRUMENTS

Pollution abatement policies

A pollution abatement policy consists of an objective plus the instruments needed to attain that objective. Most often the objective is to lower the discharge from a firm or branch. There are two ways of distinguishing between abatement instruments. In the first place, one can look at the way a firm's conduct can be influenced. There are two kinds of instruments which can result in the generation of fewer discharges; first, *direct regulations* or *non-market instruments* and second, *economic instruments* or *market instruments*.[1] The essence of direct regulation is that the government decides how much each firm should be allowed to discharge and forbids discharges in excess of those amounts, subject to civil and criminal penalties. Economic instruments or market instruments refer to the use of the price mechanism. Economic instruments include fees, marketable permits, and also subsidies.

In the second place, one can consider the stage of the production process at which an instrument influencing a firm's conduct is aimed. This can be either on the input side of the production process or on the output side. If it is on the input side, this instrument is called an *input instrument* or *preventive instrument*. An example is a fee for the use of a certain resource. An instrument aiming at the output side of the production process is called an *output instrument* or *end of pipe instrument*. An example of this kind is an effluent charge. On the basis of the two distinguishing criteria (regulations versus economic instruments and input versus output instruments) it is possible to divide all possible instruments into four categories. These categories are shown in Figure 11.1.

In the following sections, we compare direct regulations with economic instruments, (fees and marketable permits), on the input and the output sides of the economic process. Because subsidies are against the polluter-pays principle and lead, generally speaking, to a misallocation of production factors, subsidies are not considered here, with the exception of the application as a means of financing research in the area of new abatement techniques or subsidies on clean inputs (*e.g.* labour).

Output instruments

Marginal abatement cost function

If more than one firm is concerned in the abatement policy, it is possible to evaluate

1 T.H. Tietenberg, 1985. *Emissions trading*. Resources for the future, Washington. W.J. Baumol and W.E. Oates, 1989. *The theory of environmental policy*. Cambridge University Press, Cambridge. D.W. Pearce and R.K. Turner, 1990. *Economics of natural resources and the environment*. Harvester Wheatsheaf, New York.

	non-market instruments	market instruments
end of pipe instruments	1	2
preventive instruments	3	4

Figure 11.1: Four categories of instruments.

the efficiency of abatement policies with the help of the marginal abatement cost (MAC) function. This concept is based on the assumption that marginal abatement costs are a rising function of the pollution abatement. In this case efficiency means that a given reduction in pollution must be reached at the lowest possible costs. To reach this, marginal abatement costs of all firms must be equal. This can be proved as follows.

Assume that the abatement of firm j equals a_j. Total abatement must be a, at the minimum, which is a quantity set by the government. Further we know that total abatement costs c of the given amount of pollution a equal the sum of the abatement costs c_j of all the individual firms together. This means that:[2]

$$\sum_{j=1}^{n} a_j = a, \quad \sum_{j=1}^{n} c_j = c.$$

It is assumed that individual abatement costs as well as individual marginal abatement costs are an increasing function of abatement. This means that:

2 In fact, the real constraint is $\sum_{j=1}^{n} a_j \geq a$. Such a problem can be solved with the help of the Kuhn-Tucker conditions. For simplicity we use the equal sign here.

$c_j = c(a_j)$ with

$$\frac{dc_j}{da_j} > 0, \quad \frac{d^2c_j}{da_j^2} > 0.$$

To solve the problem we form the Lagrange function

$$L = c_1(a_1) + c_2(a_2) + \ldots + c_j(a_j) + \ldots + c_n(a_n) - \lambda\left(\sum_{j=1}^{n} a_j - a\right).$$

The first-order conditions are

$$\frac{dL}{da_j} = \frac{dc_j}{da_j} - \lambda = 0, \quad (j = 1, \ldots, n).$$

From this it follows that in the optimum

$$\frac{dc_1}{da_1} = \frac{dc_2}{da_2} = \ldots = \frac{dc_j}{da_j} = \ldots = \frac{dc_n}{da_n}.$$

Thus the efficient fee p_a must be such that

$$p_a = \frac{dc_1}{da_1} = \frac{dc_2}{da_2} = \ldots = \frac{dc_j}{da_j} = \ldots = \frac{dc_n}{da_n}.$$

Figure 11.2 gives a picture of the marginal abatement cost approach. In Figure 11.2 we see two firms, I and II. Both firms are characterized by a marginal abatement cost function: MAC_I and MAC_{II}. The minimum of the total abatement costs is found where $MAC_I = MAC_{II}$. So, in the case of the efficient tax p_a Firm I abates a_1 and Firm II abates a_2 units. In total they abate the prescribed a units of pollution determined by policy makers.

Now, if the marginal abatement cost curve is known for every firm, then one can determine the efficient abatement via direct regulations for every separate firm. In practice this is impossible, which means that a fee will be a more efficient instrument.

Marginal revenue of pollution

The concept of MAC concentrates on the abatement by firms, which is useful. However, often, environmental policy aims at a maximum pollution level. To

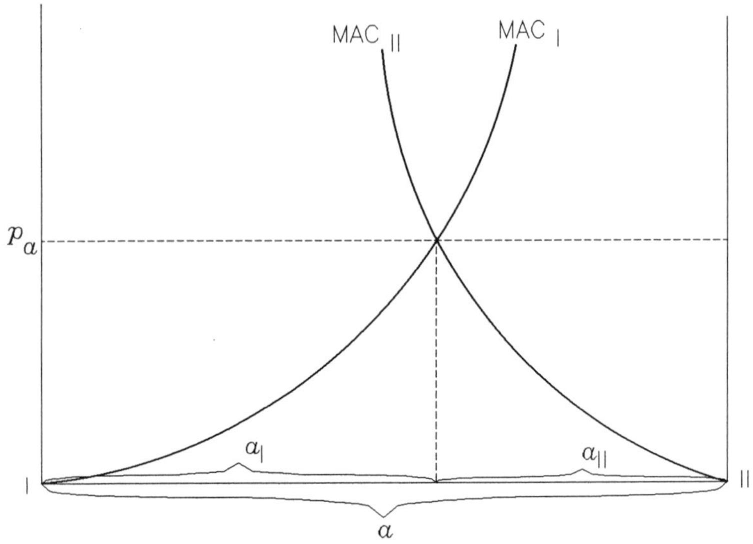

Figure 11.2: Marginal abatement cost approach.

evaluate the different instruments with respect to this target we need another concept: marginal revenue of pollution (MRP), which equals the revenue of each extra unit of pollution emitted.[3]

Suppose that total emission of a certain polluting matter is restricted by the government to v.[4] Further assume that a firm j pollutes to the amount of v_j. Total production q equals the sum of the individual outputs q_j. Price of the final product of each firm equals p_j. We assume further that

$$\frac{dq_j}{dv_j} > 0, \quad \frac{d^2q_j}{dv_j^2} < 0.$$

3 In this case we consider the right to pollute unpolluted nature as an input in the production function with labour and capital being constant. This is an output approach in the sense of Figure 11.1, because we are concentrating on the output (pollution) side of production.

4 In fact, the real constraint here is that the polluters are not allowed to exceed the total level of pollution v set by the government. This would imply an unequal sign (less than or equal to) in the constraint. Such a problem can be solved with the help of the Kuhn-Tucker conditions. For simplicity we use the equal sign here, so a simple Lagrange procedure can be used.

In this case, efficiency implies maximizing the value of total output subject to the constraint of the given level of pollution v.[5]

To solve the problem we form the Lagrange function

$$L = p_1 q_1(v_1) + p_2 q_2(v_2) + \ldots + p_j q_j(v_j) + \ldots + p_n q_n(v_n) - \lambda\left(\sum_{j=1}^{n} v_j - v\right).$$

The first-order conditions are

$$\frac{dL}{dv_j} = p_j \frac{dq_j}{dv_j} - \lambda = 0, \quad (j = 1, \ldots, n).$$

From this it follows that in the optimum

$$p_1 \frac{dq_1}{dv_1} = p_2 \frac{dq_2}{dv_2} = \ldots = p_j \frac{dq_j}{dv_j} = \ldots = p_n \frac{dq_n}{dv_n}.$$

So, the fee p_v should be

$$p_v = p_1 \frac{dq_1}{dv_1} = p_2 \frac{dq_2}{dv_2} = \ldots = p_j \frac{dq_j}{dv_j} = \ldots = p_n \frac{dq_n}{dv_n}.$$

with $p_j \frac{dq_j}{dv_j}$ for the MRP of firm j. If the government knows the MRP function of each individual firm, it is possible to reach efficiency by regulations set for each individual firm. In practice this is impossible, so a fee or a system of marketable permits is more efficient than direct regulations.

An important difference between direct regulations and fees is the effect of inflation. Inflation does not affect the direct regulations. However, because the fee is expressed as an amount of money per unit of pollution, it has to be adjusted periodically.

---

5 In fact, under conditions of perfect competition this is the same as stating that welfare must be maximized. This can be explained as follows:

$$\text{Max } u = \sum_{j=1}^{n} u_j(q_j(v_j)), \text{ s.t. } \sum_{j=1}^{n} v_j = v.$$

With Lagrange it can be shown that in the optimum $\frac{\partial u_j}{\partial q_j}\frac{dq_j}{dv_j}$ or $p_j \frac{dq_j}{dv_j}$ must be equal for all j.

A promising way of introducing the market when dealing with environmental problems is to create a marketable permit system. This means that a firm buys the right to pollute, the maximum level of a certain kind of pollution being set by the government. The price of the pollution permit functions as an efficient fee for the firms. An advantage of this kind of measure is that it is not susceptible to inflation.

A restriction on the application of a system of marketable permits is the number of firms. To create a real market with competition on the demand side the number of firms must be considerable.

At least for the greenhouse-effect an internationally coordinated marketable permit system for the emission of greenhouse gasses such as carbon dioxide seems to be a promising alternative. In this respect, an internationally agreed input fee for energy is also promising. We will deal with that later.

An important way of reducing discharges is technical innovation. The problem is how to get this started. To the extent that technical innovations are induced by the high costs of emission for polluting agencies, fees might have a stronger effect than regulations on the firm's innovating conduct. Besides, to avoid too heavy a financial burden on the average firm, the returns on these fees might be spent on research projects on abatement techniques. In this way two economic instruments, fees and subsidies, can be used at the same time.

Input instruments

We consider next input instruments. Input instruments can be used for saving resources as well as for the abatement of pollution, if there is a direct link between the input of a resource and emission.[6] Also in this case it can be proved that a fee is more efficient than direct regulations.

Suppose that the use of a resource is restricted by the government to r and that a firm j uses this resource to the amount of r_j.[7] Further we assume

$$\frac{dq_j}{dr_j} > 0, \quad \frac{d^2q_j}{dr_j^2} < 0.$$

In this case, efficiency means maximizing the value of production subject to the given constraint of the restricted resource use r.[8] To solve the problem we form the Lagrange function

6 The expression *double-edged sword* might be used here.
7 Capital and labour are kept constant. In fact, the real constraint here is that the firms are not allowed to exceed the total level of resource input r set by the government. This would imply an unequal sign (less than or equal to) in the constraint. Such a problem can be solved with the help of the Kuhn-Tucker conditions. For simplicity we use the equal sign here.
8 Under conditions of perfect competition this means that welfare is maximized.

$$L = p_1 q_1(r_1) + p_2 q_2(r_2) + \ldots + p_j q_j(r_j) + \ldots + p_n q_n(r_n) - \lambda\left(\sum_{j=1}^{n} r_j - r\right).$$

The first-order conditions are

$$\frac{dL}{dr_j} = p_j \frac{dq_j}{dr_j} - \lambda = 0, \quad (j = 1, \ldots n).$$

From this it follows that in the optimum

$$p_1 \frac{dq_1}{dr_1} = p_2 \frac{dq_2}{dr_2} = \ldots = p_j \frac{dq_j}{dr_j} = \ldots = p_n \frac{dq_n}{dr_n}.$$

So, the price (including the efficient fee) p_r of the resource should be

$$p_r = p_1 \frac{dq_1}{dr_1} = p_2 \frac{dq_2}{dr_2} = \ldots = p_j \frac{dq_j}{dr_j} = \ldots = p_n \frac{dq_n}{dr_n},$$

with $p_j \frac{dq_j}{dr_j}$ for the Value of Marginal Product of the Resource (VMPR) function for every individual firm. The introduction of an efficient fee in this case is especially difficult because of the price effects. The fee may cause a drop in the rent of the resource because of a drop in demand.

Under competition a marketable permit would produce the same price as p_r, which equals the price of the resource plus the efficient fee. Again, it appears that a fee or a marketable permit is an efficient instrument, while it is practically impossible for a government to impose an efficient system of direct regulations, because then the government would have to know all individual VMPR functions.

A good example of an input fee is the energy charge which is under consideration by the EU at present in order to reduce the CO_2 emission. Because there is a direct link between the use of energy and the emission of CO_2, this instrument might be very successful when it is applied internationally. An even more promising alternative would be a marketable permit system for the use of energy.

Choosing a policy instrument

Economic instruments are not always preferable to direct regulations. There are many cases in which direct regulations are the only way of dealing with the danger of acute environmental problems and locational problems. Shipwrecking of oil tankers and disasters with chemical mills, for example, can only be prevented by safety standards imposed by national and international authorities.

Another important aspect connected with the choice of an instrument is the transaction costs involved. These costs relate to the need for information and to the application of an instrument. In general, they differ from instrument to instrument.

However, where economic instruments can be applied, these instruments, charges and marketable permits are more efficient than direct regulations. In most cases they will also be more effective. The reason for this might be that a charge is a permanent pressure on a firm to reduce emission of polluting materials, whereas a prescribed level is not. Because when the level is met, the pressure is relieved.

Which of the two instruments, charges or marketable permits is more efficient will depend on the specific case. If the number of polluters is large enough, marketable permits can be introduced. If not, a fee will be a better choice. If both instruments can be applied, introduction of a marketable permit system is preferable because then the efficient fee is determined immediately by the market, whereas introduction of a fee will take a period of trial and error to establish the efficient charge. Besides, a fee is susceptible to inflation, whereas a marketable permit is not. Indeed, it will take a considerable period of time to work out smoothly functioning marketable permit systems.

From the discussions above it must be clear that to decide on which policy option is best depends very much on the circumstances. However, one thing is clear, economic instruments can be applied in a much wider range than is generally done. In the case of Dutch water pollution, for example, it has been shown that effluent charges can work.[9] Also in other cases, as for instance in reducing CO_2 and SO_2 emissions, an emission tax can be useful.

An argument against direct regulations and in favour of economic instruments is the supposedly less bureaucratic procedure with fees and marketable permits. This argument does not always seem correct. In order to control whether the maximum emission level is exceeded or to collect the fee and to check whether the fee is effective or not, it is necessary to have a bureaucratic apparatus, for application of economic instruments as well as for regulations. It is not immediately clear in which of either category of policy options this apparatus is smallest.

It seems that the best arguments in favour of economic instruments rather than direct regulations to control relatively low polluting economic activities are: first, that it is more efficient than regulations; second, that it places permanent pressure on a firm to change its way of production; third, that it does justice to the polluter-pays principle; fourth, that it provides the financial means for the authorities to maintain the bureaucratic apparatus and to construct cleansing installations; and sixth, that technical innovations might be initiated by the fees, or financial means are generated

---

9 See: Bressers H., 1988. Effluent charges can work: the case of the Dutch water quality policy. In: F.J. Dietz and W.J.M. Heijman, *Environmental policy in a market economy*. Pudoc, Wageningen.

to carry out scientific research in the field of preventive technology. Especially in the case of national budget deficits the last two arguments might be decisive in the future.

In the seventh place the revenue of the fee can be used for subsidizing clean inputs like labour. A fee on pollution combined with a subsidy on labour is often referred to as a *double-edged sword.* This means that this instument can work to solve an environmental problem as well as the problem of unemployment. If both economic instruments, fees and marketable permits, can be applied, marketable permits are preferable.

Finally, if emissions are closely linked to inputs as in the energy sector and government aims at both reducing emissions and the saving of resources, an input instrument is more feasible than an output one. Therefore, for example in the case of global warming, the best option might be a worldwide marketable permit system for the use of energy resources.

12. MACROECONOMIC ENVIRONMENTAL ASPECTS

Economy without cleansing sector

Stock of nature

Nature is a stock that can renew itself within certain bounds. On the one hand, stock increases because of ecological processes, while on the other hand, it decreases because of the economic process. This decrease can be called *damage*. If increase equals decrease there is an *ecological equilibrium*.

Total production

Initially production or income y as a whole, expressed in money, is generated within sectors that are polluting more or less. Now, welfare w must be corrected for environmental damage s:[1] It is assumed that environmental damage, expressed in money terms is a positive function of money income, so that we can state:

$$w = y - s(y), \quad \frac{ds}{dy} > 0, \quad \frac{d^2s}{dy^2} > 0.$$

The first-order condition for maximum welfare is:

$$\frac{dw}{dy} = 1 - \frac{ds}{dy} = 0, \quad \text{so:} \quad \frac{ds}{dy} = 1.$$

Suppose, for example, the following macroeconomic damage function: $s = \alpha y^2$. The optimum income then is:

$$\frac{ds}{dy} = 2\alpha y = 1, \quad \text{so:} \quad y = \frac{1}{2\alpha}.$$

It is important that economic equilibrium coincides with ecological equilibrium. I will now prove that, if externalities are internalized in the welfare function, this will happen in the long run. We know that in the optimum:

---

1 R. Hueting, 1974. *Nieuwe schaarste en economische groei*. Agon Elsevier, Amsterdam. J.J. Krabbe, 1974. *Individueel en collectief nut*. Veenman, Wageningen. J.J. Krabbe and W.J.M. Heijman, 1986. *Economische theorie van het milieu*. Van Gorcum, Assen. R. Hueting, 1992. Correcting national income. In: J.J. Krabbe and W.J.M. Heijman (eds), 1992. *National income and nature: externalities, growth and steady state*. Kluwer, Dordrecht.

$$s = \alpha y^2 = \alpha\left(\frac{1}{2\alpha}\right)^2 = \frac{1}{4\alpha}.$$

Suppose that the yearly increase of nature equals o. When $o < s$, stock of nature decreases, which causes an increase of nature's value per unit, because scarcity of nature increases. This will, *ceteris paribus*, cause an increase of α, because the damage per monetary unit of production increases. In turn, this will cause a decrease in the optimum production y and damage s. If $o > s$, stock of nature increases. This causes a decrease of α, because nature becomes less scarce. This implies an increase in the optimum production. So, in the long run, there is a mechanism working towards a simultaneous realization of economic equilibrium and ecological equilibrium. The long-run equilibrium of the stock of nature can be computed. By definition, the stock of nature h develops as follows:

$$h_t = h_{t-1} - s_t + o_t$$

Further I assume that natural renewal is a fixed percentage σ of total stock and that there is an ecological equilibrium, so: $o_t = s_t$.

$$o_t = \sigma h_{t-1}, \quad s_t = \alpha y_t^2, \quad s_t = o_t, \quad \text{so:} \quad h_t = h_{t-1}, \quad \text{so:}$$

$$\sigma h_t = \alpha y_t^2, \quad \text{or:} \quad y_t = \sqrt{\frac{\sigma}{\alpha} h_t}.$$

Then, because at the optimum $y = 1/2\alpha$, in the long run: $h = \frac{1}{4\sigma\alpha}$.

It should be realized that with these computations the results all depend on the assumption that damage to nature is included in the social welfare function and that welfare is maximized.

Economy with cleansing sector

Total production

Total production y expressed in money terms now consists of production of the polluting sectors y_v, together with production of the cleansing sector y_z. In the cleansing sector, goods and services are produced for cleansing of the environment or to prevent pollution. In the remaining (polluting) sectors all other goods and services are produced, so:

$$y = y_v + y_z.$$

Macro-economic environmental damage function

Total environmental damage s is a function of production of the cleansing sector and production of the polluting sectors:

$$s = s(y_v, y_z), \quad \frac{\partial s}{\partial y_v} > 0, \quad \frac{\partial s}{\partial y_z} < 0.$$

Welfare function

Total welfare w equals production of the polluting sectors minus the environmental damage.

$$w = y_v - s(y_v, y_z).$$

Maximization of welfare

When total production y is known, the optimum distribution of production between the cleansing sector and the polluting sectors can be computed. For this purpose I form the following Lagrange function:

$$\text{Max} \quad L = w(y_v, y_z) + \lambda(y - y_v - y_z) \quad \text{or}$$

$$\text{Max} \quad L = y_v - s(y_v, y_z) + \lambda(y - y_v - y_z).$$

First-order conditions for maximum welfare are:

$$\frac{\partial L}{\partial y_v} = 1 - \frac{\partial s}{\partial y_v} - \lambda = 0,$$

$$\frac{\partial L}{\partial y_z} = - \frac{\partial s}{\partial y_z} - \lambda = 0$$

So, in the optimum:

$$\frac{\partial s}{\partial y_z} = \frac{\partial s}{\partial y_v} - 1.$$

Suppose, for example, the following macroeconomic damage function:

$$s = \alpha y_v^2 - \beta y_z y_v, \quad \alpha, \beta > 0.$$

Now, in the optimum:

$$-\beta y_v = 2\alpha y_v - \beta y_z - 1,$$

$$y = y_v + y_z, \quad \text{so:}$$

$$y_v = \frac{\beta y + 1}{2\alpha + 2\beta}, \quad y_z = \frac{(2\alpha + \beta)y - 1}{2\alpha + 2\beta}.$$

Also in this model, in the long run, the ecological equilibrium will coincide with the economic equilibrium, if damage costs are internalized.

Optimization of the production process

Allocation

When the production process is to be optimized, production factors should be allocated in such a way that welfare is maximized. We assume two sectors with two production functions:

$$y_v = y_v(f_v^0, f_v^1, \ldots, f_v^i, \ldots f_v^n), \quad \frac{\partial y_v}{\partial f_v^i} > 0, \quad \frac{\partial^2 y_v}{\partial f_v^{i\,2}} < 0,$$

$$y_z = y_z(f_z^0, f_z^1, \ldots, f_z^i, \ldots f_z^n), \quad \frac{\partial y_z}{\partial f_z^i} > 0, \quad \frac{\partial^2 y_z}{\partial f_z^{i\,2}} < 0,$$

with f_v^i for the amount of production factor i allocated in the polluting sector and f_z^i for production factor i allocated in the cleansing sector. The welfare function to be maximized is:

$$\text{Max} \quad w = y_v(f_v^0, f_v^1, \ldots, f_v^i, \ldots, f_v^n) - s(y_v(f_v^0, f_v^1, \ldots, f_v^i, \ldots, f_v^n), y_z(f_z^0, f_z^1, \ldots, f_z^i, \ldots, f_z^n)) \quad (*).$$

Further the amount of every production factor is known, so: $f^i = f_v^i + f_z^i$.

The optimization problem can be solved by way of a Lagrange procedure:

$$L = w(f_v^0, f_v^1, \ldots, f_v^i, \ldots, f_v^n, f_z^0, f_z^1, \ldots, f_z^i, \ldots, f_z^n) + \lambda_1(f^1 - f_v^1 - f_z^1) + \lambda_2(f^2 - f_v^2 - f_z^2) + \ldots + \lambda_i(f^i - f_v^i - f_z^i) + \ldots + \lambda_n(f^n - f_v^n - f_z^n).$$

The first-order conditions for a maximum are:

$$\frac{\partial L}{\partial f_v^i} = \frac{\partial w}{\partial f_v^i} - \lambda_i = 0,$$

$$\frac{\partial L}{\partial f_z^i} = \frac{\partial w}{\partial f_z^i} - \lambda_i = 0, \quad \text{so:} \frac{\partial w}{\partial f_v^i} = \frac{\partial w}{\partial f_z^i}.$$

Taking into account the welfare function (*), the optimum condition can now be written as:

$$\frac{\partial w}{\partial f_v^i} = \frac{\partial y_v}{\partial f_v^i} - \frac{\partial s}{\partial y_v}\frac{\partial y_v}{\partial f_v^i}, \quad \frac{\partial w}{\partial f_z^i} = -\frac{\partial s}{\partial y_z}\frac{\partial y_z}{\partial f_z^i}, \quad \text{so:}$$

$$\frac{\partial s}{\partial y_z}\frac{\partial y_z}{\partial f_z^i} = \frac{\partial y_v}{\partial f_v^i}\left(\frac{\partial s}{\partial y_v} - 1\right).$$

Input-output analysis

Input-output table

An input-output table gives an overview of deliveries from sectors to consumers and from sectors to other sectors,[2] which is shown in Table 12.1 for three sectors: Agriculture (1), Industry (2) and Services (3).

Table 12.1: Input-output table in absolute values.

sectors → ↓	Agriculture (1)	Industry (2)	Services (3)	Final demand	Turnover
Agriculture (1)	A_{11}	A_{12}	A_{13}	f_1	x_1
Industry (2)	A_{21}	A_{22}	A_{23}	f_2	x_2
Services (3)	A_{31}	A_{32}	A_{33}	f_3	x_3
Value added	TW_1	TW_2	TW_3		
Turnover	x_1	x_2	x_3		x

In Table 12.1 A_{ij} is the delivery from sector i to sector j. TW_i is the value added of sector i, f_i representents the consumer's final demand for products of sector i and x_i is sector i's turnover. Final demand f, which equals $f_1 + f_2 + f_3$, must, of course, be equal to value added TW, which equals $TW_1 + TW_2 + TW_3$.

2 W. Leontief, 1941. *The structure of the American economy.* Harvard University Press, Cambridge (Mass.).

Analysis of changes in demand

An input-output table in absolute values (like the one in Table 12.1) may be transformed into an input-output table with fixed technical coefficients. This transformation is based on the idea that each interdelivery between sectors is a fixed proportion of turnover. In Table 12.2 an input-output table with fixed technical coefficients is shown. Because the value added does not play a significant role in this analysis, it has been left out.

Table 12.2: Input-output table with fixed technical coefficients.

sectors → ↓	Agriculture (1)	Industry (2)	Services (3)	Final demand	Turnover
Agriculture (1)	$a_{11}x_1$	$a_{12}x_2$	$a_{13}x_3$	f_1	x_1
Industry (2)	$a_{21}x_1$	$a_{22}x_2$	$a_{23}x_3$	f_2	x_2
Services (3)	$a_{31}x_1$	$a_{32}x_2$	$a_{33}x_3$	f_3	x_3

Table 12.2 can be written in matrix form as follows:

$$\begin{pmatrix} a_{11} & a_{12} & a_{13} \\ a_{21} & a_{22} & a_{23} \\ a_{31} & a_{32} & a_{33} \end{pmatrix} \begin{pmatrix} x_1 \\ x_2 \\ x_3 \end{pmatrix} + \begin{pmatrix} f_1 \\ f_2 \\ f_3 \end{pmatrix} = \begin{pmatrix} x_1 \\ x_2 \\ x_3 \end{pmatrix},$$

or:

$$\mathrm{AX} + \mathrm{F} = \mathrm{X} \quad \text{or:} \quad (\mathrm{I} - \mathrm{A})\mathrm{X} = \mathrm{F},$$

in which A represents the matrix of fixed technical coefficients, $\mathbf{I}$ the three-by-three unity matrix, X the vector of turnovers and F the vector of the final demand.

Now I want to see how changes in the final demand influence the turnover of the three sectors. We can analyse this problem by writing the last equation as:

$$\mathrm{X} = (\mathrm{I} - \mathrm{A})^{-1}\mathrm{F},$$

with $(\mathrm{I} - \mathrm{A})^{-1}$ as the inverse matrix of $(\mathrm{I} - \mathrm{A})$. The consequences of the change in the final demand pattern can now be computed. This can be illustrated with an example. Suppose the following matrices and vector:[3]

3 Computation of inverse matrices and multiplication of matrices has been done with the help of a spread sheet programme.

$$I = \begin{pmatrix} 1 & 0 & 0 \\ 0 & 1 & 0 \\ 0 & 0 & 1 \end{pmatrix}, \quad A = \begin{pmatrix} 0.2 & 0.3 & 0.1 \\ 0.25 & 0.15 & 0.4 \\ 0.1 & 0.2 & 0.3 \end{pmatrix}, \quad \text{so:}$$

$$I - A = \begin{pmatrix} 0.8 & -0.3 & -0.1 \\ -0.25 & 0.85 & -0.4 \\ -0.1 & -0.2 & 0.7 \end{pmatrix} \quad \text{and:}$$

$$(I-A)^{-1} \approx \begin{pmatrix} 1.54 & 0.69 & 0.61 \\ 0.64 & 1.65 & 1.03 \\ 0.40 & 0.57 & 1.81 \end{pmatrix}, \quad F = \begin{pmatrix} 40 \\ 50 \\ 30 \end{pmatrix}.$$

The inverted matrix $(I-A)^{-1}$ multiplied by the final demand matrix F gives the turnover of the three sectors:

$$\begin{pmatrix} x_1 \\ x_2 \\ x_3 \end{pmatrix} = \begin{pmatrix} 1.54 & 0.69 & 0.61 \\ 0.64 & 1.65 & 1.03 \\ 0.40 & 0.57 & 1.81 \end{pmatrix} \begin{pmatrix} 40 \\ 50 \\ 30 \end{pmatrix} = \begin{pmatrix} 114.4 \\ 139.0 \\ 98.8 \end{pmatrix}.$$

Now suppose that the final demand for agricultural products rises by 20. In that case the output vector X changes as follows:

$$\begin{pmatrix} x_1 \\ x_2 \\ x_3 \end{pmatrix} = \begin{pmatrix} 1.54 & 0.69 & 0.61 \\ 0.64 & 1.65 & 1.03 \\ 0.40 & 0.57 & 1.81 \end{pmatrix} \begin{pmatrix} 60 \\ 50 \\ 30 \end{pmatrix} = \begin{pmatrix} 145.2 \\ 151.8 \\ 106.8 \end{pmatrix}.$$

Input-output analysis and pollution

To determine the environmental effects of a certain production pattern, it is necessary to make a second matrix of coefficients B. This matrix gives the emission of the polluting agencies per unit of production of a certain sector. Suppose there are three polluting agencies: v_1, v_2, and v_3. The relation between vector V and vector X can now be written as follows: $BX = V$. Assume the following B–matrix:

$$B = \begin{pmatrix} 0.38 & 0.23 & 0.06 \\ 0.28 & 0.33 & 0.06 \\ 0.11 & 0.33 & 0.22 \end{pmatrix}.$$

Multiplying by X (before the change in demand) gives the following levels of pollution:

$$V = \begin{pmatrix} v_1 \\ v_2 \\ v_3 \end{pmatrix} = BX = \begin{pmatrix} 0.38 & 0.23 & 0.06 \\ 0.28 & 0.33 & 0.06 \\ 0.11 & 0.33 & 0.22 \end{pmatrix} \begin{pmatrix} 114.4 \\ 139.0 \\ 98.8 \end{pmatrix} = \begin{pmatrix} 81.4 \\ 83.8 \\ 80.2 \end{pmatrix}.$$

If the final demand changes, the levels of pollution also change:

$$V = \begin{pmatrix} v_1 \\ v_2 \\ v_3 \end{pmatrix} = BX = \begin{pmatrix} 0.38 & 0.23 & 0.06 \\ 0.28 & 0.33 & 0.06 \\ 0.11 & 0.33 & 0.22 \end{pmatrix} \begin{pmatrix} 145.2 \\ 151.8 \\ 106.8 \end{pmatrix} = \begin{pmatrix} 96.5 \\ 97.2 \\ 89.6 \end{pmatrix}.$$

Now, suppose that the government wants to reduce emission levels. The effects of this policy can be computed as follows:

$$V = BX, \text{ so: } X = B^{-1}V.$$

Assume that the maximum emission levels are given by the following vector:

$$V = \begin{pmatrix} 70 \\ 70 \\ 70 \end{pmatrix}.$$

To compute the effects on production the B−matrix must be inverted:[4]

$$B^{-1} = \begin{pmatrix} 4.90 & -2.86 & -0.56 \\ -5.10 & 7.14 & -0.56 \\ 5.20 & -9.29 & 5.66 \end{pmatrix}.$$

When the maximum emission levels are reached, the levels of production and final demand equal:

$$X = \begin{pmatrix} 4.90 & -2.86 & -0.56 \\ -5.10 & 7.14 & -0.56 \\ 5.20 & -9.29 & 5.66 \end{pmatrix} \begin{pmatrix} 70 \\ 70 \\ 70 \end{pmatrix} = \begin{pmatrix} 103.6 \\ 103.6 \\ 109.9 \end{pmatrix},$$

$$F = (I - A)X = \begin{pmatrix} 0.8 & -0.3 & -0.1 \\ -0.25 & 0.85 & -0.4 \\ -0.1 & -0.2 & 0.7 \end{pmatrix} \begin{pmatrix} 103.6 \\ 103.6 \\ 109.9 \end{pmatrix} = \begin{pmatrix} 40.8 \\ 18.2 \\ 45.9 \end{pmatrix}.$$

4 A necessary condition for the inversion of a matrix is that the number of columns equals the number of rows. This implies that the number of maximum pollution levels should equal the number of sectors, or, in other words: the number of political goals must equal the number of political instruments.

Economy with cleansing sector

Up till now I have assumed that in input-output analysis there is no cleansing sector in the economy. I shall now abandon this assumption by adding a fourth sector to the economy. This fourth sector aims at cleansing the environment. Matrix A has now become a four-by-four matrix. Matrix B must be expanded by one column in which there are also negative coefficients, showing that pollution diminishes as a consequence of the production of this sector. Assume that the A- and B-matrices are as follows:

$$A = \begin{pmatrix} 0.2 & 0.3 & 0.1 & 0.05 \\ 0.25 & 0.15 & 0.4 & 0.03 \\ 0.1 & 0.2 & 0.3 & 0.02 \\ 0.05 & 0.06 & 0.08 & 0.02 \end{pmatrix}, \quad B = \begin{pmatrix} 0.38 & 0.23 & 0.06 & -0.2 \\ 0.28 & 0.33 & 0.06 & -0.3 \\ 0.11 & 0.33 & 0.22 & -0.3 \end{pmatrix}.$$

In constructing the F-matrix I assume that the cleansing sector only delivers to the other sectors, so there is no final demand for the products of this sector.

$$F = \begin{pmatrix} 40 \\ 50 \\ 30 \\ 0 \end{pmatrix}$$

The consequences for production and pollution can now be computed as follows:

$$X = (I - A)^{-1}F, \quad V = BX, \quad \text{so:} \quad V = B(I - A)^{-1}F,$$

$$X = \begin{pmatrix} 117.0 \\ 141.4 \\ 100.6 \\ 22.8 \end{pmatrix}, \quad V = \begin{pmatrix} 78.5 \\ 78.6 \\ 74.8 \end{pmatrix}.$$

13. CONDITIONS FOR SUSTAINABLE RESOURCE USE

Sustainable depletion of a non-renewable resource

Suppose, at time 0, an economy disposes of an exhaustible resource with stock Q_0. The use of this resource at time t is known to be q_t. In case of sustainability, on the one hand, depletion time should be infinite, while on the other hand, there should be an amount R left in the deposit that may not be depleted, because this might affect nature too much. Now, with n for the number of periods, I can compute the necessary yearly relative decrease b, with $b < 0$, of the resource use as follows:[1]

$$Q_0 = q_0 + q_1 + q_2 + \ldots + q_h + \ldots + q_n + R,$$

$$Q_0 = q_0 + q_0(1+b) + q_0(1+b)^2 + \ldots + q_0(1+b)^h + \ldots + q_0(1+b)^n + R,$$

$$Q_0 = q_0\{1 + (1+b) + (1+b)^2 + \ldots + (1+b)^h + \ldots + (1+b)^n\} + R.$$

For $n \to \infty$ this results in $Q_0 = q_0\left(\frac{1}{-b}\right) + R$, or: $b = \frac{-q_0}{Q_0 - R}$, so: $b \le -\frac{q_0}{Q_0}$.

Figure 13.1 shows sustainable depletion of a non-renewable resource stock Q_t at time t of an imaginary resource with $Q_0 = 1000$, $q_0 = 100$ and $R = 100$. So: $b \approx -0.1111$.

Sustainable depletion of a renewable resource

Renewable resources may be divided into biological renewable resources and non-biological ones. In the case of biological resources, such as forests and fish, the renewal is a certain percentage of the stock. Normally, the renewal percentage is a function of the total stock available. With non-biological renewable resources, *e.g.* ground water, the renewal A_t in period t is independent of total available stock. Now I can write, with v_t for the use of the resource in period t:

$$Q_0 = q_0 + q_1 + q_2 + \ldots + q_h + \ldots + q_n + R,$$

$$Q_0 = (v_0 - A_0) + (v_1 - A_1) + (v_2 - A_2) + \ldots + (v_h - A_h) + \ldots + (v_n - A_n) + R,$$

1 In fact, the following computation keeps depletion time constant for every period. This is arranged by keeping the depletion speed $q_t/(Q_t - R)$ constant.

$$Q_0 = (v_0 - A_0) + (v_0 - A_0)(1+b) + (v_0 - A_0)(1+b)^2 +$$

$$\ldots + (v_0 - A_0)(1+b)^h + \ldots + (v_0 - A_0)(1+b)^n + R,$$

$$Q_0 = (v_0 - A_0)\{1 + (1+b) + (1+b)^2 + \ldots + (1+b)^h + \ldots + (1+b)^n\} + R,$$

So: for $n \to \infty$: $Q_0 - R = (v_0 - A_0)\dfrac{1}{-b}$, $\quad b = \dfrac{A_0 - v_0}{Q_0 - R}$, for $v_0 \geq A_0$ and $R < Q_0$.

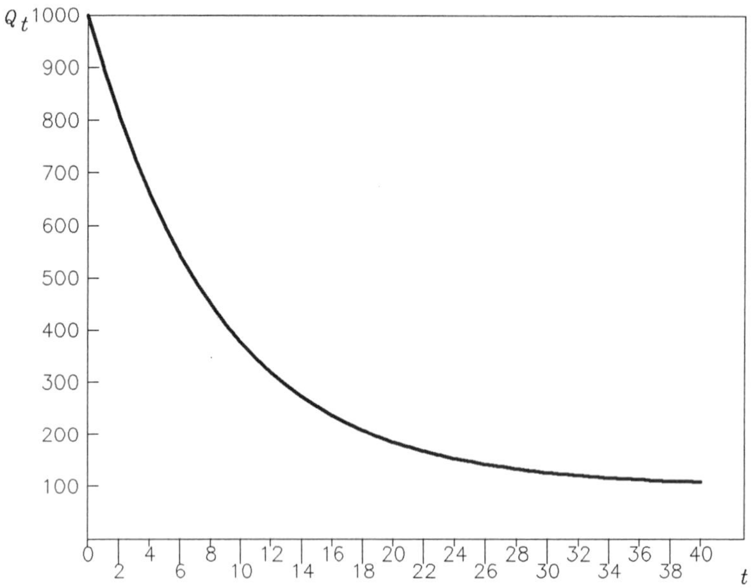

Figure 13.1: Sustainable depletion of a stock: $Q_0 = 1000$, $q_0 = 100$, $R = 100$, $b = -0.1111$.

So, in the case of ground water: if precipitation A_0 in period 0 exceeds the use of ground water v_0 in period 0 and when the rest R is smaller than the initial amount Q_0, then b might even be positive. However, this does not seem to occur in reality.

In case of a biological renewable resource the resource renews itself by a factor a, which is assumed to be fixed. With v_t for the use of the resource in period t and assuming sustainable resource use with R for the (for ecological reasons) untouched part of the renewable resource, I can write

$$Q_0 = q_0 + q_1 + q_2 + \ldots + q_h + \ldots + q_n + R,$$

$$Q_0 - R = v_0 + \frac{v_1}{1+a} + \frac{v_2}{(1+a)^2} + \ldots + \frac{v_h}{(1+a)^h} + \ldots + \frac{v_n}{(1+a)^n},$$

$$Q_0 - R = v_0 + \frac{v_0(1+b)}{1+a} + \frac{v_0(1+b)^2}{(1+a)^2} + \ldots + \frac{v_h(1+b)^h}{(1+a)^h} + \ldots + \frac{v_0(1+b)^n}{(1+a)^n},$$

so: with $n \to \infty$: $Q_0 - R = v_0 \left\{ \frac{1}{1 - \frac{1+b}{1+a}} \right\}$, or, with $q_0 = v_0$,

$$b = a - \frac{(1+a)q_0}{Q_0 - R}.$$

Figure 13.2 shows the stock Q_t at time t in case of the sustainable depletion of a renewable resource with $Q_0 = 1000$, $q_0 = 100$, $R = 100$, and $a = 0.05$. So: $b = -0.0666$.

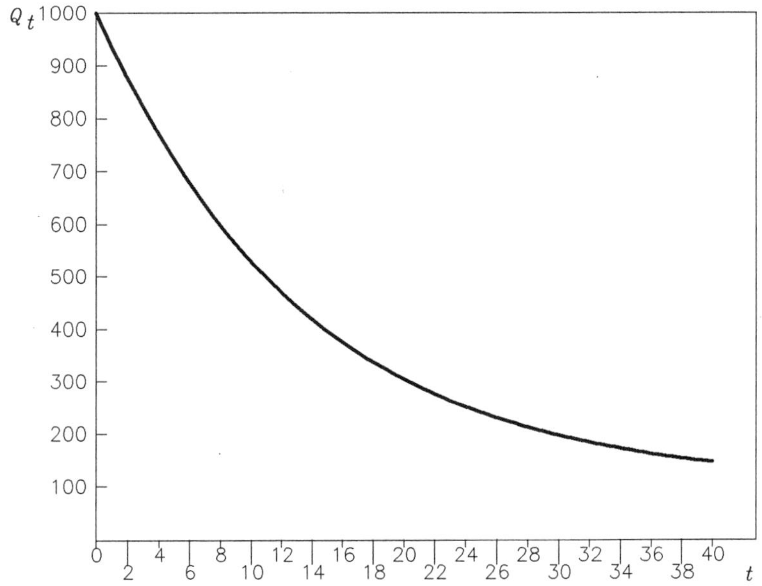

Figure 13.2: Sustainable depletion of a renewable resource: $Q_0 = 1000$, $q_0 = 100$, $R = 100$ and $a = 0.05$, so: $b = -0.055$.

Sustainability and economic growth

Suppose an economy disposes of one exhaustible resource.[2] The question to be answered is how fast the economy may grow if the exhaustible resource is not to be depleted fully, taking into account the possibility of a diminishing use per unit of product of the resource concerned. This diminishing use per unit of product can be caused by technical innovations, by substitution between other production factors and the resource, and by economies of scale. The total amount of the resource used per period is the resource output ratio μ_t multiplied by total output y_t, while in period 0, total stock equals Q_0 units. This stock is to be used over an infinite time, after which it is assumed that R units of the stock are left, with $R \geq 0$.

Further it is assumed that the resource output ratio changes by $m \times 100$ percent per period, with $m < 0$, while production grows by $c \times 100$ percent per period, with $c > 0$. This means that:

$$q_t = \mu_t y_t,$$

$$\mu_t = \mu_0 (1 + m)^t$$

$$y_t = y_0 (1 + c)^t.$$

Further I know that in the case of sustainable depletion of a resource the use of the resource should decrease as follows:

$$q_t = q_0 (1 + b)^t,$$

Now it can be deduced that in the sustainable situation:

$$q_0 (1 + b)^t = \mu_0 (1 + m)^t y_0 (1 + c)^t \approx \mu_0 y_0 (1 + m + c)^t, \text{ or: } b \approx m + c.$$

In the case of sustainable use of a biological renewable resource, I know that: $b = a - [q_0 (1 + a)/(Q_0 - R)]$, so:

$$m + c = a - \frac{q_0 (1 + a)}{Q_0 - R}, \text{ so: } m = a - c - \frac{q_0 (1 + a)}{Q_0 - R}.$$

---

2 *Exhaustible resource* is a synonym for *non-renewable* resource. See: W.J.M. Heijman, 1991. *Depletable resources and the economy*. Wageningen Economic Studies (WES), nr 21. Pudoc, Wageningen.

This equation shows the necessary decrease in the resource output ratio μ given sustainable use of the renewable resource. The result can be transferred to the case of an exhaustible resource by equalizing a to 0:

$$m = -c - \frac{q_0}{Q_0 - R}.$$

Finally, for the non-biological renewable resource, I can derive:

$$m = -c + \frac{A_0 - v_0}{Q_0 - R}.$$

The conclusion of this chapter is that to ensure both economic growth and a sustainable resource use, decoupling in the strong sense is necessary.[3] This means that the use of resources per unit of product must decrease.

3 Decoupling in the weak sense means that the resource output ratio decreases while total use of the resource still increases because of economic growth. Decoupling in the strong sense means that total use of the resource decreases while there is economic growth. Sustainable resource depletion together with economic growth presupposes decoupling in the strong sense.

14. ECONOMIC GROWTH[1]

Harrod-Domar growth model

Two important growth models are the post-Keynesian Harrod-Domar growth model and the neoclassical growth model developed mainly by Robert Solow.[2] In this section I give a brief description of the Harrod-Domar model and in the following sections the neoclassical growth model is described. The main assumptions for the Harrod-Domar model are:

a. a constant price level;
b. no lags are present;
c. savings and investment refer to income of the same period;
d. both savings and investment are net, i.e. over and above depreciation;
e. depreciation is measured not in terms of historical costs, but in terms of the cost of replacement of the depreciated asset by another one *of the same productivity;*
f. productive capacity of an asset or of the whole economy is a measurable concept.

The essential part of the model can be presented in 5 equations. The first equation states that there must be income equilibrium in the economy, which means that ex ante net investment i equals savings s:

$$i = s.$$

Net investment is to be considered the expansion of the capital stock Δk:

$$i = \Delta k.$$

Since it is possible that depreciation of the stock of capital exceeds gross investment, net investment can be negative.

Total savings equals the marginal propensity to save σ multiplied by the net national income y:

$$s = \sigma y.$$

Total capital k equals a given capital output ratio κ multiplied by production capacity $\hat{y}$:

---

1 Chapter 14 and Chapter 15 are a revised version of Chapter 6 of Heijman W.J.M, 1991. *Depletable resources and the economy*. Wageningen Economic Studies (WES) 21. Pudoc, Wageningen.

2 E. Domar, 1946. Capital expansion, rate of growth and employment. In: A. Sen, 1971. *Growth economics*. Penguin, Harmondsworth. R.M. Solow, 1956. A contribution to the theory of economic growth. In: A. Sen, 1971. *Growth economics*. Penguin, Harmondsworth. R.M. Solow, 1988. Growth theory and after. *The American Economic Review*, 78, nr 3, pp. 307-317.

$$k = \kappa \hat{y}.$$

Apart from income equilibrium, it is also required that production capacity is fully utilized:

$$y = \hat{y}.$$

From these 5 equations, the growth rate of the capital stock $\bar{k}$ can be derived:[3]

$$\bar{k} = \frac{\Delta k}{k} = \frac{i}{k} = \frac{\sigma y}{\kappa y} = \frac{\sigma}{\kappa}.$$

From these equations it can be concluded:

$$\bar{k} = \bar{y} = \bar{\hat{y}} = \frac{\sigma}{\kappa}.$$

Total income consists of consumption c and net investment i:

$$y = c + i.$$

If the absolute values of the variables in this equation are changed into relative ones, i.e. growth rates, then:[4]

$$\bar{y} = (1 - \sigma)\bar{c} + \sigma\bar{i}.$$

Because $\bar{c} = \bar{y}$, it follows that $\bar{y} = \bar{i}$. It can finally be concluded that, in the Harrod-Domar growth model, in a path of steady growth, all variables increase by the same growth rate:

$$\bar{k} = \bar{y} = \bar{\hat{y}} = \bar{c} = \bar{i} = \frac{\sigma}{\kappa}.$$

So it is possible to have a state of steady growth within the Harrod-Domar model. The growth rate σ / κ is called the warranted rate of growth. This result has been reached under the assumption of a constant marginal propensity to save and a constant capital output ratio.

---

3 If f is a function of time, then I define $\bar{f} = f'/f$, which is the relative growth speed or *growth rate*. See appendix to this chapter for a calculus for growth rates.
4 see appendix to this chapter.

The Harrod-Domar model does not guarantee full employment;[5] it only gives the condition under which full employment can be maintained. If, with a given labour output ratio, there is full employment at point of time 0, then full employment will be maintained as long as the labour force does not grow faster than the warranted rate of growth σ/κ. Unemployment occurs when the labour force grows faster than the warranted rate of growth, while if the labour force grows at a rate less than the warranted rate of growth, there will be a shortage of labour.[6]

This rule holds so long as there is no labour-saving technical development. If there is Harrod-neutral technical change, then productivity per unit labour will grow each year, say by rate ρ. In that case, if there is a situation of full employment, then to maintain it, the labour force has to grow each year by the warranted rate of growth minus ρ. In other words, with π for the growth rate of labour, in equilibrium:

$$\pi = \frac{\sigma}{\kappa} - \rho, \quad \text{or} \quad \frac{\sigma}{\kappa} = \pi + \rho.$$

This equation shows that, in equilibrium, the warranted rate of growth σ/κ must equal the rate of growth of the population π plus the rate of growth of the productivity of labour ρ. The rate $\pi + \rho$ is called the natural rate of growth.[7] In the Harrod-Domar model, attaining growth equilibrium, which means a state of steady growth together with full employment, is just a matter of luck; there is no mechanism to restore the equilibrium if it is broken. This is the first cause of instability in the Harrod-Domar model. The second cause arises when the production capacity does not equal production. In that case, the expected rate of growth does not equal the warranted rate of growth and this will cause an unstable development of production.

Finally, with regard to income distribution, the ratio of total wages to total income λ is:

$$\lambda = \frac{p_l l}{p y}.$$

In this equation, p_l represents the nominal wage level, p the general price level, l employment, which is assumed to be equal to the labour force, and y real national income. The real wage level is equal to p_l/p and l/y is equal to the labour output

5 We are assuming full capacity of capital, not of labour.
6 In that case, the actual growth rate will be lower than the warranted rate of growth.
7 This *natural rate of growth* is completely different from the physical concept *growth rate of nature*, which equals the growth rate of the total amount of biomass in the biosphere. In fact, the natural rate of growth postulates some kind of natural order in which the economy is to grow according to this growth rate. To me it seems that this natural order is some kind of relic from the era of the Enlightenment, during which time this type of thinking came into being.

ratio, which is the reciprocal of the average productivity of labour. If the average productivity per unit of labour is represented by y/l and real wage by w, the last equation can be rewritten as:

$$\lambda = \frac{w}{y/l}.$$

This equation rewritten in terms of growth rates gives:

$$\bar{\lambda} = \bar{w} - (\bar{y} - \bar{l}).$$

This result means that income distribution remains unchanged $(\bar{\lambda} = 0)$ if real wage $\bar{w}$ increases by the same rate as the rise in average productivity of labour $(\bar{y} - \bar{l})$.

Neoclassical growth model

In the post-Keynesian Harrod-Domar growth model discussed in the previous section, full employment is not attained automatically. Starting from a situation of full employment, if supply of labour grows faster than production minus labour-saving technical change, then unemployment ensues. Since prices are fixed, the only way the government can attain full employment is by manipulating effective demand. Thus steady growth in the Harrod-Domar growth model is not a sufficient condition for the growth equilibrium since full employment is not guaranteed.

In contrast to the Harrod-Domar model, the neoclassical growth model, developed mainly by Solow, assumes that the price mechanism will clear all markets including the labour market. This means that in this model there is no room for unemployment and thus there is no role for government to play, since the price mechanism is supposed to function efficiently. In the Harrod-Domar model, the question to be answered was under what conditions there would be growth equilibrium. It appeared that there could be steady growth maintaining full employment, although there seemed to be two causes for instability. The expected rate of growth might not equal the warranted rate of growth and the warranted rate of growth might not equal the natural rate of growth. This model has no mechanism to restore growth equilibrium once it is disturbed. However, in the neoclassical growth model, there is, by definition, full employment so the only questions left to be answered are whether there will be a steady growth path and by what circumstances this growth path will be determined.

Another difference between the Harrod-Domar growth model and the neoclassical growth model is the explicit presence in the latter of a production function with substitution possibilities. To show the consequences of this, I have used a Cobb-Douglas production function, which allows production factors to be substituted for each other with a substitution elasticity of 1. In general terms, a Cobb-Douglas production function presents a specified relation between the output or production y and the input or the production factors labour l and capital k. Written in an equation (α and δ being parameters):

$$y = \alpha l^{\delta} k^{1-\delta}.$$

The specific form of this production function implies that there are no economies of scale. It can be proved that, in this case, the marginal productivity theory gives a complete solution for the distribution of income (or production) assuming that the market form is characterized by perfect competition. Assuming only Harrod-neutral technical change, the production function written in terms of growth rates is:

$$\bar{y} = \bar{\alpha} + \delta \bar{l} + (1 - \delta)\bar{k}.$$

The growth rate of capital equals net investment i divided by the stock of capital. Since investment is supposed to be a constant fraction σ of production, the growth rate of capital can be written as:

$$\bar{k} = \frac{\sigma y}{k}.$$

The double growth rate of capital $\bar{\bar{k}}$ equals:

$$\bar{\bar{k}} = \bar{y} - \bar{k}.$$

This result implies that with a normal production function like a Cobb-Douglas production function, there is a mechanism working towards a constant capital output ratio. During this adaptation process, the capital output ratio is variable. If income grows faster than capital, the double growth rate of capital is positive, which means that the growth rate of capital is increasing. So, in equilibrium, the growth rate of income equals the growth rate of capital. This is illustrated by Figure 14.1. Equilibrium is found when $\bar{y} = \bar{y}^*$ and $\bar{k} = \bar{k}^*$.

The growth rate of production (income) equals both the growth rate of investment and the growth rate of consumption, since investment as well as consumption are constant fractions of production, σ and $1 - \sigma$ respectively. Written in a different way:

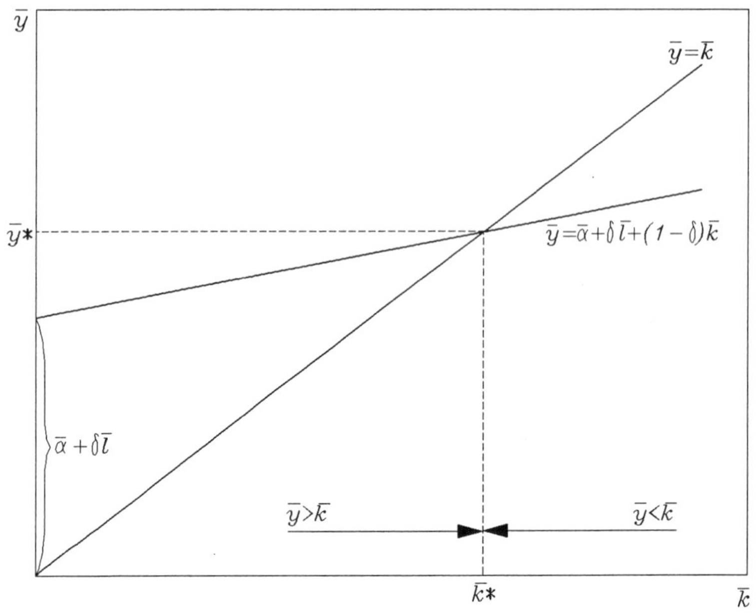

$$\bar{y} = \bar{k} = \bar{i} = \bar{c} = \frac{\sigma}{\kappa}.$$

It can be concluded that in the neoclassical model, a steady-state growth is automatically maintained by the price mechanism and the variable capital-output ratio. Therefore, the two causes of instability in the Harrod-Domar model are absent in the neoclassical model. Assuming that in equilibrium $\bar{y}$ can be substituted for $\bar{k}$ in the production function, the following result can be reached:

$$\bar{y} = \frac{\bar{\alpha}}{\delta} + \bar{l}.$$

$\bar{\alpha}$ as well as $\bar{l}$ are exogenous and $\bar{\alpha}$ is a measure of technical development. This type of technical change is called Harrod-neutral technical change. $\bar{\alpha}/\delta$ equals ρ, while $\bar{l}$ equals π. This means that, in equilibrium, production will grow at the natural rate of growth. In this case, the Harrod neutral technical change is a purely labour-saving type of technical change. It is remarkable that in this model the permanent rate of growth of output per unit of labour input depends entirely on the rate of technological progress and is totally independent of the savings (investment) rate.

Turning to income distribution, it is possible to define the wage share and the profit share as follows (with w for real wage and r for real interest) and, further, ϵ for the labour output ratio and κ for the capital output ratio:

$$\lambda = \frac{wl}{y}, \qquad 1-\lambda = \frac{rk}{y} \quad \text{so:} \quad \lambda = \epsilon w, \qquad 1-\lambda = r\kappa .$$

Wage level and interest rate are determined by the marginal productivity of labour and capital respectively:

$$\frac{\partial y}{\partial l} = w, \quad \frac{\partial y}{\partial k} = r .$$

This equation can be rewritten as:

$$\frac{l}{y}\frac{\partial y}{\partial l} = \lambda, \qquad \frac{k}{y}\frac{\partial y}{\partial k} = 1 - \lambda .$$

Using the production function to determine the partial derivatives, the last equation can be rewritten as

$$\lambda = \delta, \quad 1 - \lambda = 1 - \delta .$$

It can be concluded that, because $\bar{y} = \frac{\bar{\alpha}}{\delta} + \bar{l}$ and $\lambda = \delta$, the rise in average productivity of labour during the growth process $(\bar{y} - \bar{l})$ equals the percentage of technical change divided by the wage share λ..

Since there is only Harrod-neutral technical change in the neoclassical growth model, which means that δ is a constant, it can be concluded that during the process of steady growth there will be no change in income distribution, because λ is a constant too.

After this brief description of the neoclassical growth model with two production factors, it can be concluded that the neoclassical growth model provides a stable and steady growth together with full employment, which implies growth equilibrium.

Appendix: Calculus for growth rates
Define growth rate $\bar{y}$ of function y_t as

$$\bar{y} = \frac{dy_t}{dt}\frac{1}{y_t} .$$

(0) If $y_t =$ constant, $\bar{y} = 0$.

(1) If $y_t = \alpha x_t$, then $\bar{y} = \bar{x}$.

Proof: $\frac{dy_t}{dt} = \alpha \frac{dx_t}{dt}$, so: $\bar{y} = \bar{x}$.

(2) If $y_t = \alpha x_t + \beta$, then $\bar{y} = \frac{\alpha x_t}{\alpha x_t + \beta} \bar{x}$.

Proof: $\bar{y} = \alpha \frac{dx_t}{dt}$, so: $\bar{y} = \frac{\alpha x_t}{\alpha x_t + \beta} \bar{x}$.

(3) If $y_t = x_t^\alpha$, then $\bar{y} = \alpha \bar{x}$.

Proof: $\frac{dy_t}{dt} = \alpha x_t^{\alpha - 1} \frac{dx_t}{dt}$, so: $\bar{y} = \alpha \bar{x}$.

(4) If $y_t = x_t z_t$, then $\bar{y} = \bar{x} + \bar{z}$.

Proof: $\frac{dy_t}{dt} = \frac{dx_t}{dt} z_t + x_t \frac{dz_t}{dt}$, so: $\bar{y} = \bar{x} + \bar{z}$.

(5) If $y_t = \frac{x_t}{z_t}$, then $\bar{x} - \bar{z}$.

Proof: $y_t = x_t z_t^{-1}$, so from (3) and (4): $\bar{y} = \bar{x} + \overline{z^{-1}} = \bar{x} - \bar{z}$.

(6) If $y_t = x_t + z_t$, then: $\bar{y} = \frac{x_t}{x_t + z_t} \bar{x} + \frac{z_t}{x_t + z_t} \bar{z}$.

Proof: $\frac{dy_t}{dt} = \frac{dx_t}{dt} + \frac{dz_t}{dt}$, so: $\bar{y} = \frac{x_t}{x_t + z_t} \bar{x} + \frac{z_t}{x_t + z_t} \bar{z}$.

(7) If $y_t = x_t - z_t$, then from (3) and (6) $\bar{y} = \frac{x_t}{x_t - z_t} \bar{x} + \frac{z_t}{x_t - z_t} \bar{z}$.

Proof: $\bar{y} = \overline{x + (-z)} = \frac{x_t}{x_t - z_t} \bar{x} + \frac{-z_t}{x_t - z_t} (-\bar{z})$

$$= \frac{x_t}{x_t - z_t} \bar{x} + \frac{z_t}{x_t - z_t} \bar{z}.$$

15. RESOURCE DEPLETION AND ECONOMIC GROWTH

Harrod-Domar growth model and an exhaustible resource

In this chapter, I continue with the integration of depletable resources into two growth theories: the Harrod-Domar growth theory and the neoclassical growth theory. It try to determine whether a state of steady growth can be combined with a steady depletion of exhaustible resources on the one hand, and sustainable use of renewable resources on the other. This combination of steady growth, steady depletion and sustainable use is called *sustainable growth.* Within this framework, special attention is paid to the critical role of interest rate and technical change.[1]

Suppose an economy has at its disposal one exhaustible resource. The question I examine is whether steady growth is possible for an infinite time. At first glance, this question does not make sense since there is an exhaustible resource at stake. This means that the resource cannot renew itself, so that any use of it leads to a decrease of the total stock. However, there is a way out of this dilemma.

The depletion rate of total stock of the exhaustible resource $\bar{n}_\epsilon$ per period equals the use of the resource g_ϵ, which is a flow, divided by total stock n_ϵ at the beginning of the period:[2]

$$\bar{n}_\epsilon = \frac{-g_\epsilon}{n_\epsilon}.$$

From this equation it follows:

$$\bar{\bar{n}}_\epsilon = \bar{g}_\epsilon - \bar{n}_\epsilon.$$

So the relative change of the depletion rate $\bar{\bar{n}}_\epsilon$ will equal 0 if the growth rate of the use of the resource $\bar{g}_\epsilon$ equals the depletion rate $\bar{n}_\epsilon$. This means, of course, a steady depletion of the resource stock.

Since the rate of depletion is negative, in order to be able to use the resource over an infinite time period, the growth rate of the use of the resource must also be negative. The reason for this is simply that if a stock of an exhaustible resource decreases over each period by the same percentage, total stock will approach zero when time approaches infinity. This result implies that, if a constant amount of the

---

1 W.J.M. Heijman, 1991. *Depletable resources and the economy*. Wageningen Economic Studies (WES) 21. Pudoc, Wageningen.
2 See Chapter 13.

resource μ is needed per unit of product and if the resource is to be used over an infinite time, total production y must decrease over each period by the same percentage as the use of the resource. To put it differently:

$$g_\epsilon = \mu y, \quad \overline{g}_\epsilon = \overline{\mu} + \overline{y}.$$

If $\overline{\mu}$ equals 0, which is the case if a constant amount of the resource is needed per unit of product, it follows that

$$\overline{y} = \overline{g}_\epsilon.$$

It can also be concluded that a steady depletion of the resource stock can be combined with a growing production if $\overline{\mu}$ is negative and $|\overline{\mu}|>|\overline{y}|$. This implies that it is possible to have a steady depletion of the resource combined with a growing production if the relative decrease in the resource use per unit of product exceeds the growth of production. If production, together with capital, investment, and consumption, grows each year according to the warranted rate of growth σ/κ, and if there is a steady depletion of the resource stock $\overline{g}_\epsilon = \overline{n}_\epsilon$, then the necessary annual relative decrease in resource use per unit of product can be derived:

$$\overline{\mu} = \overline{n}_\epsilon - \frac{\sigma}{\kappa}$$

In equilibrium, the price of the exhaustible resource must rise by the interest rate.

The income distribution is now considered. Suppose that the proportion of the national income going to royalties is represented by ζ. Then, with p_n representing real royalty per unit:

$$\zeta = \frac{p_n g_\epsilon}{y}, \quad \overline{\zeta} = \overline{p}_n + \overline{g}_\epsilon - \overline{y}.$$

If the royalty share is constant, while $\overline{p}_n$ is equal to the interest rate r and $\overline{g}_\epsilon = \overline{y} + \overline{\mu}$, the last equation can be rewritten as:

$$r = -\overline{\mu}.$$

This outcome means that if the interest rate equals the yearly relative decrease in resource use per unit of product, then there will be a steady growth together with a steady depletion of the non-renewable resource. What will happen to the resource stock if the rate of interest rises while a steady growth path is maintained? We then have:

$$\bar{n}_{\epsilon} = \frac{\sigma}{\kappa} - r \qquad r > \frac{\sigma}{\kappa}.$$

The resource stock decreases proportionately at a more rapid pace as the rate of interest rises. This result is in agreement with the one reached by Hotelling in 1931.

Harrod-Domar growth model and a renewable resource

If a renewable resource is growing at rate a, an appreciation in value is not the only source of current return to its owner. Indeed, the renewal rate of the stock as a return to the owner of the stock should also be taken into consideration. The rate of depletion can then be written as:

$$\bar{n}_{\rho} = a - \frac{\mu y}{n_{\rho}}.$$

In this case, instead of a steady depletion, sustainable depletion of the renewable resource must be the aim. This implies that the annual use of the renewable resource is exactly the same as the production of nature. This implies that, in equilibrium, $\bar{n}_{\rho}$ must be zero while a is constant. This means that:

$$a = \frac{\mu y}{n_{\rho}}, \qquad \bar{y} = -\bar{\mu}.$$

Since the renewal rate of the renewable resource has to be considered part of the return for the owner, the price of the renewable resource in equilibrium must increase each year by the difference between the rate of interest and the rate of renewal (see Chapter 10). This can be seen in the income distribution, which is considered to be constant on the steady growth path:

$$\zeta = \frac{p_n \mu y}{y}$$

$$\bar{p}_n + \bar{\mu} + \bar{y} - \bar{y} = 0$$

$$r - a + \bar{\mu} = 0$$

$$r = a - \bar{\mu}.$$

This last equation describes a necessary condition for a steady growth path.

Exhaustible resource in a neoclassical growth model

An efficient depletion means that interest rate has to equal the proportional rise in royalty. Formerly, this rule was called the Hotelling efficiency rule. Since in the neoclassical growth model, the price of the natural resource (p_n) equals its marginal product $\partial y / \partial g_\epsilon$, then:

$$\frac{\partial y}{\partial k} = \overline{\frac{\partial y}{\partial g_\epsilon}} = r = \bar{p}_n .$$

Put like this, the rule is called the Solow-Stiglitz efficiency rule.

Introducing an exhaustible resource into the neoclassical growth model means that the number of production factors in the production function is expanded by one, that is, by the amount of exhaustible resource which is used in the production process. This flow is referred to as g_ϵ. The production function can now be formulated as follows:

$$y = y(l, k, g_\epsilon).$$

Specified as a linearly homogenous Cobb-Douglas production function, it can be formulated in the following way:

$$y = \alpha l^\delta k^\beta g_\epsilon^{1-\delta-\beta}.$$

This last equation rewritten in growth rates gives:

$$\bar{y} = \bar{\alpha} + \delta \bar{l} + \beta \bar{k} + (1 - \delta - \beta)\bar{g}_\epsilon .$$

Assuming that the capital output ratio and the labour output ratio are constant ($\bar{y} = \bar{l}$, $\bar{y} = \bar{k}$), this implies that production grows according to a steady growth path and that the Harrod-neutral technical change is purely resource saving. In this case the last equation can be rewritten as:

$$\bar{g}_\epsilon = \bar{y} - \frac{\bar{\alpha}}{1 - \delta - \beta}.$$

The depletion rate of the non-renewable resource ($\bar{n}_\epsilon$) equals $-g_\epsilon / n_\epsilon$. From this the double depletion rate $\left(\bar{\bar{n}}_\epsilon\right)$ can be calculated as:

$$\bar{\bar{n}}_{\epsilon} = \bar{g}_{\epsilon} - \bar{n}_{\epsilon}.$$

So in equilibrium $\bar{g}_{\epsilon} = \bar{n}_{\epsilon}$. On a steady growth path, the royalty share in income must be stable. So:

$$r + \bar{g}_{\epsilon} - \bar{y} = 0, \quad \bar{g}_{\epsilon} = \bar{y} - r.$$

This implies that:

$$r = \frac{\bar{\alpha}}{1 - \delta - \beta}.$$

For both a steady depletion and a steady growth, the rate of interest must equal the rate of technical change divided by the production elasticity of the exhaustible resource, which is equal to the royalty share.

If a steady depletion of the resource stock is assumed, then it can be deduced that:

$$\bar{n}_{\epsilon} = \frac{\sigma}{\kappa} - r.$$

This implies that on a steady growth path which is combined with a steady depletion of the resource stock, the depletion rate of the stock depends on the rate of interest, and also that the interest must depend on the resource-saving technological change. The overall conclusion is that a steady depletion together with a steady growth path is also possible within the neoclassical growth model.

Renewable resource in the neoclassical growth model

If a renewable resource rather than an exhaustible resource is introduced, the production function can be represented as follows:

$$y = y(k, l, g_{\rho}).$$

The production function is specified as a linearly homogenous Cobb-Douglas production function:

$$y = \alpha l^{\delta} k^{\beta} g_{\rho}^{1-\delta-\beta}.$$

This equation can be rewritten in growth rates as follows:

$$\bar{y} = \bar{\alpha} + \delta\bar{l} + \beta\bar{k} + (1 - \delta - \beta)\bar{g}_p.$$

Assuming a steady growth process with constant capital output and labour output ratios it can be deduced that:

$$\bar{y} = \bar{g}_p + \frac{\bar{\alpha}}{1 - \delta - \beta}.$$

With a renewable resource, the question is whether sustainable depletion is possible. There is sustainable depletion when human use of the renewable resource g_p/n equals the production of nature a, and further, when the growth of human use equals zero $\bar{g}_p = 0$. These assumptions combined with the last equation give:

$$\bar{y} = \frac{\bar{\alpha}}{1 - \delta - \beta}.$$

So on the one hand, steady growth depends completely on the resource saving technical change. On the other hand, an economy without resource-saving technical change completely depending on a renewable resource can be sustainable if the population growth equals zero.

In equilibrium, the rise of royalty has to equal interest rate minus the natural renewal rate, while the royalty share is constant. This means:

$$r - a - \bar{y} = 0.$$

So, the rate of interest is given by

$$r = \frac{\bar{\alpha}}{1 - \delta - \beta} + a.$$

Now, suppose that the renewal rate of the renewable resource a is a linear decreasing function of total stock: $a = \psi - \phi n_p$. After having substituted this expression for a in the last equation, the equilibrium value n_p^* for the renewable resource stock is found:

$$n_p{}^* = \frac{\bar{\alpha}}{(1 - \delta - \beta)\phi} + \frac{\psi}{\phi} - \frac{r}{\phi}.$$

It can be concluded that, for steady growth, the total stock should be constant $(n_\rho*)$, which means that $\bar{g}_\rho$ equals zero. From this it follows that a steady growth path implies sustainable use of the renewable resource. Or, formulated a little differently, sustainable use of the renewable resource is a necessary condition for steady growth. Another conclusion is that total stock n_ρ in a state of steady growth will decrease as the rate of interest increases. Again, in this case, it should be noticed that the possibility of sustainable use together with a state of steady growth does not guarantee that society will follow such a path. Also the social rate of time preference appears to be crucial.

Simultaneous use of exhaustible and renewable resources

Assume there are four production factors: labour, capital, an exhaustible resource and a renewable resource. The production function can now be written as follows:

$$y = y(l, k, g_\epsilon, g_\rho).$$

This production function is specified as a Cobb-Douglas production function:

$$y = \alpha l^\delta k^\beta g_\epsilon^\gamma g_\rho^{(1-\delta-\beta-\gamma)}.$$

If steady growth is assumed, then both the capital-output ratio and labour-output ratio are constant. In that case, the last equation can be rewritten in growth rates as follows:

$$\bar{y} = \frac{\bar{\alpha}}{1-\beta-\gamma} + \frac{\delta}{1-\beta-\gamma}\bar{g}_\epsilon + \frac{(1-\beta-\gamma-\delta)}{1-\beta-\gamma}\bar{g}_\rho.$$

Since during the steady growth path, royalty shares are constant:

$$\bar{g}_\epsilon + r - \bar{y} = 0, \quad \bar{g}_\rho + r - a - \bar{y} = 0.$$

So:

$$\bar{g}_\rho = \bar{g}_\epsilon + a.$$

This can also be shown through the substitution elasticity (η_s), which, with a Cobb-Douglas production function, equals 1:

$$\eta_s = \frac{\bar{g}_\epsilon - \bar{g}_\rho}{r - a - r} = 1, \quad \bar{g}_\rho = \bar{g}_\epsilon + a.$$

The last three equations give:

$$r = \frac{\bar{\alpha}}{1-\beta-\gamma} + \frac{1-\beta-\gamma-\delta}{1-\beta-\gamma} a.$$

This implies that in an economy with both renewable and exhaustible resources there can be a state of steady growth and a steady depletion of the exhaustible resource. Further, it proves that in this situation there can be a positive rate of interest even without resource-saving technical change.

A state of steady growth and a steady depletion of the exhaustible resource do not imply sustainable use of the renewable resource. A necessary condition for sustainable growth is a constant use of the renewable resource $\bar{g}_\rho = 0$. It can be determined from the last equation that, in that case, $\bar{g}_\epsilon = -a$. This implies the following expression for the growth rate of net production:

$$\bar{y} = \frac{\bar{\alpha}}{1-\beta-\delta} - \frac{\delta}{1-\beta-\delta} a.$$

From this equation it can be concluded that, in an economy depending on exhaustible and renewable resources and fixed capital output and labour output ratios, resource-saving technical change is indispensable, even in a non-growth situation. In that case, $\bar{\alpha}$ must be equal to δa.

Since a is a decreasing function of n_ρ, there are now two consequences of a moderate rate of interest. First, the renewable resource stock will remain relatively large, and second, the depletion rate of the exhaustible resource will be relatively low. The first part of the conclusion can be verified with the help of $a = \psi - \phi n_\rho$:

$$r = \frac{\bar{\alpha}}{1-\beta-\gamma} + \frac{1-\beta-\gamma-\delta}{1-\beta-\gamma} a,$$

$$a = \psi - \phi n_\rho, \quad \text{so:}$$

$$n_\rho = \frac{\bar{\alpha}}{\phi(1-\beta-\gamma-\delta)} + \frac{\psi}{\phi} - \frac{1-\beta-\gamma}{\phi(1-\beta-\gamma-\delta)} r.$$

As can be seen, the renewable resource stock will decrease if there is an increase in the rate of interest.

16. SPATIAL ASPECTS OF THE ENVIRONMENTAL PROBLEM

Input-output analysis of interregional environmental problems

Interregional input-output table

When more regions are included in the construction of an input-output table, the table is called an *interregional* input-output table. Table 16.1 shows an interregional input-output table with two sectors, two regions and four polluting agencies (V^1, V^2, V^3 en V^4). The term (11) refers to sector 1 in Region 1, the term (12) to sector 1 in Region 2, *etcetera*.

Table 16.1: Interregional input-output table in absolute values.

sectors → ↓	(11)	(21)	(12)	(22)	Final demand	Turnover	Emission
(11)	$A^{(11)}_{(11)}$	$A^{(21)}_{(11)}$	$A^{(12)}_{(11)}$	$A^{(22)}_{(11)}$	f_{11}	x_{11}	
(21)	$A^{(11)}_{(21)}$	$A^{(21)}_{(21)}$	$A^{(12)}_{(21)}$	$A^{(22)}_{(21)}$	f_{21}	x_{21}	
(12)	$A^{(11)}_{(12)}$	$A^{(21)}_{(12)}$	$A^{(12)}_{(12)}$	$A^{(22)}_{(12)}$	f_{12}	x_{12}	
(22)	$A^{(11)}_{(22)}$	$A^{(21)}_{(22)}$	$A^{(12)}_{(22)}$	$A^{(22)}_{(22)}$	f_{22}	x_{22}	
					f	x	
V^1	V^1_{11}	V^1_{21}	V^1_{12}	V^1_{22}			v_1
V^2	V^2_{11}	V^2_{21}	V^2_{12}	V^2_{22}			v_2
V^3	V^3_{11}	V^3_{21}	V^3_{12}	V^3_{22}			v_3
V^4	V^4_{11}	V^4_{21}	V^4_{12}	V^4_{22}			v_4

In Table 16.1 $A^{(kl)}_{(ij)}$ refers to sector i in region j's deliverance to sector k in region l. The term V^m_{ij} refers to the emission of polluting agency m by sector i in region j. The term f^n_{ij} represents final demand for goods in region n delivered by sector i located in region j. Finally, v_m refers to the total emission of the polluting agency m.

Assuming fixed technical coefficients and that matrix $(\mathrm{I}-\mathrm{A})$ may be inverted, Table 16.1 can be written as:

$$\mathrm{AX}+\mathrm{F}=\mathrm{X} \quad \text{so:} \quad \mathrm{X}=(\mathrm{I}-\mathrm{A})^{-1}\mathrm{F},$$

$$\mathrm{V}=\mathrm{BX},$$

with A for the matrix of technical coefficients concerning inter-deliverances, F for the vector of final demand, X for the vector of production, V for the vector of emissions, and B for the matrix of pollution coefficients. Consider an example with two sectors and two regions in the following matrices and vectors:

$$A = \begin{pmatrix} 0.063 & 0.1 & 0.1 & 0.075 \\ 0.25 & 0.1 & 0.2 & 0.15 \\ 0.125 & 0.075 & 0.133 & 0.1 \\ 0.25 & 0.2 & 0.2 & 0.15 \end{pmatrix}, \quad \text{so:}$$

$$(I - A)^{-1} = \begin{pmatrix} 1.19 & 0.19 & 0.22 & 0.16 \\ 0.48 & 1.27 & 0.42 & 0.32 \\ 0.27 & 0.18 & 1.28 & 0.21 \\ 0.53 & 0.40 & 0.46 & 1.35 \end{pmatrix}.$$

If:

$$F = \begin{pmatrix} 400 \\ 500 \\ 350 \\ 275 \end{pmatrix}, \quad \text{then:} \quad X = \begin{pmatrix} 690.60 \\ 1060.71 \\ 703.64 \\ 941.78 \end{pmatrix}.$$

To compute the environmental effects, I need matrix B:

$$B = \begin{pmatrix} 0.125 & 0.1 & 0.34 & 0.24 \\ 0.25 & 0.05 & 0.02 & 0.15 \\ 0.067 & 0.1 & 0.8 & 0.77 \\ 0.133 & 0.125 & 0.95 & 0.3 \end{pmatrix}, \quad \text{so:} \quad V = BX = \begin{pmatrix} 657.66 \\ 381.02 \\ 1440.42 \\ 1175.42 \end{pmatrix}.$$

Environmental policy

Now, I shall deal with the effects of environmental policy in Region 1. Because there are only two sectors, sector 1 and sector 2, the government has only two instruments: production size of the two sectors in Region 1: x_{11} and x_{21}. Because of this, the government of Region 1 can only concentrate on two emissions, for example: V^1 and V^2. To analyse the consequences I need one other matrix: B_1, and three other vectors: V_1, X_1, and X_2:

$$B_1 = \begin{pmatrix} V^1_{11} & V^1_{21} \\ V^2_{11} & V^2_{21} \end{pmatrix}, \quad X_1 = \begin{pmatrix} x_{11} \\ x_{21} \end{pmatrix}, \quad X_2 = \begin{pmatrix} x_{12} \\ x_{22} \end{pmatrix},$$

$$V_1 = B_1 X_1.$$

In our example:

$$B_1 = \begin{pmatrix} 0.125 & 0.1 \\ 0.25 & 0.05 \end{pmatrix}, \quad X_1 = \begin{pmatrix} 690.60 \\ 1060.71 \end{pmatrix}, \quad X_2 = \begin{pmatrix} 703.64 \\ 941.78 \end{pmatrix}, \quad \text{so:}$$

$$V_1 = B_1 X_1 = \begin{pmatrix} 192.40 \\ 225.69 \end{pmatrix}.$$

The following model can now be formulated:

$$A_1 X_1 + A_2 X_2 + F_1 = X_1,$$

$$A_3 X_1 + A_4 X_2 + F_2 = X_2,$$

$$F_1 + F_2 = C,$$

$$X_1 = B_1^{-1} V_1,$$

with:

$$A_1 = \begin{pmatrix} a_{(11)}^{(11)} & a_{(11)}^{(21)} \\ a_{(21)}^{(11)} & a_{(21)}^{(21)} \end{pmatrix}, \quad A_2 = \begin{pmatrix} a_{(11)}^{(12)} & a_{(11)}^{(22)} \\ a_{(21)}^{(12)} & a_{(21)}^{(22)} \end{pmatrix},$$

$$A_3 = \begin{pmatrix} a_{(12)}^{(11)} & a_{(12)}^{(21)} \\ a_{(22)}^{(11)} & a_{(22)}^{(21)} \end{pmatrix}, \quad A_4 = \begin{pmatrix} a_{(12)}^{(12)} & a_{(12)}^{(22)} \\ a_{(22)}^{(12)} & a_{(22)}^{(22)} \end{pmatrix}.$$

The values for the coefficients $a_{(ij)}^{(kl)}$ can be derived from the original matrix A.

$$A_1 = \begin{pmatrix} 0.063 & 0.1 \\ 0.25 & 0.1 \end{pmatrix}, \quad A_2 = \begin{pmatrix} 0.1 & 0.075 \\ 0.2 & 0.15 \end{pmatrix},$$

$$A_3 = \begin{pmatrix} 0.125 & 0.075 \\ 0.25 & 0.2 \end{pmatrix}, \quad A_4 = \begin{pmatrix} 0.133 & 0.1 \\ 0.2 & 0.15 \end{pmatrix}.$$

Further, I define:

$$F_1 = \begin{pmatrix} f_{11} \\ f_{21} \end{pmatrix}, \quad F_2 = \begin{pmatrix} f_{12} \\ f_{22} \end{pmatrix}.$$

It is assumed that total final demand for the goods from the two regions is constant. This implies that if a sector in Region 1 cannot deliver goods any more because of environmental regulations, the same sector in Region 2 will do it. Vector $\mathbf{C}$ contains two numbers, reflecting constant demand for the goods from both sectors. In our example:

$$C = F_1 + F_2 = \begin{pmatrix} f_{11} \\ f_{21} \end{pmatrix} + \begin{pmatrix} f_{12} \\ f_{22} \end{pmatrix} = \begin{pmatrix} 400 \\ 500 \end{pmatrix} + \begin{pmatrix} 350 \\ 275 \end{pmatrix} = \begin{pmatrix} 750 \\ 775 \end{pmatrix}.$$

Now, it can be deduced that:

$$(A_1 + A_3)X_1 + (A_2 + A_4)X_2 + F_1 + F_2 = X_1 + X_2,$$

$$(A_2 + A_4 - I)X_2 = (I - A_1 - A_3)X_1 - C,$$

$$X_2 = (A_2 + A_4 - I)^{-1}(I - A_1 - A_3)B^{-1}V_1 - (A_2 + A_4 - I)^{-1}C,$$

$$F = (I - A)\begin{pmatrix} X_1 \\ X_2 \end{pmatrix}, \quad V = B\begin{pmatrix} X_1 \\ X_2 \end{pmatrix}.$$

If Region 1 reduces its emissions of V^1 and V^2 by 20%, then:

$$V_1 = \begin{pmatrix} 153.92 \\ 180.55 \end{pmatrix},$$

$$X_1 = B_1^{-1}V_1 = \begin{pmatrix} -2.67 & 5.33 \\ 13.33 & -6.67 \end{pmatrix}\begin{pmatrix} 153.92 \\ 180.55 \end{pmatrix} = \begin{pmatrix} 552.48 \\ 848.60 \end{pmatrix}.$$

The results in our example are:

$$X = \begin{pmatrix} 345.33 \\ 530.33 \\ 847.02 \\ 1137.50 \end{pmatrix}, \quad F = \begin{pmatrix} 262.80 \\ 285.59 \\ 487.91 \\ 489.63 \end{pmatrix}, \quad V = \begin{pmatrix} 344.81 \\ 163.18 \\ 813.51 \\ 681.05 \end{pmatrix}.$$

The conclusion is that production, final demand and total pollution have decreased.

However, production (together with employment and pollution) has moved for the greater part to Region 2. If Region 2 uses backward technologies the effect of that might even be that total pollution increases.[1] So, in the end, Region 1 could be left with less employment and higher pollution levels (because pollution might be

1 This is not the case in the example.

of a transboundary nature) because of its environmental policies. This might be the reason why countries are so reluctant to carry out strict environmental policies on their own.

Game theory

The *prisoner dilemma* game situation has been described by the American mathematician A.W. Tucker. In this situation two prisoners have committed a crime together. They are being interrogated separately. If they both keep silent, they will get one year detention on remand. If both prisoners accuse each other, they get 15 years in jail. If only one prisoner speaks accusing the other of the crime, the speaker goes free, while the other will get 30 years in prison. Table 16.2 shows the alternatives schematically.

Tabel 16.2: Prisoner dilemma.

		Prisoner B	
		Silent	Speak
Prisoner A	Silent	A: 1; B: 1	A: 30; B: 0
	Speak	A: 0; B: 30	A: 15; B: 15

The best solution is that both prisoners keep silent. Indeed, they will only be sentenced to one year in prison. However, the individual interest of both is that they will speak. Both prisoners choose between sentences of 1 or 30 years (if they keep silent) or 0 or 15 years (if they speak). The equilibrium found in a prisoner dilemma game is a so called *Nash equilibrium* not coinciding with the Pareto optimum.[2] This prisoner dilemma may also occur with international environmental policies.

Table 16.3: Prisoner dilemma in international environmental policy.

		Country B	
		High cleansing budget	Low cleansing budget
Country A	High cleansing budget	A: 6; B: 6	A: 1; B: 8
	Low cleansing budget	A: 8; B: 1	A: 2; B: 2

2 A *Nash equilibrium* is a game-theoretical equilibrium based on purely individualistic motives. It is a characteristic for this kind of equilibrium that it does not necessarily coincide with the Pareto optimum. Both players can improve their position by increasing their cleansing budget simultaneously.

If countries feel responsible for all environmental damage they cause, including the damage caused by them abroad by transboundary pollution, then they act cooperatively. Otherwise they act individualistically. Acting cooperatively means a high abatement budget, acting individualistically means a low abatement budget. Net benefits of abatement policies in the case of transboundary pollution are for an important part gained abroad. This is illustrated in Table 16.3. In this table there are two countries, A and B, that can choose between a high abatement budget and a low abatement budget. As with the pure prisoner dilemma situation a country profits most from a high abatement budget of the other. The cooperative strategy, which implies a high budget for both countries gives (A: 6, B: 6). However, in this example, both countries will pursue an individualistic policy. Indeed, this policy gives both countries net benefits at a value of 8 or 2 against 6 or 1 for the cooperative strategy.

Efficiency in abatement

It is often assumed that benefits as well as costs can be expressed in money terms. Generally speaking, this is not a realistic assumption. For the cases in which the benefits cannot be calcultated in money terms, minimization of the abatement costs for an amount of pollution b agreed upon offers a workable alternative for the distribution of the costs over the participating countries.

Suppose that the abatement cost functions as well as the collective target function for n countries are given:

$$\text{Min} \quad c = \sum_{i=1}^{n} c_i,$$

$$c_i = c_i(b_i), \quad \frac{dc_i}{db_i} > 0,$$

$$b = \sum_{i=1}^{n} b_i.$$

This minimization problem can be solved by using a Lagrange function:

$$L = c(c_1(b_1), c_2(b_2), \ldots, c_i(b_i), \ldots, c_n(b_n)) + \lambda\left(b - \sum_{i=1}^{n} b_i\right).$$

The first-order conditions for the minimum are:

$$\frac{\partial L}{\partial b_i} = \frac{\partial c}{\partial c_i}\frac{\partial c_i}{\partial b_i} - \lambda = 0.$$

Because total costs c equal the summing up of the costs c_i of all individual countries, it can be deduced that:

$$\frac{\partial c}{\partial c_i} = 1, \quad \text{so:} \quad \frac{\partial c_i}{\partial b_i} - \lambda = 0, \quad \text{so:}$$

$$\frac{\partial c_1}{\partial b_1} = \frac{\partial c_2}{\partial b_2} = \ldots = \frac{\partial c_i}{\partial b_i} = \ldots = \frac{\partial c_n}{\partial b_n}.$$

Suppose that two countries agree that they will abate 1000 units of a certain pollution agency. The cost functions for both countries are:

$$c_1 = 100 + 5b_1 + 0.5b_1^2,$$

$$c_2 = 150 + 10b_2 + 0.25b_2^2,$$

$$b_1 + b_2 = 1000.$$

With the help of the optimization rule, I can now compute the optimum distribution of the costs between the countries:

$$\frac{dc_1}{db_1} = \frac{dc_2}{db_2}, \quad \text{so:} \quad 5 + b_1 = 10 + 0.5b_2, \quad \text{while:}$$

$$b_1 + b_2 = 1000, \quad \text{so:} \quad b_1 = 336.67, \quad b_2 = 663.33.$$

After assessment of the efficient distribution of abatement efforts, the matter of financing must be considered. A solution might be that both countries establish a fund and that the money from this fund is allocated according to the principle of cost minimization.[3] The money for the fund would be paid by the countries involved in pollution abatement. The payment could be arranged according to the 'polluter pays principle'. However, sometimes the polluters are countries which are in an economically bad way. In that case it can be decided upon that countries profiting most by the abatement also pay the most. This principle could be called 'profiteer pays principle'. Instead of continuing installing cleansing installations in their own country, it could, for example, be a good alternative for the Netherlands, to pay for

3 Another option is to set up a system of tradeable emission permits. For an extensive discussion about the application of such a system to the problem of SO_2 emissions, see S. Kruitwagen, 1996. *An Economic Analysis of Tradeable Emission Permits for Sulphur Dioxide Emissions in Europe.* PhD-Thesis, Wageningen Agricultural University.

cleansing installations for acid emissions in Poland. The advantage of doing so is that for a relatively small amount of money a relatively large decrease in the acid emission can be achieved.

Effects of an increase in the oil price on a non-oil-producing small open economy[4]

Instead of an environmental problem, in this section I would like to deal with a resource problem: the effect of oil price fluctuations on a small oil-importing economy. I want to begin by looking at the KLEM-production function. In this, production is a function of capital k, labour l, energy e, and materials m. Since the measurement of input of m is generally considered too difficult a task, I have assumed that k, l, and e are separable from m.[5]

The effects of an oil price rise are studied using a linearly homogenous Cobb-Douglas production function with the three inputs mentioned above:[6]

$$q = \alpha k^{\beta} l^{\gamma} e^{1-\beta-\gamma}. \tag{1}$$

In equation (1), q, k, l and e stand for production, capital, labour and energy respectively, while α, β, and γ are coefficients. Equation (1) written in percentages gives:[7]

$$\bar{q} = \bar{\alpha} + \beta\bar{k} + \gamma\bar{l} + (1-\beta-\gamma)\bar{e}. \tag{2}$$

Since in equilibrium the production elasticities β, γ and $(1-\beta-\gamma)$ also determine the distribution of production over the three production factors, the return to labour, capital and energy can be written as:

$$kr = \beta q, \quad lp_l = \gamma q, \quad ep_e = (1-\beta-\gamma)q. \tag{3}$$

In equation (3), r is the rate of return, p_l represents real wage and p_e equals the real oil price. Further it is assumed that the balance of payment is continually in equilibrium. National income, which would then equal national spending, can be written as:

---

4 This section is a revised version of Heijman W.J.M., 1991. *Depletable resources and the economy,* Section 7.III: Effects of an increase in the oil price on a non-oil-producing small open economy. Wageningen Economic Studies 21. Pudoc, Wageningen.

5 The separability assumption strictly implies that if $w = f(k,l,e,m) = mg(k,l,e)$, then $q = w/m = g(k,l,e)$, with w for total production and q for the production per unit of material.

6 'Production' here equals national income plus exports, that equals imports of oil.

7 For the meaning of variables indicated with a bar, like $\bar{q}$, see the appendix to Chapter 14.

$$y = kr + lp_l. \tag{4}$$

From equations (3) and (4) it can be derived

$$y = (\beta + \gamma)q. \tag{5}$$

Equations (3) and (5) written in percentages give:

$$\bar{k} = \bar{q} - \bar{r}, \quad \bar{l} = \bar{q} - \bar{p}_l, \quad \bar{e} = \bar{q} - \bar{p}_e, \quad \bar{y} = \bar{q}. \tag{6}$$

In the next part of this section I want to look at four cases: (a) the short-term effects of a sudden rise in the oil price, assuming flexible real wages, (b) the short-term effects of a sudden rise in the price of oil, assuming non-flexible wages, (c) the long-term effects of a sudden rise in the price of oil, assuming no technical innovation and (d) the long-term effects of a sudden rise in the price of oil, assuming technical innovation.

In the first case it is assumed that real wage is so flexible that employment does not change $(\bar{l} = 0)$, that capital stock will not change in the short run $(\bar{k} = 0)$ and that there are no technical innovations $(\bar{\alpha} = 0)$. These assumptions, together with equations (2) and (6), lead to the effects on the economy as shown in Column (a) of Table 16.4.[8]

In the second case, real wage is non-flexible, which means that $\bar{p}_l = 0$, the capital stock is still unchanged $(\bar{k} = 0)$ and there are no technical innovations $(\bar{\alpha} = 0)$. These assumptions give the results shown in Column (b) of Table 16.4.

In the long term, wages are assumed to be flexible $(\bar{l} = 0)$, while capital owners are assumed to restore real rate of return before the oil crisis $(\bar{r} = 0)$. Also in Case (c) it is assumed that there are no technical innovations $(\bar{\alpha} = 0)$. These assumptions give the results shown in Column (c) of Table 16.4.

In the last case it is assumed that in the long term, energy-saving technical innovations are sufficient to compensate for the negative effects of the oil price rise. This means that $\bar{l} = 0$, $\bar{r} = 0$, and $\bar{q} = 0$. Based on these assumptions, it appears that the necessary saving in energy per unit of output equals the production elasticity of oil multiplied by the relative rise in the price of oil (see Column d of Table 16.4).

To give a numerical example, I have taken the same production elasticities as Van de Klundert *et al.* (1983). This means: $\beta = 0.3$, $\gamma = 0.6$ and $(1 - \beta - \gamma) = 0.1$, the increase in the oil price being 10%. The results have been collected in Table 16.5.

---

8 See also: Th. van de Klundert, 1983. The energy problem in a small open economy. *Journal of Macroeconomics,* 5, nr 2, pp. 211-222.

Table 16.4: The short-term and long-term effects of an oil price shock (percentages/100).

Variable	Cases			
	short-term, flexible real wages ($\bar{k}=0$, $\bar{l}=0$, $\bar{\alpha}=0$) (a)	short-term, non-flexible wages ($\bar{k}=0$, $\bar{p}_l=0$, $\bar{\alpha}=0$) (b)	long-term, no technical innovations ($\bar{r}=0$, $\bar{l}=0$ $\bar{\alpha}=0$) (c)	long-term, technical innovations, ($\bar{l}=0$, $\bar{r}=0$, $\bar{q}=0$) (d)
$\bar{q}$	$\frac{-(1-\beta-\gamma)}{\beta+\gamma}\bar{p}_e$	$\frac{-(1-\beta-\gamma)}{\beta}\bar{p}_e$	$\frac{-(1-\beta-\gamma)}{\gamma}\bar{p}_e$	0
$\bar{y}$	$\frac{-(1-\beta-\gamma)}{\beta+\gamma}\bar{p}_e$	$\frac{-(1-\beta-\gamma)}{\beta}\bar{p}_e$	$\frac{-(1-\beta-\gamma)}{\gamma}\bar{p}_e$	0
$\bar{e}$	$\frac{-1}{\beta+\gamma}\bar{p}_e$	$\frac{-(1-\gamma)}{\beta}\bar{p}_e$	$\frac{-(1-\beta)}{\gamma}\bar{p}_e$	$-\bar{p}_e$
$\bar{p}_e$	$\bar{p}_e$	$\bar{p}_e$	$\bar{p}_e$	$\bar{p}_e$
$\bar{p}_l$	$\frac{-(1-\beta-\gamma)}{\beta+\gamma}\bar{p}_e$	0	$\frac{-(1-\beta-\gamma)}{\gamma}\bar{p}_e$	0
$\bar{r}$	$\frac{-(1-\beta-\gamma)}{\beta+\gamma}\bar{p}_e$	$\frac{-(1-\beta-\gamma)}{\beta}\bar{p}_e$	0	0
$\bar{l}$	0	$\frac{-(1-\beta-\gamma)}{\beta}\bar{p}_e$	0	0
$\bar{k}$	0	0	$\frac{-(1-\beta-\gamma)}{\gamma}\bar{p}_e$	0
$\bar{\alpha}$	0	0	0	$(1-\beta-\gamma)\bar{p}_e$

In general, one may conclude that the effects of an oil price rise in the short term on income and employment can be mitigated by the possibilities of substitution between the production factors and flexibility of real wages. In the long term, flexible wages, substitution between production factors, and the possibilities of energy-saving technical innovations might even cause a zero effect on the main parameters of the economy, *i.e.* income and employment.

Table 16.5: The short-term and long-term effects of an oil price shock (percentages).[9]

Variable	Cases			
	short-term, flexible real wage ($\bar{k}=0$, $\bar{l}=0$, $\bar{\alpha}=0$) (a)	short-term, non-flexible real wage ($\bar{k}=0$, $\bar{p}_l=0$, $\bar{\alpha}=0$) (b)	long-term, no technical innovations ($\bar{r}=0$, $\bar{l}=0$, $\bar{\alpha}=0$) (c)	long-term, technical innovations ($\bar{l}=0$, $\bar{r}=0$, $\bar{q}=0$) (d)
$\bar{q}$	-1.11	-3.33	-1.67	0.00
$\bar{y}$	-1.11	-3.33	-1.67	0.00
$\bar{e}$	-11.11	-13.33	-11.67	-10.00
$\bar{p}_e$	+10.00	+10.00	+10.00	+10.00
$\bar{p}_l$	-1.11	0.00	-1.67	0.00
$\bar{r}$	-1.11	-3.33	0.00	0.00
$\bar{l}$	0.00	-3.33	0.00	0.00
$\bar{k}$	0.00	0.00	-1.67	0.00
$\bar{\alpha}$	0.00	0.00	0.00	+1.00

9 The results of the first three columns in this table can also be found in Th. van de Klundert en H. Peer, 1983. *Energie: een economisch perspectief.* Stenfert-Kroese, Leiden.

17. STEADY-STATE ECONOMICS[1]

Steady-state concept

There are at least three basic definitions of the steady state:

1. The steady state as a situation in which both production measured through Gross Domestic Product (GDP) and population are constant over time. I call this situation the *stationary state*.[2]
2. The steady state defined as a physical concept. For renewable resources the term indicates a situation in which human use of nature (expressed in physical terms) equals natural production.[3] For non-renewable resources, this situation is one in which the stock-depletion ratio is constant.[4] I use the term *physical steady state* to refer to a situation in which both the stock of renewable resources and the stock-depletion ratio for non-renewable resources are constant.[5]
3. The steady state as a situation in which production, consumption and investment grow by a constant percentage, resulting in a constant capital-output ratio. In this definition, which is the one economists are most familiar with, production is measured in terms of GDP. I refer to this situation as a *state of steady growth*. In this chapter I will look at the stationary state and the physical steady state respectively.

These three definitions are often combined. For example, the concept of *sustainable growth* is a combination of the state of steady growth and the physical steady state. In other words, the physical steady state is a necessary condition to maintain sustainable growth. This implies that a physical steady state is not the same as a no-growth economy in terms of GDP.

Stationary state

In classical, neoclassical and also Marxist theories, in the absence of population growth and technological innovations, the stationary state will generally be reached

1 This chapter is a revised version of Chapter 3 from Heijman W.J.M., 1991. *Depletable resources and the economy*. Wageningen Economic Studies (WES) 21. Pudoc, Wageningen.
2 J.S. Mill, 1973 (1848). *Principles of political economy*. Kelley, Clifton.
3 In terms of Chapter 13, this means that, after infinite time of depletion, rest R of the renewable natural resource stock equals the initial stock.
4 Regardless of a rest R of the resource after an 'infinite time' of depletion. See Chapter 13.
5 K.E. Boulding, 1966. The economics of the coming spaceship earth. In: W.A. Johnson and J. Hardesty (eds), 1971. *Economic growth vs. the environment*. Wadsworth, Belmont (Cal.). N. Georgescu-Roegen, 1971. *The entropy law and the economic process*. Harvard University Press, Cambridge (Mass.). H.E. Daly, 1977. *Steady-state economics: the economics of biophysical equilibrium and moral growth*. Freeman, San Francisco.

more or less automatically because of the decreasing marginal productivity of capital.[6] This can be shown as follows. In the situation described, total production y is a function of the input of capital k:

$$y = y(k), \quad \frac{dy}{dk} > 0, \quad \frac{d^2y}{dk^2} < 0.$$

Savings s, which equal gross investment, are assumed to be a fixed proportion σ of the total product:

$$s = \sigma y(k), \quad \frac{dy}{dk} > 0, \quad \frac{d^2y}{dk^2} < 0.$$

Depreciation b is assumed to be a fixed proportion π of capital stock:

$$b = \pi k.$$

Net investment in a certain period dk/dt, which is the extension of the capital stock, equals gross investment minus depreciation:

$$\frac{dk}{dt} = \sigma y(k_t) - \pi k_t.$$

From the last equation the equilibrium value of capital k^* can be calculated.

If $k_t < k^*$, gross investment (s) exceeds depreciation b. This implies that net investment dk/dt exceeds zero and, as a consequence, the stock of capital will grow. If $k_t > k^*$, net investment is less than zero, implying that capital stock will decrease. This means that $k*$ is a stable equilibrium of the capital stock. In this equilibrium, capital, production, consumption, investment and population will be stationary. Indeed, it has to be admitted here that the model above reflects a rather specific situation since zero population growth and no technological development are both assumed. Besides, in the model there is no relation between depletable resources and capital stock.

6 In fact the *tendency of the rate of profit to fall* is the Marxist counterpart of the *tendency of the marginal product of capital to decrease* in usual neoclassical theory. One might even consider the latter the cause of the former.

Tinbergen's model

A more appropriate application of the stationary state concept from the viewpoint of resource conservation (input aspect) has been made by Tinbergen.[7] For his steady state model, Tinbergen assumed:

- a stable world population,
- constant consumption for all present and future generations,
- that the problem of the unequal world income distribution is solved.

Suppose in year 0 the total stock of a certain natural resource equals H_0, while the use of natural resources in this year equals h_0. The consumption then is c_0, implying a resource productivity of $c_0/h_0 = p_0$. Because of technological innovations, the amount of resource needed to produce c_0 units of consumption goods decreases each year by factor f. This gives:

$$h_t = f h_{t-1}.$$

This equation implies that all generations will use:

$$\sum_{t=0}^{\infty} h_t = \frac{h_0}{(1-f)}.$$

Since the amount indicated must equal H_0, the use of the natural resource in period 0 must equal:

$$h_0 = (1-f)H_0.$$

If, for example, factor f equals 0.976, which was approximately the case for the global productivity of labour in the period 1960-1987, then h_0 can be 1/41 part of the total stock. Though this result is fairly optimistic, it still implies the following *rules of life:*

- keep population constant,
- continue technological development at factor f,
- increase development aid, so that migration for economic reasons will not occur,
- continue exploration for new natural resources.

Tinbergen's model is based on the use of exhaustible resources. Also in his model, substitution between the resource (the non-reproductive factor) and capital (the reproductive factor) is not possible. These two circumstances imply that, in his model, for a constant population, technological innovation is necessary to maintain

---

7 J. Tinbergen, 1987. *Kunnen wij de aarde beheren?* Kok Agora, Kampen. J. Tinbergen, De verdeling van hulpbronnen over toekomstige generaties. *Economisch Statistische Berichten,* 74 (1989), nr 3715, p. 677.

a constant level of consumption per head. It can be shown that under certain assumptions, in the case of substitution between a non-renewable resource and capital, a constant consumption per head can be maintained even without innovations.[8]

Zoeteman's model

An interesting contribution to thinking in terms of physical steady state was made by Zoeteman.[9] His model does not deal directly with the use of resources, but with the abatement of environmental damage (output aspect). His central idea is that for the attainment of a steady state with respect to a certain polluting agency, for instance the emission of CO_2, the cleansing capacity for that agency has to equal yearly emissions. The cleansing capacity in tons Z equals the density of the earthly biomass in tons per square mile d present on the natural area of the surface of earth multiplied by the cleansing productivity in tons per ton of biomass weight z, multiplied by the natural area of the surface of the earth. This natural area equals total area O minus the indurated part. The indurated part equals the necessary infrastructure per head i multiplied by the world population B. The total cleansing capacity for CO_2 can now be written as follows:

$$Z = zd(O - iB).$$

The yearly emission in tons V equals total population B, multiplied by GDP per head p, multiplied by the emission factor v in tons per monetary unit GDP. The yearly emission can now be written as:

$$V = vpB.$$

In order to reach the steady state the yearly emission has, of course, to equal the cleansing capacity:

$$V = Z, \quad \text{so:} \quad vpB = zd(O - iB).$$

It is clear that in this model, population is the most important variable. If the population grows too fast, it will be very difficult to reach a steady state. To achieve

8 See, for example, Perman R., Y. Ma and J. McGilvray, 1996. *Natural resource & environmental economics*. Longman, London.
9 K. Zoeteman, 1989. *Gaiasofie: anders kijken naar evolutie, ruimtelijke ordening en milieubeheer*. Ankh-Hermes, Deventer.

this, huge emission reductions per unit of product are necessary. This can be illustrated by the following example. If time is included, then the last equation can be written as follows (with A for natural surface and t for time):

$$v_0 p_0 B_0 e^{(\bar{v}+\bar{p}+\bar{b})t} = z_0 d_0 A_0 e^{(\bar{z}+\bar{d}+\bar{a})t}.$$

In this equation the bar indicates a growth rate as usual. Now, it can be deduced that:

$$\bar{v} = \bar{z} + \bar{d} + \bar{a} - \bar{p} - \bar{b} - \frac{1}{t}\ln\frac{v_0 p_0 B_0}{z_0 d_0 A_0}.$$

In a moderate scenario from 1975 till 2075, the world population will grow by 0.75% a year ($\bar{b} = 0.0075$). I have assumed further moderate values for $\bar{z}$, $\bar{d}$ and $\bar{a}$, -0.1%, -0.05%, -0.05% respectively, and a zero growth in the output per head ($\bar{p} = 0$). I have also assumed that the emission-cleansing capacity ratio of the world equals 6 in the year 1990 and that a worldwide steady state must be reached in the year 2050. These assumptions give a necessary emission reduction per unit of output of about 3.9% each year. This means that, relative to 1990, by the year 2050 the emission per unit of product must be reduced by over 90%. Even if it is assumed that the emission-cleansing capacity ratio equals 1 in 1990, an emission reduction per unit of output of almost 1% each year would be necessary. This implies that, by the year of 2050, total reduction of the emission per unit of output must equal 45% of the 1990 emission. This example shows that if a physical steady state has to be reached within about sixty years even moderate assumptions may make a huge reduction in the emission per unit of product necessary in the next fifty or sixty years.

Renewable resources

Importance of renewable resources
Both exhaustible and renewable resources are depletable. Human production reduces the total stock of depletable resources. Renewable resources have a limited renewal capacity, so that the change in the total stock of depletable resources is the result of both human production and natural renewal. If natural renewal equals human expenditure of nature, then one condition for a physical steady state is fulfilled (the other is a constant stock-depletion ratio for exhaustible resources).

As the stock of non-renewable resources diminishes and the prices of these resources increase, the use of renewable resources becomes more important in an economic sense. However, the unlimited exploitation of these resources easily leads to overexploitation and exhaustion. Indeed, overexploitation of renewable resources is as great a danger today as the exhaustion of non-renewable resources. Therefore it is important to investigate the possibilities of ensuring an efficient and lasting use of renewable resources.

Natural production, human production and the optimum steady state

In laboratory culture models of succession, the development of the amount of biomass of an ecosystem n_t in time t from the first stage onwards can be expressed in a so-called 'logistic curve'. In such a model, net natural production[10] in a certain period of time dn_t/dt can be approximately described as a parabolic function of the existing total stock of biomass at the beginning of this period. This function is given with:

$$\frac{dn_t}{dt} = \alpha(n_c - n_t)n_t.$$

In this equation, α is a positive constant.[11] The parabolic shape of the function can easily be explained. In the climax stage, net natural production equals zero. The same holds for a situation in which the total stock of nature equals zero. Net natural production is at a maximum when the stock of nature reaches the volume connected with the point of inflexion of the logistic curve. Net natural production is to be interpreted here as the increase of the volume of biomass. In laboratory models, no account is taken of the use of nature originating from human respiration. Indeed, the 'growth of nature' in the real world is defined as net natural production minus the volume of the human use of nature.

If net natural production equals human use of nature g_t, a physical steady state exists, since the volume of biomass is then constant. This is given with

$$g_t = \alpha(n_c - n_t)n_t.$$

---

10 The 'net natural production' of an ecosystem during a certain period is the difference between gross natural production, i.e. the production by photosynthesis and the respiration by plants and animals, excluding respiration by man. The 'growth of nature' is the difference between net natural production and man's respiration, i.e. the human process of production and consumption.

11 The solution of this differential equation is:

$$n_t = \frac{n_c}{1 + \frac{n_c - n_0}{n_0} e^{-\alpha n_c t}}.$$

Further dn_t/dt is at the maximum for:

$$t = \frac{\ln\left(\frac{n_c - n_0}{n_0}\right)}{n_c \alpha}.$$

and $n = \frac{1}{2} n_c$.

In this situation, the growth of nature equals zero, which implies a physical steady state. The optimum steady state can be defined as the physical steady state in which the human use of nature is at a maximum. This is when net natural production reaches the top of the parabolic function. This maximum implies that the first derivative of the human use of dn_t/dt with respect to n_t must be zero, so:

$$\frac{d(\alpha(n_c - n_t)n_t)}{dn_t} = -2\alpha n_t + \alpha n_c = 0, \quad \text{so} \quad n^* = \frac{1}{2} n_c.$$

The outcome of n^* can be substituted in the second last equation. This gives the optimum human use of nature g^*:

$$g^* = 0.25 \alpha n_c^2.$$

For human production per unit of time, e.g. a year, a certain amount of energy is necessary. The total human need for energy g_t equals the need for energy per unit of product β multiplied by total human production y_t:

$$g_t = \beta y_t.$$

The optimum use of nature g^* substituted in the last equation gives the optimum human production y^*: [12]

$$y^* = 0.25 \frac{\alpha}{\beta} n_c^2.$$

From this equation it follows that, without affecting total stock, human production can increase to a maximum level determined by the regeneration speed of nature, the need for energy per unit of product and the volume of biomass in the climax stage.

---

12 As long as the optimum steady state has not been reached, human use of nature should be less than natural production. In that case there will be a positive growth of nature if:

$$\frac{dn_t}{dt} > g_t \quad \text{for} \quad n_t < n_c.$$

Suppose, for example:

$$g_t = \gamma \alpha (n_c - n_t) n_t \quad \text{with} \quad 0 < \gamma < 1 \quad \text{for} \quad n_t < n_c \quad \text{and} \quad \gamma = 1 \quad \text{for} \quad n_t = n_c.$$

From this it follows:

$$\frac{dn_t}{dt} = \alpha (n_c - n_t) n_t - \gamma \alpha (n_c - n_t) n_t = \alpha (1 - \gamma)(n_c - n_t) n_t.$$

Further it is assumed that the optimum steady state will have been reached within T years. So, by using $n^* = n_T = \frac{1}{2} n_c$,

$$T = \frac{\ln\left(\frac{n_c - n_0}{n_0}\right)}{n_c \alpha (1 - \gamma)}, \quad \text{which means} \quad \gamma = 1 - \frac{\ln\left(\frac{n_c - n_0}{n_0}\right)}{\alpha T n_c}$$

In this way human production need not affect future means of support in an irresponsible way, so that humanity may survive with enough power for as long as the sun shines (on estimate, another 5 billion years). The last equation gives a very strict prescription for human production. However, there are many kinds of (bio)technological innovations which may widen the ecological borders. These are studied in the next sections.

Technological change

No doubt, it is the technological developments which have caused the large-scale exhaustion of natural resources for a great deal. However, it is also clear that technology is an indispensable instrument in solving the ecological crisis which the world faces today. So, a strict anti-technology attitude makes no sense. In fact, there is a distinction between 'nature-conserving' and 'nature-affecting' technological innovations.

Throughout human history most technological innovations have meant a further assault on the stock of depletable resources. When man first practised agriculture several thousands of years ago, he profoundly influenced the ecological system. Even more influential were the industrial revolutions in the eighteenth, nineteenth and twentieth centuries, when a great number of inventions and innovations made it possible to process large amounts of resources. Because of rapidly diminishing stocks of resources, a point has now been reached where it is realized that technological innovations ought to have a nature-conserving rather than a nature-affecting character. In economic terms, nature has become a scarce commodity.

Nature-conserving technological change can be subdivided into 'nature-sparing' and 'nature-creating' technological changes. Nature-sparing technological innovations are aimed at using less energy per unit of human production. This is represented mathematically by a reduction of parameter β in the last equation. This type of technological change can be demonstrated by several examples. The use of sun, wind and water as energy sources is one of them. Another is the invention of the fuel cell.

The discovery of the super conductivity of certain materials at moderate temperatures is another promising development in this field. In the future the loss of electric energy through the transport system might be eliminated by using materials which are super conductive even at normal temperatures. One should realize that these possible future innovations diminish the scarcity of energy sources. It is even conceivable that a future invention might abolish the scarcity of a specific resource, which would mean that the rent for this resource becomes zero.

The total amount of organic matter generated by plants each year is enormous. It is the equivalent of one hundred billion (10^{11}) tons of carbon. This natural production needs only 1 per cent of all sunlight shed on earth. *Nature-creating* technological development could try to retain a greater part of sunlight in plants and vegetables each year. Think, for example, of fast-growing trees. Nature-creating technological innovations are expressed by an increase in parameter α in the last equation. It may also be possible to enlarge the possible volume of biomass in the climax stage by introducing new energy crops which can be grown in regions where climate and soil are less suitable for traditional crops. This type of biotechnological change is represented by an increase of n_c in the last equation.

The need for nature-conserving technological innovations is obvious. How quickly technology will develop in this direction is hard to predict, since political decisions and public opinion play a major role in the process.

Economic growth and nature-conserving technological change

The aim of this section is to determine a sustainable growth rate of human production considering the possibilities of nature-conserving technological change. The starting point of this calculation is the last equation. Now suppose that we start in period 0 and that the growth rate of production equals $\bar{y}$. Further let us assume that in period 0 mankind lives in the optimum steady state. If no technological changes occur, there can be no economic growth if the optimum steady state is to be maintained.

Next, nature-sparing and nature-creating innovations are assumed. This means that the last equation can be rewritten as follows:

$$y_0 e^{\bar{y}t} = 0.25 \frac{\left(n_{c,0} e^{\bar{n}_c t}\right)^2 (\alpha_0 e^{\bar{\alpha}t})}{(\beta_0 e^{\bar{\beta}t})}.$$

$\bar{\alpha}$ and $\bar{n}_c$ represent the nature-creating technological changes, while $\bar{\beta}$ represents the nature-sparing technological change. Now it can be deduced that:

$$\bar{y} = 2\bar{n}_c + \bar{\alpha} - \bar{\beta}.$$

It can be concluded that human production can grow, maintaining an optimum steady state, if growth equals the difference between the nature-creating technological changes and the nature-sparing technological ones. Indeed, in nature-sparing technological innovations, $\bar{\beta}$ will be negative, while in nature-creating technological innovations, $\bar{\alpha}$ and $\bar{n}_c$ will be positive.

Necessity of technological change

Normally economists define a steady state as being the same as the *state of steady growth*. This means a state of the economy with a constant capital-output ratio, and a constant rate of growth of output, consumption and wages. Because of depletable resources some economists have reconsidered this definition. In this type of analysis, a steady state is characterized by a constant population, a constant output etc.; in other words, as a stationary state. Tinbergen concluded that this state can be maintained if technological innovation sufficiently increases the productivity of the exhaustible resource. Other economists showed that this technological innovation is not a necessary condition if the exhaustible resource can sufficiently be substituted for by capital. Another approach is that of making use of the productivity of nature. In this case, the focus is on the renewable resources instead of exhaustible resources.

Since the stock of non-renewable resources is decreasing, the stock of renewable resources is becoming more important. It is clear that a steady state with the use of renewable resources is possible without the assumption of technological change. Only if one assumes a growing population combined with a constant or growing production per head is technological change necessary. The same conclusion can be reached when substitution between capital and an exhaustible resource is assumed. In this case, use is made of the productivity of capital, instead of the productivity of nature.

If a constant population with a constant income per head is to be maintained indefinitely without technological progress, two conditions must be fulfilled. First, the substitution possibilities of capital and the limited stock of exhaustible resources must be sufficient.[13] Second, for renewable resources, a physical steady state must be maintained, which means that there will be a balance between natural production and human respiration.[14]

However, world population is not constant, but is expected to grow. This immediately implies that to assure a sufficient level of income per capita (bio)technological innovations are unavoidable. The overall conclusion must be that, even under the assumption of a growing population, dismal forecasts, done for example in *the limits to growth*[15], need not materialize provided that technological change sufficiently increases productivity of both renewable and non-renewable natural resources.

---

13 If the elasticity of substitution between capital and a non-renewable resource is greater than or equal to unity, it is possible to sustain a positive level of consumption. This is known in the literature as the Hartwick rule.
14 This is based on the assumption that the stock of renewable resources can not be substituted by the stock of man-made capital or the stock of non-renewable resources.
15 Meadows D.L., D. Meadows, J. Randers and W. Behrens, 1972. *The limits to growth: a report for the Club of Rome Project on the predicament of mankind.* Dutch version, Het Spectrum, Utrecht.

18. Sustainable growth and economic metabolism

Economic metabolism

The principle of economic metabolism is demonstrated in Figure 18.1.

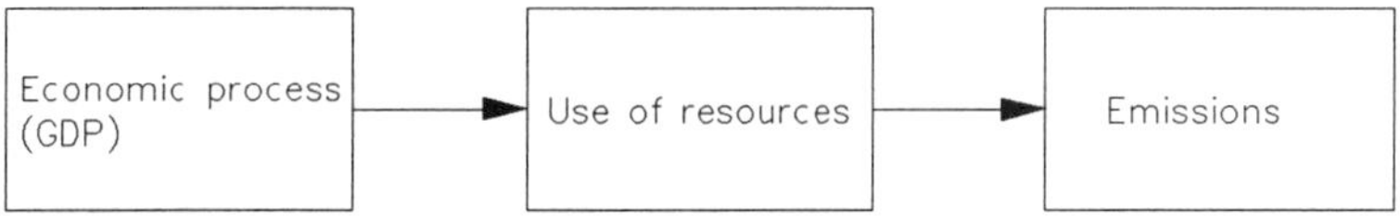

Figure 18.1: Economic metabolism.

In essence economic metabolism is the conversion of physical resources R to economic activity measured by the Gross Domestic Product Y, and physical emissions H, for example CO_2. The resource use over time t equals the resource output ratio α times the GDP Y. The emission H of a particular polluting agency equals the emission resource ratio β times resource use R. So:

$$R_t = \alpha_t Y_t, \quad H_t = \beta_t R_t.$$

Further, I use the following definitions, the small letters indicating growth rates:

$$Y_t = Y_0 e^{yt}, \quad R_t = R_0 e^{rt}, \quad H_t = H_0 e^{ht}, \quad \alpha_t = \alpha_0 e^{at}, \quad \beta_t = \beta_0 e^{bt}.$$

Sustainability

The standard of sustainability for a non-renewable resource is that the use R of the resource divided by stock S must be constant:[1]

$$\frac{\Delta S_t}{S_t} = \frac{R_t}{S_t} = c.$$

In that case, stock S develops as follows:

$$S_t = S_0 e^{-ct},$$

1 See Chapter 13. However, here we assume that after infinite time the stock will be completely exhausted. Besides, in this chapter we concentrate on a non-renewable resource. Of course, the same procedure can be applied to renewable resources.

From substitution it follows:

$$\frac{\alpha_t Y_t}{S_0 e^{-ct}} = c,$$

$$\frac{\alpha_0 Y_0 e^{(a+y)t}}{S_0 e^{-ct}} = c,$$

$$e^{(a+y+c)t} = \frac{cS_0}{\alpha_0 Y_0} = 1, \text{ so: } (a+y+c)t = 0 \text{ and } a = -c-y.$$

This is the sustainability condition for the input side of the economy for a specific natural resource.

If $H_t = \beta_t R_t$, then:

$$H_0 e^{ht} = \beta_0 e^{bt} R_0 e^{rt}, \quad \text{so:}$$

$$H_0 e^{ht} = \beta_0 e^{bt} \alpha_0 e^{at} Y_0 e^{yt}, \quad \text{so:}$$

$$h = b + a + y.$$

With $a = -c - y$ (sustainability condition for the input side), this gives:

$$h = b - c, \text{ so: } b = h + c.$$

When h is considered the wanted (sustainable) rate of emission reduction, this can be considered the sustainability condition for the whole economy for a particular polluting agent and a specific natural resource.

Figure 18.2 gives a picture of a situation in which the economy grows by 2% each year ($y = 0.02$), $c = 0.025$, so $a = -0.025 - 0.02 = -0.045$. Further, the sustainable reduction of the polluting agent is assumed to be minus 3% each year ($h = -0.03$),[2] so $b = -0.03 + 0.025 = -0.005$. The picture shows GDP Y_t, the sustainable resource use $R_t = \alpha_t Y_t$, and the sustainable development of pollution $H_t = \beta_t R_t$. All three variables in index figures (period 0 = 100).

In Figure 18.2 a growing economy together with a decreasing use of a resource is shown. The sustainable amount of resource that can be used in each period together with the allowed output of pollution agents may be called *ecospace* or *ecoscope*. Of course, the analysis presented in this chapter is based on the assumption that substitution between resource-intensive and resource-extensive economic sectors, substitution between capital and natural resources and resource-saving technology

---

2 This implies that the initial amount of pollution should be halved in about 23 years.

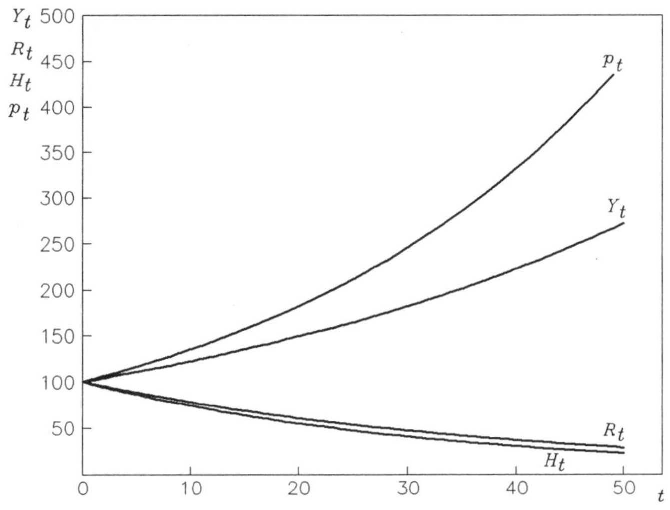

Figure 18.2: Example of sustainable resource use together with a growing economy.

will allow the economy to grow, and, at the same time, the resource use to decrease. This *dematerialization process* or *decoupling process* is essential for sustainable growth.[3]

Sustainability and efficiency

Can sustainability be combined with efficiency? The Hotelling efficiency rule implies that the rent p of a non-renewable resource should rise by the rate of interest. If the rate of interest i and the price elasticity of demand ϵ are known, we can determine an efficient and sustainable depletion path as follows (with $\bar{r}$ for the relative change in depletion of a non-renewable resource, $\bar{p}$ for the relative change in the rent of the resource, i for the interest rate, R_0 for the resource use in period 0 and S_0 for the resource stock at time 0).[4]

$$\bar{r} = \epsilon \bar{p}, \quad \bar{p} = i, \quad \bar{r} = -\frac{R_0}{S_0}.$$

3 In literature this is known as the environmental Kuznets curve (see Chapter 9). A distinction is possible between *relative decoupling* and *absolute decoupling*. The first concept refers to a decrease of pollution and resource use per unit production, while total poolution and resource use is still rising, the second concept refers to an absolute decrease of pollution and resource use together with a growing production.

4 Here, price elasticity of demand is assumed to be constant.

After substitution it can be derived that:

$$R_0 = -\epsilon i S_0.$$

For example, if $S_0 = 1000$, $\epsilon = -0.75$ and $i = 0.03$, then:

$$R_0 = 0.75 \times 0.03 \times 1000 = 22.5.$$

Finally, if we know quantity R_0 and the demand function, *e.g.* $R_t = p_t^{\epsilon}$, it is possible to compute p_0:

$$\ln p_0 = \frac{\ln R_0}{\epsilon}, \text{ so: } \ln p_0 = \frac{\ln 22.5}{-0.75} = -4.151, \text{ and } p_0 \approx 0.016.$$

The efficient rent path p_t is presented in Figure 18.2. The conclusion is that the efficiency rule provides us with the necessary relative change in price. Combined with the sustainability rule and elasticity of demand it gives us the necessary price level in period 0. The efficiency rule and the sustainability rule together determine the efficient and sustainable depletion path of the resource.

Conclusion

A number of (natural) scientists seem to think that production growth combined with decreasing pollution and a slower rate of resource depletion is not possible. This idea is based upon the two laws of thermodynamics:[5] the law of of conservation of energy (the first law) and the law of maximum entropy (the second law). According to them, more production (economic growth) inevitably causes an increase in entropy (more pollution and use of natural resources). However, they may be defining the concept of production incorrectly. In economics, production means 'value added'. This value added may be created by the production of material goods like cars or by a scientist sitting behind his desk and trying to solve an environmental problem. Both activities generate value added and contribute to production. The idea that the production is only production of material goods is obsolete.[6]

5 See, for example, W. Norde, 1997. Energy and entropy: a thermodynamic approach to sustainability. *The environmentalist*, 17, pp. 57-62.

6 The discussion about the measurement of production goes back to the physiocrats and the times of the classical economists. Adam Smith, for example, distinguished between productive and unproductive labour. He held the view that labour producing a service is unproductive. "As late as John Stuart Mill, it lead to the most fruitless controversies over the precise qualities which make one kind of labor productive and another the reverse" (quotation from R. Lekachman, 1976 (1959). *A History of Economic Ideas*. McGraw-Hill, New York). See also: H. Landreth and D.C. Colander, 1994. *History of Economic Thought*. Houghton Mifflin, Boston.

Therefore, it is possible that there is a decoupling between economic growth and environmental damage. Four reasons can be given for that:

1. In countries with a relatively high income per head, population growth tends to decline, leading to less environmental damage. This phenomenon is called the *demographic transition.*
2. In a highly developed economy the basic needs are satisfied. Therefore, production of the agricultural and industrial sector will remain more or less constant or may even decline. The growth of the economy will take place in the service sector, which is less polluting and uses less resources per unit output. This process is called the *economic transition.*[7]
3. Besides, in such an economy, the public's awareness of environmental affairs is relatively high. The demand for a clean environment will increase. Therefore, production itself will be increasingly aimed at the generation of 'environmental goods'.[8] The willingness to change lifestyles, normally speaking, is linked to a sufficient level of income per head. This may be called the *environmental transition.*
4. In growing economies there are financial resources available for education and research. This enhances the public's environmental awareness, and, more important, it enables the development of relatively cheap environmental-friendly technology. While technology is one of the key factors in the origin of pollution and the abuse of natural resources, it now becomes the main factor in solving these problems. This change may be called the *technological transition.*

The overall conclusion must be that decoupling is a real option.[9] Of course there is no economic law which says that economic development will move in that direction. That depends on the speed of the various transition processes we have mentioned. However, one thing is certain: poverty is bad for the environment.

7 This change in the product mix is also called the *composition effect.*
8 This may be the strongest argument against pessimistic future watchers. Nature building and recycling and reuse of resources contribute to production and, at the same time, decrease pollution and the use of primary resources.
9 Instead of increasing entropy, we might experience decreasing entropy or increasing *negentropy* in future.

LITERATURE

Allen R.G.D., 1973 (1956). *Mathematical economics*. MacMillan, London.

Ayres R.U. and U.E. Simonis, 1994. *Industrial Metabolism: Restructuring for Sustainable Development*. United Nations University Press, Tokyo.

Baumol W.J. and W.E. Oates, 1989. *The theory of environmental policy*. Cambridge University Press, Cambridge.

Blaug M., 1985. *Great Economists since Keynes: An introduction to the life & works of one hundred modern economists*. Wheatsheaf, Brighton.

Böhm-Bawerk E. von, 1921 (1889). *Kapital und Kapitalzins II, 1: Positive Theorie des Kapitales,* 4th edition. Fischer, Jena.

Böhm-Bawerk E. von, 1921 (1889). *Kapital und Kapitalzins II, 2: Kapital und Kapitalzins: Exkurse,* 4th edition. Fischer, Jena.

Boulding, K.E., 1966. The economics of the coming spaceship earth. In: W.A. Johnson and J. Hardesty (eds), 1966. *Economic growth vs. the environment*. Wadsworth, Belmont (Cal.).

Bressers H.Th., 1988. Effluent charges can work: the case of the Dutch water quality policy. In: F.J. Dietz and W.J.M. Heijman, *Environmental policy in a market economy*. Pudoc, Wageningen.

Callan S.J. and J.M. Thomas, 1996. *Environmental Economics and Management*. Irwin, Chicago.

Clark C.W., 1990. *Mathematical bioeconomics*. John wiley, New York.

Coase R., 1960. The problem of social cost. *Journal of law and economics,* 3, October, pp. 1-44.

Coase R.H. and F.F. Fowler, 1935. Bacon production and the pig-cycle in Great Britain. *Economica*, 2, May, pp. 142-167.

Cournot A.A., 1929 (1838). *Researches into the mathematical principles of the theory of wealth*, translated from the original French into English by N.T. Bacon. MacMillan, New York.

Daly H.E., 1977. *Steady-state economics: the economics of biophysical equilibrium and moral growth*. Freeman, San Francisco.

Dietz F.J., W.J.M. Heijman and E.P. Kroese, 1996. *Micro-economie: aanvullingen en uitwerkingen*. Stenfert Kroese, Houten.

Domar E., 1946. Capital expansion, rate of growth and employment. In: A. Sen, 1971. *Growth economics*. Penguin, Harmondsworth.

Douglas P.H., 1948. Are there laws of production? *American Economic Review,* 38, March, pp. 1-41.

Eatwell J., M. Milgate, and P. Newman, 1987. *The new Palgrave: a dictionary of economics*. Macmillan, London.

Engel E., 1857. *Die Productions und Consumptionsverhaeltnisse des Koenigreichs Sachsen*.

Faustmann M., 1968 (1849). *Calculation of value which forest land and immature stands possess for forestry*. Commonwealth Forestry Institute (CFI), Institute paper nr 42.

Fisher I., 1954 (1930). *The theory of interest*. Kelley and Millman, New York.

Georgescu-Roegen N., 1971. *The entropy law and the economic process.* Harvard University Press, Cambridge (Mass.).

Gini C., 1912. Variabilità e mutibilità. In: C. Gini, 1955. *Memorie di metodologia statistica: Vol. 1: Variabilità e concentrazione.* Libreria Eredi Virgilio Veschi, Rome.

Goodwin R.M., 1947. Dynamical coupling with especial reference to markets having production lags. *Econometrica,* 15, nr 3, pp. 181-204.

Gossen H.H., 1889 (1853). *Entwickelung der Gesetze des menschlichen Verkehrs, und der daraus fließenden Regeln für menschliches Handeln.* Prager, Berlin.

Hartwick J.M. and N.D. Olewiler, 1986. *The economics of natural resource use.* Harper Collins, New York.

Heijman W.J.M., 1990. Natural resources and market forms. *Wageningen Economic Papers.* Wageningen Agricultural University.

Heijman W.J.M., 1990. The neoclassical location model of firms. In: Dietz F., W. Heijman and D. Shever. *Location and Labor considerations for regional development.* Avebury, Aldershot.

Heijman W.J.M., 1991. *Depletable resources and the economy.* Wageningen Economic Studies (WES), nr 21. PUDOC, Wageningen.

Heijman W.J.M., 1995. Austrian sustainability. In: G. Meijer, *New Perspectives on Austrian Economics.* Routledge, London.

Henderson J.M. and R.E. Quandt, 1980 (1958), 3rd edition. *Microeconomic theory: a mathematical approach.* Mcgraw-Hill, Auckland.

Hirschmann A.O., 1964. The paternity of an index. *American Economic Review,* 54, September, p. 761.

Hotelling H., 1931. The economics of exhaustible resources. *The journal of political economy* 39, nr 2, pp. 137-175.

Hueting R., 1974. *Nieuwe schaarste en economische groei.* Agon Elsevier, Amsterdam

Hueting R., 1992. Correcting national income. In: Krabbe J.J. and W.J.M. Heijman (eds). *National income and nature: externalities, growth and steady state.* Kluwer, Dordrecht.

Isard W., 1956. *Location and Space-Economy.* John Wiley, New York.

Keynes J.M., 1951 (1936). *The general theory of employment, interest and money.* MacMillan, London.

Klaassen L.H. and A.C.P. Verster, 1974. *Kosten-batenanalyse in regionaal perspectief.* Tjeenk willink, Groningen.

Klundert Th. van de, 1983. The energy problem in a small open economy. *Journal of Macroeconomics,* 5, nr 2, pp. 211-222.

Klundert Th. van de and H. Peer, 1983. *Energie: een economisch perspectief.* Stenfert-Kroese, Leiden 1983.

Komen R., S. Gerkin and H. Folmer, 1997. Income and environmental RD: some empirical evidence from OECD countries. *Environment and Development Economics.* (to be expected).

Krabbe J.J., 1974. *Individueel en collectief nut.* Veenman, Wageningen.

Krabbe J.J. and W.J.M. Heijman, 1986. *Economische theorie van het milieu.* Van Gorcum, Assen.

Kruitwagen S., 1996. *An Economic analysis of Tradeable Emission Permits for Sulphur Dioxide Emissions in Europe.* PhD thesis, Wageningen Agricultural University.

Kula E., 1992. *Economics of natural resources and the environment.* Chapman and Hall, London.

Lancaster K.J., 1966. A new approach to consumer theory. *Journal of Political Economy*, 74, pp. 132-157.

Landreth H. and D.C. Colander, 1994. *History of Economic Thought.* Houghton Mifflin, Boston.

Lekachman R., 1976 (1959). *A History of Economic Ideas.* McGraw-Hill, New York.

Leontief W., 1941. *The structure of the American economy.* Harvard University Press, Cambridge (Mass.).

Lorenz M.O., 1905. Methods for measuring concentration of wealth. *Journal of the American Statistical Association,* 9, pp. 209-219.

Marshall A., 1920 (1890). *Principles of economics.* MacMillan, London.

Meadows D.L., D. Meadows, J. Randers and W. Behrens, 1972. *The limits to growth: a report for the Club of Rome Project on the predicament of mankind.* Dutch version, Het Spectrum, Utrecht.

Mill J.S., 1973 (1848). *Principles of political economy.* Kelley, Clifton.

Mills E.S., 1978. *The economics of environmental quality.* Norton, New York.

Norde W., 1997. Energy and entropy. *The environmentalist,* 17, pp. 57-62.

Ott A.E., 1968. Grundzüge der Preistheorie: p. 39. Vandenhoeck & Ruprecht, Göttingen.

Paelinck J.H.P. and P. Nijkamp, 1975. *Operational theory and method in regional economics.* Saxon House, Westmead.

Pareto V.F.D., 1966 (1909). *Manuel d'économie politique.* Genève. Originally published by Girard et Brière, Paris.

Pearce D.W., 1983 (1971). *Cost-Benefit analysis.* Macmillan, London.

Pearce D.W. and R.K. Turner, 1990. *Economics of natural resources and the environment.* Harvester Wheatsheaf, New York.

Perman R., Y. Ma and J. McGilvray, 1996. *Natural resource and environmental economics.* Longman, London.

Pigou A.C., 1952 (1920). *The economics of welfare.* Macmillan, London

Predöhl A., 1925. Das Standortsproblem in der Wirtschaftstheorie. *Weltwirtschaftliches Archiv* 21, pp. 294-331.

Price Gittinger J., 1982 (1973). *Compounding and discounting tables for project evaluation.* Johns Hopkins University Press, Baltimore.

Ricardo D., 1978 (1817). *The principles of political economy and taxation.* Everyman's library, London.

Schumacher E.F., 1975 (1973). *Small is beautiful: economics as if people mattered.* Harper and Row, New York.

Solow R.M., 1956. A contribution to the theory of economic growth. In: A. Sen, 1971. *Growth economics*. Penguin, Harmondsworth.
Solow R.M., 1988. Growth theory and after. *The American Review,* 78, nr 3, pp. 307-317.
Solow R.M., 1988. The economics of resources or the resources of economics. *The American economic review* 78, nr 2, pp. 1-14.
Thünen J.H. von, 1921 (1826). *Der isolierte Staat*. Fischer, Jena.
Tietenberg T.H., 1985. *Emissions trading*. Resources for the future, Washington.
Tinbergen J., 1943. *Economische bewegingsleer.* Noord-Hollandsche Uitgevers Maatschappy, Amsterdam.
Tinbergen J., 1987. *Kunnen wij de aarde beheren?* Kok Agora, Kampen.
Tinbergen J., 1989. De verdeling van hulpbronnen over toekomstige generaties. *Economisch Statistische Berichten,* 74 (1989), nr 3715, p. 677.
Walras M.L., 1926. *Éléments d'économie politique pur: Édition Définitive*. Pichon, Paris.
Weber A., 1929 (1909). *Theory of the Location of Industries*. Chicago Press, Chicago.
Wicksell K., 1954 (1893). *Value, Capital and Rent*. Allen & Unwin, London.
Zoeteman K., 1989. *Gaiasofie: anders kijken naar evolutie, ruimtelijke ordening en milieubeheer*. Ankh-Hermes, Deventer.

INDEX

ad valorem tax, 27, 28
ad valorem tax, 33, 34
aim of a firm, 13
allocation, 47, 134
attribute, 9, 10
average fixed costs, 24
average product, 73, 75
average total costs, 24
average variable costs, 24, 27

bilateral polypoly, 61
biomass, 178, 180, 181, 183
break-even point, 23, 24

capital, 13, 17, 18, 20, 75 - 79
cash flow, 55, 56, 59, 77, 78
chaos, 39
cleansing sector, 131 - 134, 139
climax population, 112
Coase theorem, 32, 35, 36
Cobb-Douglas production function, 13, 14, 16, 17, 43, 80, 82, 89, 150, 158, 159, 161
Cobb-Douglas utility function, 2, 9, 43
cobweb model, 37 - 40
collective demand function, 31
collective supply function, 27, 31
complementary good, 5
consumer's expansion path, 44, 45, 47
consumer's optimum, 3, 9
consumer surplus, 51
cost-benefit analysis, 51, 53, 54
costs, 23
Cournot-Nash equilibrium, 99
Cournot point, 63, 66
cross-price elasticity, 5

damage function, 131, 133
decoupling, 145, 187
decreasing marginal product, 73
demand, 3 - 7
demand for labour, 75
demand function, 31, 44, 46, 47, 103, 106
dematerialization, 187
demographic transition, 189
depletion speed, 103
depletion time, 101 - 104
direct price elasticity, 4
direct regulations, 121, 123, 125 - 128
discount rate, 105
discounting, 54, 55
distance, 79, 80, 82, 85
double-edged sword, 129
double dividend, 15
durability, 11, 12
duration of capital, 76, 78, 79

ecological equilibrium, 131, 132, 134
economic growth, 144, 145
economic instruments, 121, 126 - 129
economic metabolism, 185
economic transition, 189
ecoscope, 186
ecospace, 186
efficiency, 13, 16, 97, 98, 101, 115
elasticity, 4 - 8
elasticity of demand, 34
elasticity of production, 17
elasticity of supply, 34
emission resource ratio, 185
Engel, 3, 4, 7, 8
environmental costs, 21
environmental damage, 21
environmental Kuznets curve, 93 - 95
environmental policy, 27, 121, 123, 164, 167
environmental risk, 59
environmental transition, 189
excess supply, 32
exhaustible resource, 103, 108, 141, 144, 145, 155, 156, 158, 159, 161, 162
experience coefficient, 38 - 40
externality, 21, 22, 52, 131

Faustmann rule, 109
fee, 19 - 21, 121, 123, 125 - 129
fishery effort, 112, 113
fishery model, 112, 115
fixed costs, 23, 24

game theory, 167
general equilibrium, 43, 48
Giffen good, 4
Gini coefficient, 87, 88, 90
good of luxury, 5
Gossen's laws, 1, 2
greenhouse-effect, 126
ground water, 141, 142
growth equilibrium, 149, 150, 153
growth rate, 148, 150, 151, 153
heterogeneous good, 9, 10
Harrod-Domar growth model, 147 - 150, 152, 155, 157
Harrod-neutral technical change, 149, 151 - 153
Herfindahl-Hirschmann-index, 61

Hotelling rule, 97, 98, 100, 101, 103, 187

income distribution, 87, 88, 92, 93, 149, 150, 153, 156, 157
income elasticity, 5
income equilibrium, 147, 148
independent good, 5
inflation, 125, 126, 128
input-output analysis, 135 - 137, 139, 163
input-output table, 163
input instruments, 121, 126
internalization, 53
iso-utility curve, 2

KLEM production function, 170
Kuznets curve, 93
labour, 13, 17, 18, 20, 73 - 75, 79 - 82, 84
Lagrange procedure, 14, 15
land, 80, 81
land rent, 79 - 81
location, 82 - 85
Lorenz curve, 87, 88

marginal abatement cost, 121, 122 - 124
marginal costs, 23 - 25, 27
marginal efficiency of capital, 76
marginal product, 13, 14, 17, 18, 74, 78
marginal revenue, 105, 106
marginal revenue of pollution, 123, 124
market dynamics, 36
market equilibrium, 31, 35, 36
market forms, 61, 70
market instruments, 121
marketable permit, 126 - 129
Marshall, 6, 7, 51
maximum price, 32
maximum sustainable yield, 113, 115
minimum price, 32, 39, 40
monopoly, 61, 62, 64 - 66, 69, 100, 103, 105, 107, 108, 113, 114
monopsony, 61, 62, 66, 69

Nash equilibrium, 167
natural rate of growth, 149, 150, 152
natural renewal, 132
natural renewal rate, 160
nature, 19 - 22, 131, 132, 180
neoclassical growth model, 147, 150, 153, 158, 159
non-renewable resource, 141, 157, 158
numeraire, 45, 47

oil price, 170
oligopoly, 61, 63, 64
oligopsony, 61
open access resource, 112
optimization, 9
optimum catch, 117
optimum harvesting time, 110
optimum income distribution, 88, 94
optimum product, 10, 11
optimum rotation period, 108 - 112
output instruments, 121

Pareto, 51
Pareto optimum, 167
perfect competition, 61, 62, 65, 69, 70, 97, 100, 101, 103, 106 - 108, 113 - 115
physical steady state, 175
Pigou, 51
Pigovian tax, 52, 53
policy, 8
polipsony, 61, 62, 66
polluter-pays principle, 121, 128
polluting sectors, 132, 133
polypoly, 61
precipitation, 142
primary good, 5
prisoner dilemma, 167, 168
producer's expansion path, 78, 79
producer surplus, 51
production factors, 13, 18, 20, 134
production function, 13, 14, 16 - 18, 20
productivity of capital, 56, 58, 75, 76
profit, 23 - 25
profit maximization, 43, 44
property rights, 35, 36, 103

rate of depletion, 155, 157
rate of interest, 103
rate of renewal, 109
recycling, 117, 118
recycling multiplier, 119
relative growth speed, 110
renewable resource, 141 - 145, 155, 157, 159 - 162
rent, 97 - 101, 116
resource, 97, 98, 101 - 103, 108, 112, 117 - 119
resource output ratio, 185
risk management, 60
risk policy, 59
royalty, 101, 103, 105

scale of production, 16 - 19
shut-down point, 26, 27
social welfare, 52, 88
Solow, 108
Solow-Stiglitz efficiency rule, 158
spatial production function, 84
spatial profit curve, 85, 86

specific tax, 27, 28, 32, 33
state of steady growth, 175, 183
stationary state, 175, 177, 184
steady-state growth, 152
steady depletion, 155 - 157, 159, 162
steady growth, 148 - 150, 153, 155 - 162
steady state, 175, 177 - 181, 183, 184
subsidies, 121, 126
substitute, 5
supply elasticity, 27 - 29
supply function, 31
sustainability, 185 - 188
sustainable depletion, 141 - 144, 157, 160
sustainable growth, 155, 162, 175, 183, 185, 187

taxation, 32, 34
technical change, 149 - 153, 155, 158 - 160, 162
technical innovations, 126, 128, 177
technological innovations, 175 - 177, 182 - 184
technological transition, 189
time preference, 56, 58
Tinbergen's model, 177
transaction costs, 35, 128
transportation costs, 79, 82, 84, 85
turnover, 23
turnover elasticity, 5

utility, 1, 10
utility function, 1 - 3, 5, 8, 9
utility maximization, 43, 44

value of land, 81
variable costs, 23

warranted rate of growth, 148 - 150, 156
welfare, 89, 90, 131 - 135
welfare economics, 51
willingness to pay, 51

Zoeteman's model, 178